LIGHT AT EVENING TIME

SOLID GROUND CHRISTIAN BOOKS
BIRMINGHAM, ALABAMA USA

LIGHT AT EVENING TIME:

A BOOK OF

SUPPORT AND COMFORT

FOR

THE AGED.

At evening time it shall be light.
Zech. xiv., 7.

EDITED BY

JOHN STANFORD HOLME, D.D.

NEW YORK:
HARPER & BROTHERS, PUBLISHERS,
FRANKLIN SQUARE.
1874.

Solid Ground Christian Books
PO Box 660132
Vestavia Hills, AL 35266
205-443-0311
sgcb@charter.net
www.solid-ground-books.com

Light at Evening Time
A Book of Support and Comfort for the Aged

Edited by John Stanford Holme

First Solid Ground Edition, December 2007

Cover image is a photograph of the setting sun silhouettes the lighthouse on Lake Michigan in Muskegon, Michigan, taken by Ric Ergenbright. View all his images at ricergenbright.com

Cover design by Borgo Design in Tuscaloosa, Alabama. Contact them at borgogirl@bellsouth.net

ISBN: 1-59925-126-4

NEW EDITION
DEDICATED TO
MY MOTHER

DOROTHY JONES GAYDOSH PETTITT

FROM THE PUBLISHER

CHRISTMAS 2007

PREFATORY NOTE.

CICERO, in his justly celebrated treatise on Old Age, says "it can not be supposed that Nature, after having wisely distributed to all preceding periods of life their peculiar and proper enjoyments, should have neglected, like an indolent poet, the last act of the human drama, and left it destitute of suitable advantages."

If this term Nature, as here used by Cicero, might be so defined as to include the God of nature as revealed in the Bible, the sentiment is not only eminently true, but in singular harmony with the spirit of divine revelation; for in the light of the Bible, old age is not without its especial sources of enjoyment and its own peculiar rewards.

The calmness and tranquillity of this period of life enable the believer, as from an eminence, to

PREFATORY NOTE.

look back over the past with great spiritual profit, and to look forward with clear vision to an eternity of bliss not far distant. While those in advanced years may be incapable of fixed and long-continued attention, yet this period of life is not unfavorable to meditation. In its exercise, the truths of religion and the promises of the divine Word grow more precious, and yield great spiritual refreshment and comfort. Thus the aged are not only enabled to forget many of their infirmities, but they are frequently more than compensated for the absence of many of the hurrying and bustling pleasures of earlier life.

As far as may be, to assist the aged in the performance of their duties and in the enjoyment of their privileges, this volume has been prepared. It contains such religious truth as is adapted to the wants of the aged, and is printed in such type as is best suited to their use. The articles are generally brief, and the work is designed to be a sort of Manual, to be taken up at odd moments for occasional perusal.

PREFATORY NOTE.

In the selection of materials for the volume, we have aimed to secure the greatest variety both of matter and form, and to gather them from the widest range of authorship. We have admitted nothing which is not eminently evangelical in sentiment, and nothing, as we suppose, offensively sectarian in doctrine.

It is hoped that there may be found in the book something suitable for every frame of mind and every experience incident to the decline of life, and that it may be to the spirit of the aged pilgrim what the staff of myrtle, according to Pliny, was to the traveler, infusing such an energy that during the longest day he never grew faint or weary.

Especial thanks are due to Rev. John Hall, D.D., Rev. Howard Crosby, D.D., Rev. George B. Cheever, D.D., and Rev. William Adams, D.D., for original contributions to the volume, and to Rev. Stephen H. Tyng, D.D., for services kindly proffered in the examination of the manuscripts.

J. S. H.

NEW YORK, *September*, 1870.

INTRODUCTION.

I AM desired to write an Introduction to this valuable compilation. I have looked through it with care and pleasure. It presents an aggregate of religious experience, wisdom, and genius, which gives to it the weight of authority and the attraction of delight. The selection displays an equal extent of information and discernment of skill in the industrious compiler. He will be rewarded, personally, in the assurance of the fact, and commemoratively in the continuance of its influence, that he has been the instrument, in divine and gracious hands, for giving comfort, encouragement, and strength to thousands of the people of God in their years of debility, solitude, and earthly decay. The mind which so skillfully provides true comfort for age, may enjoy the cheering reflection that its objects will never fail, and that the Savior who loves them will

INTRODUCTION.

surely bless the one who so willingly and cheerfully does them good.

The title of the work is well selected. There is but one LIGHT to this dark and sinful world. That is the gracious Savior, who visited this world for its full redemption, and who gave to its fallen, wandering ones the infallible assurance that whosoever "followeth him shall not walk in darkness, but shall have the light of life." Jesus Christ, the Lamb of God, and the Lord of man, is the one living, adequate, glorious light on earth, for the aged and the young. To embrace him in the heart, with a living, loving faith, is to be brought out of darkness into light. To walk with him in the fellowship of mutual trust and love, is to "walk in the light, and to have no darkness at all." To do this in youth, to abide in this through all of active life on earth, is to provide a sunshine for the evening, as effective as the wonder of victorious Joshua, and as real and sure as the promise of a covenant-keeping God. "Thy sun shall no more go down, neither shall thy moon withdraw itself. The Lord shall be thine everlasting light, and the days of thy mourning shall be ended."

This is the "light at evening time," in a twofold

INTRODUCTION.

sense of application—in *retrospection* and in *anticipation*—the light of memory in the past, and the light of hope in the future.

The aged believer has a precious light of retrospection and memory. The whole path of the past, perhaps from the days of youth, shines illuminated by the light of Jesus, a Savior already accepted, enjoyed, and loved. None but the aged can really understand this, with what delight the meditations rest upon the grace which has been given in all the years gone by. The memory is a divine repository of joys. And age is wonderfully quickened and aided in the power of recalling them, and contemplating them in the most minute analysis of particulars, and in the clearest display of connections between individual facts.

The day of one's conversion, the period of life when Jesus first came to claim his abode in the heart—how vividly all its facts, its relations, its developments, its influences, rise up then to view. It was the time of a divine espousal. Jesus appeared, the loving bridegroom of the waiting soul. He aroused the thought; he awakened the conscious needs; he displayed his own attractions to the heart distressed; he entered into his chamber of repose;

INTRODUCTION.

he assumed his abiding dwelling there; and the darkness had passed, and the true light was now shining, to go out no more.

In this precious light of a Savior, received, accepted, and loved, the converted soul has walked; believing, trusting, grateful, happy, perfectly satisfied, and perfectly at rest; filled with joy in such companionship, and desiring none other than this Angel of the Covenant, who hath redeemed him from all evil, and hath led him all his life through in perfect security and perfect peace.

And now, at evening time, in the remembrance of all this life of divine acceptance and of self-renouncing faith in Jesus, there is a sweet and assuring light. As old John Newton said in such a time, "I am not what I ought to be, I am not what I wish to be, I am not what I shall be, but, by the grace of God, I am not what I was. And by that grace, I am what I am." Thus may the aged Christian say. Born of God, living in Christ, walking in the Spirit, kept in the faith, abiding in the love of God, and rejoicing in him who was "the guide of my youth," and is "all my salvation, and all my desire." I bless God from the ground of my heart that, according to his promise, "at evening time there is light."

INTRODUCTION.

But it is the light of anticipation, as well as the light of memory. Jesus is very near to aged companions with himself. He has laid out their journey; he has attended them in all their passage through the wilderness of earth; and now he shines before them in the solitude of peculiar attractions, and with the power of peculiar encouragement.

Never before did human goodness and man's sufficiency appear so worthless or vanish so completely. Never was the soul brought so low or so dependent. Never was the heart so weaned from earth and earthly things. Never were obstructions so completely removed from the path of the believing soul. And never did the absolute and incomparable sufficiency of Jesus, as an all-sufficient Savior, appear so supreme, so complete, so appropriate, so attractive, so sure, as he now seems to the soul believing at evening tide.

The aged pilgrim really sees but one thing, desires but one thing, possesses but one thing. That is JESUS, an all-conquering, all-supplying Savior; bringing every thing, giving every thing, having every thing, securing every thing. Never was hope so clear, so adequate, or so glorified. "I am a great sinner. I have a great Savior." The past is filled

INTRODUCTION.

with his grace. The future is flowing with his glory. And JESUS, JESUS ONLY, is "the Light at evening time."

Such are the views, such are the emotions with which the evening of the soul on earth is blessed by its great Redeemer. These principles, thus illustrated, shine through this affecting and encouraging compilation. And in the sure enjoyment of such blessings, through infinite grace, I commend the work to all my fellow-pilgrims in this evening time of life.

STEPHEN H. TYNG.

ST. GEORGE'S RECTORY, NEW YORK, *June*, 1873.

Cast me not off in the time of old age; forsake me not when my strength faileth.

*　　*　　*　　*　　*　　*

I will go in the strength of the Lord God: I will make mention of thy righteousness, even of thine only.

O God, thou hast taught me from my youth: and hitherto have I declared thy wondrous works.

Now also when I am old and gray-headed, O God, forsake me not; until I have showed thy strength unto this generation, and thy power to every one that is to come.

(71st Psalm.)

LIGHT AT EVENING TIME.

YOUTH RENEWED IN AGE.
BY JAMES W. ALEXANDER, D.D.

CHRISTIAN confidence and hope in God give freshness, strength, and joy even in the period of old age. "They that wait on Jehovah"—or, in modern English, they that wait for him, who evince their trust in his goodness and power by patiently awaiting the fulfillment of his promises, they, though no longer young (mark the contrast with ver. 30)—"shall renew their strength: they shall mount up on wings like eagles; they shall run and not be weary, and they shall walk and not faint."* The same thought is in the thanksgiving of the one hundred and third Psalm, verse 5: "Bless the Lord, O my soul, who satisfieth thy mouth with good things, so that thy youth is renewed like the eagle's." From both we may conclusively gather that Divine grace has influences to bestow which can counteract and often annul the debilitating tendencies of old age. We are not au-

* Isaiah xlix., 31.

thorized, it is true, to teach that any degree of religious affection can turn back the shadow on the dial-plate, restore its auburn beauty to the gray head, or neutralize the physical causes of distress; though even here, such is the power of spirit over matter, that history shows marvels of an almost youthful gladness in blessed Christian old age. But we may and can assert that he whose habits have been formed in a perpetual waiting upon God receives a hallowed unction of grace, which, so to speak, makes him young again, or, more properly, keeps him from waxing old within. In the most rapid survey, we have considered some of the causes which makes this season of life formidable. All ages have observed them; all philosophies have sought to destroy or lessen their force. The most accomplished of all Roman authors has left nothing more finished than his celebrated tract on Old Age (Cicero, *De Senectute*). Short of the meridian beam of revelation and its reflections, nothing ever showed more nobly; yet the ray of its consolations is but a beautiful moonlight. In vain is the venerable Cato introduced to teach us secrets which Cato never knew. In this gem-like treatise Cicero refers the troubles of age to four classes. Old age, so he tells us, is feared because (**1.**) it withdraws from the affairs of life; because (**2.**) it brings infirmity of body;

because (3.) it abridges or ends our pleasures; and (4.) because it leads to death. Already, in treating of these several heads, much is said truly, ably, and, to a certain extent, satisfactorily, on the first and third topics, but on the last there is nothing but melancholy conjecture. Even in regard to the other heads—of business, health, and pleasure—the suggestions are infinitely below those known by the humblest Christian rustic; for what did this great and eloquent Roman know of the oil which grace pours into the sinking and almost expiring lamp?

RETIRING FROM BUSINESS.

It is not to be denied, when we come with candor to the investigation, that, as a general truth, old age withdraws men from the employments of life, and seals up the active business years. In the great majority of instances, however, this retreat from labor is voluntarily sought long before the access of grave infirmity. Indeed, in prosperous communities, many retire too early, under the chimerical hope of enjoying an elegant repose, for which they have made no provision by mental culture and discipline of moral habits. There is, it is true, another sort of recession from productive labors which we occasionally observe in old men, and which arises wholly from an unchastened selfishness. Let any one grow. wealthy without the warming and expanding influences of benevolence, and he will more and more lose his interest in all that is going on in the world. Even wars and revolutions touch him only in their financial aspects, and the daily journal is to him not so much a courier of news as a barometer of loss and gain. Without religion, the circle becomes more contracted. Friends have departed, by scores if not by hundreds. What cares he for mighty movements in behalf of humanity and holiness around him? What cares he for posterity, the country, or the world, so that he can exalt his own gate, or die worth some round sum which floats before him as his heaven? In the same degree he wraps himself in his mantle, which is daily shrinking to his own poor dimensions. This is misery indeed. Take away the blessed sun, and every thing becomes wintry, frozen, all but dead; take away more blessed love, and the heart is dumb, cheerless, insulated, meanly poor, so that the Latins named such a one *Miser*.

AGED CHRISTIANS STILL IN ACTIVE LIFE.

Let us leave him, shivering in his cave, overhung with icicles, and come out into the evening sunshine to consider the aged believer. He is like Mnason, "an old disciple." He still learns. The Greek story tells us that when Solon lay dying, and overheard some conversation on philosophy in his apartment, he raised his head and said, "Let me share in your conversation, for, though I am dying, I would still be learning." Ten thousand times has this been more reasonably exemplified in dying Christians, who consider the whole of this life as but the lowest form of the school into which they have been entered. And in regard to activity, while modes of service must vary with the bodily condition, we are bold to maintain that innumerable Christians now living are, in advanced life, impressing the whole engine of human affairs with as momentous a touch as at any previous stage of existence. If there is wisdom, the proper jewel of age, and divine grace in its manifold actings, there need be no lack of influence. They still lift up the eagle pinion, and soar in such greatness as belongs to their nature. But the point to which we would ask more marked attention is this, that the aged believer, so far from being selfishly dead to what is going on in the world, is more vigilant, and more in sympathy with all, than even in his days of youth. Blessed be God, we have seen this again and again. The man who waits on God, the man of faith and hope, the man of melting benevolence, looks through the loop-holes of retreat upon a world whose vast and often terrific revolutions interest him chiefly as included in a cycle of providential arrangements calculated to develop and exhibit the glory of grace. His heart beats responsive to these. The news of Christ's kingdom is as dear to him as when he was vehemently active in the field. He looks down the ages by the lamp of prophecy, and beholds events which will take place when he shall have been long in Paradise. This connects him with the cause of Christ on earth, and redeems him from that miserable dungeon-like seclusion of soul which wastes away the aged worldling. So far is it from being true that these portraitures are figments of religious imagination, that we have been led to the choice of the subject by knowledge and recollection of this very paradox in actual example — to wit, extreme old age made light, strong, and happy by community of interest in the progressive triumphs of philanthropy and missions.

THE SOUL MOUNTING TOWARD THE SUN OF RIGHTEOUSNESS.

When, according to the Talmudic fable, the eagle soars toward the sun, he renews the plumage of his former days. As the serene disciple withdraws himself from any personal agency in the entangling plans of life, he studies more profoundly what his Master is weaving into the web of history. No longer young, he has a heart which gushes in sympathy with the young. He cheers them on. He places the weapons in their hands. He takes from the wall his sword, shield, and helmet, and rejoices that God still has younger soldiers in the field. He lives his life over again in their achievements, and pictures to himself more signal victories after he shall have gone. Like the wounded hero, Wolfe, he could even die more happy if the shout of victory should arouse his failing perception. Far from being shut up in morose, neglectful selfishness, he glories that God's cause still lives and must prevail.

CHRISTIANITY A SYSTEM OF INDEMNITIES.

But, then, you retort, there is a sad infirmity inseparable from old age. Piety, however exalted, will not remove this. Of all diseases, this is proverbially the most incurable. Brethren, we might take the high ground that godliness hath the promise of the life that now is; that temperance and other virtues prolong life and avert disease; that the righteous shall "see good days;" and that religion is the best of all medicines. But, fearing lest we should be charged with exaggeration by the inexperienced, we will pitch our cause on a lower plane, and rest content with declaring that Christian confidence and hope confer a strength which is perfectly compatible with all this bodily weakness, decay, and pain. Christianity, my readers, is a system of indemnities. It does not insure us exemption from all losses, but it guarantees that these shall be more than made up to us. True, the grand indemnification is at the recompense of the resurrection. But prelibations of glory are poured into the earthly vessels of grace. The quickening charm is not natural, but supernatural. Mark, in the twenty-eighth verse, how the eternal increate fount of good is pointed out; and learn how the fullness of God, through a Mediator, becomes the available supply of man. "Hast thou not known? hast thou not heard, that the everlasting God, Jehovah, the creator of the ends of the earth, fainteth not, neither is weary? There is no searching of his understanding. He giveth power TO THE FAINT." Here is human infirmity brought into connection with Omnipotence. Here is the solution of Paul's enigma, "When I am weak, then am I strong." Here is Christ's cordial to the aged, "My strength is made perfect in weakness." But let us return to our prophet. He represents even blooming adolescence as desponding, while the feeble are made powerful by faith. "Even the youths shall faint and be weary, and the young men shall utterly fall; but they that wait on the Lord shall renew their strength."

THE JOY OF THE LORD THE STRENGTH OF AGE.

In the return from Babylon the oldest were saddest, for they remembered the glory of the first house. Nehemiah, therefore, had peculiar reference to them when he said to the weeping assembly, "Neither be ye sorry, for the joy of the Lord is your strength." Holy joy is a spring-head of renewed youthfulness. The effects of grief and age are not unlike. How often have we seen a friend go into the house of mourning young and come out old? Such was David's experience (Psalm xxxii., 3): "My bones waxed old, through my moaning all the day long; for day and night thy hand was heavy upon me: my moisture is turned into the draught of summer." The cedars and palms of the sanctuary, planted in the house of the Lord, "shall still bring forth fruit in old age; they shall be fat and flourishing" (Psalm xcii.). Make a soul thoroughly glad, and you make it young. The effusion of divine joys has virtues to annul outward disabilities. For observe the perfect analogy of another passage concerning strength (Isaiah xxxv.): "Strengthen ye the weak hands, and confirm the feeble knees; say to them that are of a fearful heart, Be strong, fear not!" "Then shall the lame man leap as an hart, and the tongue of the dumb shall sing." Such is grace, superseding nature, conciliating contraries, making the feeble mighty, and giving youth to the aged. And oh how greatly would our experience and observation of the gift be increased if, with higher faith and expectation, we were waiting upon God!

The antechamber of the eternal abode is cold and appalling to nature. This makes old age unwelcome to the unprepared. This causes the wretched shifts by which they avert the thought of doom. So successful is the delusion, that the man of seventy plans for to-morrow as if he were not already in many senses dead. No man is so old, says Cicero, but that he thinks he may live another day. And so from day to day, as by stepping-stones in the turbid stream, they totter on, till the sudden fall plunges them into eternity.

THE FEAR OF DEATH.

The fear of death, which on the young sometimes works salutary reflection, often becomes to the aged a motive for abstracting the thoughts from the hateful subject, and so they think of something else, and are damned. I dare not undertake to say what may be the reflections of the old worldling when he lies down for the last struggle, and finds that eternity is dawning on his soul, and yet that he has not made the least provision for meeting his God. But I know, for I have often seen, how strong in faith and hope may be the old age of the true Christian. After all, it is celestial *hope* which sheds the dew of youth on his silver locks. His posture is that of waiting, as watchers expect the dawn—"more than they that watch for the morning." Fresh blood seems to course through these outworn arteries as Hope waves the hand of indication toward perpetual spring and everlasting youth. Not in the mere elysian or Mohammedan sense, though we deny the attributes and enjoyments of that bodily complement of the soul which is to be raised in incorruption, in glory, in power, a spiritual body. But the fresh breath of knowledge, of reason, of truth, therefore of beauty, of love, of universal holiness, is wafted from those gardens to the ancient believer, as he worships, leaning on the top of his staff, and sojourns a little in the land of Beulah. We have sometimes seen the clearness and vigor of former years come back. Call not that man old who is full of joys and hallelujahs, and who is eager to drop the clog, shuffle off the mortal coil, and soar like a bird set free from the snare of the fowler. Call him old who is inveterate in sin; who never prays; who dares not think of death; who is without God and without hope, and on whose hoary head no blessing ever descends. The Simeon who has Christ in his arms, has in him a well of water springing; and so the true fountain of youth. All believing and sublime exercises of Christian experience have in them something as fresh as childhood. Once, when I was supporting a very aged believer from the house of God, he turned to me and said, "I never felt younger; and I believe that promise is fulfilled in me, 'He satisfieth thy mouth with good things, so that thy youth is renewed like the eagle's.'" This persuasion, that true religion brings the soul into fellowship with all that is free, hopeful, and advancing in earth, and all that is bright and perfect in heaven, led the most distinguished of late German theologians, Schleiermacher, to say, in the close of a long life, "The true Christian is always young."

THE SUBURBS OF HEAVEN.

The racy old English of John Bunyan best sets forth this stage of pilgrimage. Here they heard continually the singing of birds, and saw every day the flowers appear in the earth, and heard the voice of the turtle in the land. In this country the sun shineth night and day. Here they were within sight of the city they were going to: also they met some of the inhabitants thereof; for in this land the shining ones commonly walked, because it was upon the borders of heaven. In this land, also, the contract between the Bride and Bridegroom was renewed; yea, here, "as the bridegroom rejoiceth over the bride, so doth their God rejoice over them." My beloved brethren, we must be submissive to God's will, even if such an evening of life be not vouchsafed to us. Yet I will maintain that it is of the nature of Christianity to produce such joys. The exceptions are not from grace, but from disturbing causes in our partially unsanctified hearts. Waiting on God is directly promotive of fresh and heavenly strength. The long-continued practice and rooted habit of waiting upon God, in confidence and expectation, are the best preparative for a serene decline and a happy end.

THE WORLDLING'S NOTION OF DEATH.

If the sentiment of the world may be safely judged from its reflection in the mirror of the fictitious literature which is seized with most avidity and reproduced in the greatest number of languages, then unquestionably the opinion is that there is no happiness in evangelical piety, and an old age of religion is one of sourness, vindictiveness, and misanthropic woe. Let the picture of a Christian matron be painted by the matchless pencil of one whose misfortune it must have been never to have beheld the original, and with whom devotion and hypocrisy are the same, and the lineaments are such as these: "Great need had the rigid woman of her mystical religion, veiled in gloom and darkness, with lightnings of cursing, vengeance, and destruction flashing through the sable clouds." I quote from the ignorant and malignant travesty of Christian old age, which mars the most widely current story of the hour; and I quote it because it will meet response in hundreds of thousands who need the grace of Christ to avert these very storm-clouds of declining day. Let a holier literature prevail in the refined world—a literature which shall honor holy wedlock, family religion, and the Church of Christ—and we shall behold other portraitures of the wife or the widow upon whom evangelical truth has shed its dews of eventide.

THE HOARY HEAD A CROWN OF GLORY.

WHILE we call old age the winter of our life, we must beware lest we derogate from the bounty of our Maker, and disparage those blessings which he accounts precious, among which old age is none of the meanest.

Had he not put that value upon it, would he have honored it with his own style, calling himself the

"Ancient of Days?" Would he have set out this mercy as a reward of obedience to himself, "I would fulfill the number of thy days?" and of obedience to our parents, "To live long in the land?" Would he have promised it as a marvelous savor to restored Jerusalem, now become a city of Truth, that "there shall yet old men and old women dwell in the streets of Jerusalem, and every man with his staff in his hand for every age?" Would he else have denounced it as a judgment to over-indulgent Eli, "There shall not be an old man in thy house forever?" Far be it from us to despise that which God doth honor, and to turn his blessing into a curse.

Yea, the same God who knows best the price of his own favors, as he makes no small estimation of age himself, so he hath thought fit to call for a high respect to be given to it, out of a holy awe to himself: "Thou shalt rise up before the hoary head, and honor the face of the old man, and fear thy God. I am the Lord." Hence it is that he hath pleased to put together the "ancient" and the "honorable," and has told us that a hoary head is a crown of glory, if it be found in the way of righteousness; and, lastly, makes it an argument of the deplored estate of Jerusalem that "they favored not the elders."—JOSEPH HALL.

AT EVENING TIME IT SHALL BE LIGHT.

BY REV. A. K. H. BOYD.

THE day of life, shall we think, is drawing to its close. It has been, on the whole, a sober day, with "the light not clear nor dark;" there has been neither unvarying sunshine nor unvarying gloom; there have been, no doubt, some great trials in it, and a host of little, insect cares, which do no worse than fret and annoy; it has seemed, perhaps, a dull and weary thing, yet we have grown to like even its dullness and commonness; it has had within it times of special elevation, love to the Redeemer, trust in God; and it has had, too, its seasons of backsliding, of coldness and worldliness, of lack of interest in spiritual engagements, of despondency, and almost of despair. For the day of grace goes by just such rules as the day of providence, and, save a few blessed and memorable believers, who have seemed to breathe the air of heaven even while they lived on earth, it is the general experience of even the earnest believer that his inward feeling, like his outward lot, is a checkered one, is in the main a sobered one—is shone upon by a light which is "not clear nor dark." But the evening of the long day is drawing on at length — the day that dawned with the sunny cheerfulness of infancy and childhood, that went on amid the growing cares of maturity, that sloped westerly amid the enfeebled powers and the flagging hopes of age; and as the evening advances, as the hours go on in which the light that had lasted through the day might naturally grow less, strange how it oftentimes is that that unwearied light does but beam brighter and clearer! It was but a cloudy day; but the Sun of Righteousness has broken through the clouds; the flaming west is all purple and gold; it is the evening time, and oh how fair its light! It has sometimes been, as in that beautiful story, that the last steps before the dark river was reached lay through the land of Beulah; that already the brightness of the golden city shone from afar upon the believer's face, and his sharpened ear could almost catch the fall of its ceaseless songs. I do not say that such a thing is common; all I say is that such a thing has been, and wherefore should it not be again with you or me? I shall not pretend to describe this happy state in my own words; I shall tell you about it in the words of one who spoke from his own experience, and who, shortly before he died, wrote as thus: "Were I to adopt the figurative language of Bunyan, I might date this letter from the land of Beulah, of which I have been for some weeks a happy inhabitant. The Celestial City is full in my view. Its glories have been upon me, its breezes fan me, its odors are wafted to me, its sounds strike upon my ears, and its spirit is breathed into my heart. Nothing separates me from it but the river of death, which now appears but as an insignificant rill, that may be crossed at a single step whenever God shall give permission. The Sun of Righteousness has been gradually drawing nearer and nearer, appearing larger and brighter as he approached, and now he fills the whole hemisphere, pouring forth a flood of glory, in which I seem to float like an insect in the beams of the sun; exulting, yet almost trembling, while I gaze on this excessive brightness, and wondering with unutterable wonder why God should deign thus to shine upon a sinful worm." There, my readers, are words dictated by experience. That is what was actually written by a dying man. And oh! what need I add to it to make you feel how glorious a sermon it is upon the blessed promise that "at the evening time there shall be light."

But then you will say to me, and say it truly, that it is not always so. Not only is it not the case that all who have "died the death of the righteous" have thus tranquilly, fearlessly, hopefully, triumphantly passed away, but has not such a thing been known as that one who was a true Christian, if true Christian ever breathed, died absolutely in despair? Oh, who can forget the story of that sweet and gentle poet, who would take nothing to himself at the last of the comfort his words have given to others; whose latest lines sadly tell us how his soul was whelmed in deeper than Atlantic depths; who regarded himself as doomed to everlasting perdition, and who shuddered at the very mention of the name of that blessed Redeemer who was looking down in kindness upon his wayward child! But, then, let me remind you that, fine as was that poet's mind, it was a mind unhinged and deranged; and however the Holy Spirit works upon the renewed soul, he no more sets himself to cure hereditary diseases of the mind than those of the body. Religion does not alter temperament: it leaves the cheerful man cheerful; it leaves the anxious, desponding man still prone to look at the future through the haze of anxiety and fear. It no more pretends to cure that hereditary taint, that overshadowing gloom that all his life had its grasp of Cowper's mind, than it pretends to weed out the family consumption or apoplexy from the Christian's body; and never let us forget that constitutional temperament, and the depressing influence of many forms of disease, may make dark and distressful the dying-bed of the very best believers. Perhaps, even with true Christians, the death is as the life was, the evening is what the day was—"not clear nor dark"—as the general rule. There are blessed hopes, but there are also distressing fears. And shall we say, then, that this text does not speak truth? No, far from that. The light *does* come, and it comes at evening; but evening is the close of day, and the light may perhaps not beam forth until the day has entirely closed. Not upon this side of time may the blessed promise find its fulfillment. The foot may be dipped in the chill dark river before the heavenly light has shone upon the face. The eye may be blind to dearest faces and forms ere the Sun of Righteousness dawns, as in the natural world the darkest, coldest hour is that before the daybreak. The tongue may never be able to tell surviving loved ones how the shadows fled away when the dark valley was past till they have passed that darkness too. Yes, to the believer, true as God liveth, "at the evening time there *shall* be light;" if not in this world, then in a better! Bowing his head to pass under the dark portal, the believer lifts it up on the other side in the presence and the light of God. It is but a single step from the darkness of death into the light of immortality; and if the evening should remain gloomy to its very end, all the brighter will seem the glory when the latest breath has parted. I told you how that Christian poet passed away almost in despair; how the gloom that overshadowed his spirit endured all but to the end; but even in the last moment there came a wonderful change, and they tell us how even on his dead face there remained, till it was hidden forever, a look of bright, and beautiful, and sudden surprise; the light at evening had been long in coming, but oh! it had come at last.

There is something very touching about the story of that eminent teacher, the most eminent of his time, who, when his mind wandered in the weakness of the dying hour, fancied himself among his pupils, engaged in his accustomed work, and whose last words, when the shadow of death was falling deeper, were, "It grows dark, boys; you may go." There is something touching, too, in the parting scene of that great poet, dying as the sun was going down in its summer glory, who bade his friends raise him that he might see the light once more—open the window that he might look upon the setting sun again before his eyes should close upon the earthly light forever. And very strange it is, indeed, to stand, as some of us may have stood, in the chamber of death, and in the west to see the summer sunset blazing, and the golden rays shining upon the still face and the closed eyes which never shall open more till the sun has ceased to shine. But it is only to us who remain that the evening darkness is growing—only for us that the sun is going down. Oh, look on the fixed features of that disciple now asleep in Jesus, and think, as the prophet spake, "Thy sun shall no more go down, neither shall thy moon withdraw itself, for the Lord shall be thine everlasting light, and the days of thy mourning shall be ended." And oh! my readers, tell me, as the evening falls on you, but not on him; as the shadows deepen on you, but not on him; as the darkness gathers on you, but not on him, if now, at last, the glorious promise has not found its perfect fulfillment, that "at the evening time there shall be light."

"REMEMBER LOT'S WIFE."

THE disobedience of Lot's wife was not that she went to Sodom, but that she looked back. Doubtless she verily thought that she was pressing unto safety; but her heart was not right in her. She was disobedient in will, and in the hankerings and longings of the mind. . . . . She looked back, and that forbidden gaze betrayed a multitude of unchastened thoughts and a world of disobedience.—H. E. MANNING.

OLD AGE. (A PARABLE.)

SIEGFRIED, a farmer of ninety years of age, sat in his arm-chair, and saw not the day, for he was blind; yet he was patient, and thought, "Soon will the day of my redemption appear." It was now spring.

His grandson, Herman, came out of the field, and with joy told the old man of the fruitfulness of the year and the hopefulness of the crops.

The old farmer asked, "Have the trees already put forth their leaves?" The youth wondered at the question, and replied, "Long ago, dear grandpa. Yesterday I brought you a twig of blossoms, and a rose too."

Siegfried smiled and said, "Yes, my dear son, your yesterday and to-day are no more for me; and your flowers have lost their fragrance for me." Afterward he asked, "Do the nightingales and larks sing?" The youth leaned down to him, for he was deaf, and said, "Yes, dear grandpa; shall I not take you into the garden?"

The old man smiled, saying, "If you can lend me also your hearing; otherwise of what use will it be to me to be taken out?" A little after he said, "Go you out again, and bring me little Trude, that some one may be with me in my dark room." The youth replied, with faltering voice, "Ah! dearest grandpa, Trude is not at home."

"Where is she, then, the dear child?" asked Siegfried; and the young man replied, with choked voice, "She has been buried three months." The old man smiled and wept at the same time, and said, "Oh, yes; she is already at home, and it is time I follow her."

When the mother of the house, the old man's daughter, who had come into the chamber, heard this, she fell on the neck of the blind father, and wet his eyes with her tears; and Herman wept too, and took the old man's hand.

Siegfried then raised himself up and said, "Children, be not troubled, and let it not distress you that the world and time to me have vanished, and I have become a child. How should it be otherwise? I stand at the entrance of my Father's house, and my weak old age is the infancy of eternity."—F. W. KRUMMACHER.

CHRISTIAN PROGRESS.

CHRISTIAN progress is only possible in Christ. It is a very lofty thing to be a Christian, for a Christian is a man who is restoring God's likeness to his character, and therefore the apostle calls it a high calling. High as heaven is the calling wherewith we are called. But this very height makes it seem impracticable. It is natural to say, "All that was well enough for one so transcendently gifted as Paul to hope for, but I am no gifted man; I have no iron strength of mind; I have no sanguine hopefulness of character; I am disposed to look on the dark side of things; I am undetermined, weak, vacillating; and then I have a whole army of passions and follies to contend with." We have to remind such men of one thing they have forgotten. It is the high calling of God, if you will; but it is the high calling of God in Christ Jesus. What the world calls virtue is a name and a dream without Christ. The foundation of all human excellence must be laid deep in the blood of the Redeemer's cross and in the power of his resurrection. First let a man know that all his past is wrong and sinful, then let him fix his eye on the love of God in Christ loving him, even him the guilty one. Is there no strength in that? no power in the knowledge that all that is gone by is gone, and that a fresh, clear future is open? It is not the progress of virtue that God asks for, but progress in saintliness, empowered by hope and love.—F. W. ROBERTSON.

SUCH A ONE AS PAUL THE AGED.

AND what was Paul in the moment here represented? Verily an aged servant of his Master, but not retired from the scene of action. Paul, though grown old in the Lord's service, was still as hotly engaged as ever in the Lord's battle. Art thou such a one, my soul, as Paul was? Then learn from hence that, however many or however heavy former campaigns have been, there is no rest for thee this side Jordan, no more than for Paul; no winter quarters for the true soldiers of Jesus Christ. Until thy Captain undress thee for the grave, the holy armor in which he hath clad thee is not to be taken off. Art thou such a one as Paul the aged? Then, like Paul, see that thou art strong in the Lord, and in the power of his might. And how sweet the thought! Thy Jesus, who hath borne thee from the womb, and carried thee from the belly, knows well the burden of thy increasing years, and all the infirmities belonging to them, and will carry both thee and them. Yes, my soul, those very infirmities which the tenderest-hearted friend sometimes feels impatient at, and even thyself thou knowest not how to bear, Jesus feels, Jesus commiserates, Jesus will soften! He that hath carried all thy sins, carrieth also thy sorrows. Doth he not say so? Even to your old age I am he; and even to hoar hairs I will carry you. I have made, and I will bear; even I will carry, and will deliver you (Isaiah xlvi., 3, 4). Precious Lamb of God! henceforth I cast all my burdens upon thee. Thou hast never called thyself *I Am* for nothing. Thou hast indeed made me, and new-made me. Thou hast borne all my sins in thine own body on the tree. Art thou not both the Alpha and Omega, both the Author and Finisher of my salvation? Oh, yes, thou hast been every thing to me, and for me, from the womb of creation; borne me on eagles' wings; made me, and new-made me; redeemed me in a thousand redemptions, and been better to me than all my fears! What, indeed, hast thou not done for me? And now, then, being such a one as Paul the aged, shall I now doubt or now fear when every pain, and every cross, and every new assault from sin and Satan bid me go to Jesus? Oh! for grace ever to keep in view what thou hast said and done, and what thou hast promised. Yes, yes, it is enough; Jesus hath said, "Even to your old age I am he. The same I have been, the same I will ever be; I will never leave thee nor forsake thee." Shout, my soul, and cry out Hallelujah! He that hast been my first will be my last — my strength, my song, my salvation forever!—ROBERT HAWKER.

HAPPINESS OF AGE.

As ripe fruit is sweeter than green fruit, so is age sweeter than youth, provided the youth were grafted into Christ. As harvest-time is a brighter time than seed-time, so is age brighter than youth—that is, if youth were a good seed-time for good. As the completion of a work is more glorious than the beginning, so is age more glorious than youth—that is, if the foundation of the work of God were laid in youth. As sailing into port is a happier thing than the voyage, so is age happier than youth—that is, when the voyage from youth is made with Christ at the helm.—J. PULSFORD.

SIMPLE FAITH.

A CHRISTIAN friend, calling upon a poor old woman in Scotland, found her in great pain, and expressed sorrow at seeing her suffer so much. "Oh," said Jeannie, "it's just an answer to prayer. You see, I've lang prayed to be conformed to the image of Christ; and since this is the means, I've naething to do wi' the choosin' o' them. That's the end I seek. It is ours to aim at meetness for his presence, and to leave it to his wisdom to do his ain way wi' us. I would rather suffer than sin, ony day."—*Anon.*

JOB. (*A PARABLE.*)

IN Job's time there lived a prophet of the Lord, in the land of Uz, named Eliud, to whom came Joram, a friend of Job, and said, "The ways of the Lord are inscrutable; but wherefore must the righteous suffer so much? Behold, Job has lost all his possessions and goods; his children have been taken from him by death, and those who should console him torment him with reproaches and bitter disease; he himself is afflicted with disease, and is full of sores from the sole of his foot even to his head."

"The hand of the Lord has touched him," answered the prophet.

"And yet," pronounced Joram, "Job is pious, and fears God more than any one in the land. Did he not save the oppressed when they cried unto him, and the orphan who had none to help? Was he not a father to the poor, eyes to the blind, and feet to the lame? Righteousness was his garment; and the eye that saw him blessed Job, and pronounced him happy."

"Blessed is the man whom the Almighty disciplines," answered the prophet.

"Is not, then, the Almighty also the All-merciful?" said Joram. "Wherefore did he need discipline, who, converting God's gifts so kindly into blessings, maintained a godly walk and conversation before all the world?"

"That he might also have a conscience void of offense before God," answered the prophet.

"What other offering could Job yet bring to him?" asked Joram.

"The most difficult and most valuable," answered the prophet—"HIS WILL."—F. W. KRUMMACHER.

REACHING FORWARD.

LET each man put this question to himself: "Dare I look on?" With an earnest Christian, it is reaching forth to those things which are before. Progress ever. And then, just as we go to rest in this world tired, and wake up fresh and vigorous in the morning, so does the Christian go to sleep in the world's night, weary with the work of life, and then on the resurrection-day he wakes in his second and his brighter morning. It is well for a believer to look on. Dare you? Remember, out of Christ, it is not wisdom, but madness to look on. You must look back, for the longest and best day is either past or passing. It will be winter soon—desolate, uncheered, hopeless winter; old age, with its dreariness, and its disappointments, and its querulous broken-heartedness; and there is no second spring for you, no resurrection-morning blessedness to dawn on the darkness of your grave. God has only one method of salvation, "the Cross of Christ." God can have only one; for the Cross of Christ means death to evil, life to good. There is no other way to salvation but that, for that in itself is, and alone is, salvation. Out of Christ, therefore, it is woe to the man who reaches forth to the things which are before. To such I say, "My unhappy brethren, Omnipotence itself can not change the darkness of your destiny."—F. W. ROBERTSON.

THE WALK OF FAITH.

.... THIS walk by faith takes in all the minute circumstances of every day's history; a walking EVERY STEP by faith, a looking above trials, above necessities, above perplexities, above improbabilities, above impossibilities, above all second causes, and, in the face of difficulties and discouragements, going forward, leaning upon God. If the Lord were to roll the Red Sea before us, and marshal the Egyptians behind us, and, thus hemming us in on every side, should yet bid us advance, it would be the duty and the privilege of faith instantly to obey, believing that, ere our feet touched the water, God, in our extremity, would divide the sea, and take us dry-shod over it. This is the only holy and happy life of a believer; if he for a moment leave this path, and attempt to walk BY SIGHT, difficulties will throng around him, troubles will multiply, the smallest trials will become heavy crosses, temptations to depart from the single and upright path will increase in number and power, the heart will sicken at disappointment, the spirit will be grieved, and God will be disappointed.—MARY WINSLOW.

"ONE IN CHRIST."

I HAVE seen a field here and a field there stand thick with corn; a hedge or two has separated them. At the proper seasons the reapers entered; soon the earth was disburdened, and the grain was conveyed to its destined resting-place, where, blended together in the barn or in the stack, it could not be known that a hedge had ever separated this corn from that. Thus it is with the Church. Here it grows, as it were, in different fields, and even, it may be, separated by different hedges. By-and-by, when the harvest is come, all God's wheat shall be gathered into the garner, without one single mark to distinguish that once they differed in outward circumstantials of form and order.—A. M. TOPLADY.

A PSALM FOR THE AGED.—THE LXXIst.

VER. 1–3. The old man, cast down by the visitations of divine Providence, appears before his God. He is supported by the promise of the Lord that those who trust in him shall never be put to confusion, and his faith, confirmed by the experience of his whole life, that the Lord is indeed a rock and a fortress.

Ver. 4–8. He has a solid foundation—the experience of a long life. He has clung to faith and hope throughout the entire period of his existence —even from his youth, when lightsomeness presents so powerful an obstacle to their exertion. His experience is of an extraordinary kind; he is as a wonder unto many; and the excellence of his experience arises from having sought in the Lord his only refuge. He did not, like most men, recognize the hand of God only when in an extraordinary manner it became manifest in life, but his eye of faith regards the ordinary works of God as miracles. The translation from his mother's womb to the light of day is to him an object of praise. . . . . Is not the reason of our finding so little to praise to be sought in our having no eyes for his daily mercies? The Psalmist *has* eyes for the daily mercies of the

Lord, and therefore his mouth is daily full of the praise of the Lord.

Ver. 9–13. If God did help in the time of youth and manhood, when our own strength aided us to overcome many difficulties, how much more will *his* strength deliver us when ours is gone—especially when the wicked challenge his mighty arm! For God will never suffer it to be said that he forsakes those who all their life long have not forsaken him.

Ver. 14, 15. But, whatever may happen, the Psalmist will not cease to persevere even in the night of tribulation. Though unable to proclaim the salvation of God as the result of actual present experience, he does it by *faith* and hope. He is sure that the continuous flow of his most ardent praise is always greatly surpassed by his salvation.

Ver. 16. Weak in himself, his faith assures him of strength through the strength of the Lord God. And as those who wait upon the Lord shall renew their strength, and mount up with wings as eagles, so the *old man* is seen walking in that strength which comes from above. The praise which youth bestows on earthly goods, because still *unacquainted* with their insufficiency, lies far behind him. The praise which manhood, in the proud consciousness of its own strength, bestows on the strength of man, he has seen turned to shame. Of all things which men are wont to praise in old age, one only is left as praiseworthy—the *righteousness and goodness* of the Lord. This is the proper employment of old age; the supports of earth must diminish in our estimate in the measure as we recede from them.

Ver. 17–19. He regards it as the chief concern of his life to proclaim the wondrous works of God; if spared any longer on earth, that shall be the end of his life. Are there better preachers of the works of God to be found than hoary parents in the circle of their children, or grandparents in that of their grandchildren?

Ver. 20, 21. The public sufferings of the nation seem to have brought low into the dust *his* greatness, but he hopes to share the elevation of his people.

Ver. 22–24. *We* think it a lovely sight to see an old man spend his days in singing the praise of God with trembling lips to the notes of the harp, and there is no more beauteous sight to God; and the notes of that harp ascend up to the highest heavens. Faith did inspire the pious old man with his confidence; his future songs of praise became therefore the foundation of his hope.—A. THOLUCK.

OBLIVION OF THE PAST.

Up to a certain period of life it is the tendency of man to look forward. There is a marvelous prodigality with which we throw away our present happiness when we are young, which belongs to those who feel that they are rich in happiness, and never expect to be bankrupts. It almost seems one of the signatures of our immortality that we squander time as if there were a dim consciousness that we are in possession of an eternity of it; but as we arrive at middle age it is the tendency of man to look back. To a man of middle life, existence is no longer a dream, but a reality. He has not much more new to look forward to, for the character of his life is generally fixed by that time. His profession, his home, his occupations will be, for the most part, what they are now. He will make few new acquaintances—no new friends. It is the solemn thought connected with middle age that life's last business is begun in earnest; and it is then, midway between the cradle and the grave, that a man begins to look back, and marvels with a kind of remorseful feeling that he let the days of youth go by so half enjoyed. It is the pensive autumn feeling; it is the sensation of half sadness that we experience when the longest day of the year is past, and every day that follows is shorter, and the lights fainter, and the feebler shadows tell that Nature is hastening with gigantic footsteps to her winter grave. So does man look back upon his youth. When the first gray hairs become visible, when the unwelcome truth fastens itself upon the mind that a man is no longer going up the hill, but down, and that the sun is already westering, he looks back on things behind. Now this is a natural feeling, but is it the high Christian feeling? In the language of the text (Philippians iii., **13, 14**), we may assuredly answer No. We who have an inheritance incorruptible and undefiled, and that fadeth not away, what have we to do with things past? When we were children, we thought as children. But now there lies before us manhood, with its earnest work; and then old age, and then the grave, and then home. And so manhood in the Christian's life is a better thing than boyhood, because it is a riper thing; and old age ought to be a brighter, and a calmer, and a more serene thing than manhood. This is a second youth for man, better and holier than his first, if he will look on and not back. There is a peculiar simplicity of heart and a touching singleness of purpose in Christian old age, which has ripened gradually and not fitfully. It is then that to the wisdom of the serpent is added the harmlessness of the dove; it is then that to the firmness of manhood is joined almost the gentleness of womanhood; it is then that the somewhat austere and sour character of growing strength, moral and intellectual, mellows into the rich ripeness of old age, made sweet and tolerant by experience; it is then that man returns to first principles. There comes a love more pure and deep than the boy could ever feel; there comes a conviction, with a strength beyond that which the boy could ever know, that the earliest lesson of life is infinite, Christ is all in all.—F. W. ROBERTSON.

SUSPENSE.

SUSPENSE has been one of the most trying features of my case. Just as I have unclasped my hand from my dear Ernest's; just as I have let go my almost frantic hold of my darling children; just as heaven opened before me, and I fancied my weariness over and my wanderings done, just then almost every alarming symptom would disappear, and life recall me from the threshold of heaven itself. Thus I have been emptied from vessel to vessel, till I have learned that he only is truly happy who has no longer a choice of his own, and lies passive in God's hands.—MRS. E. PRENTISS, "*Stepping Heavenward.*"

CHRISTIAN PERSEVERANCE.

THEN I saw in my dream that the Interpreter took Christian by the hand, and led him into a place where was a fire burning against a wall, and one standing by it, always casting much water upon it to quench it; yet did the fire burn higher and better.

Then said Christian, "What means this?" The Interpreter answered, "This fire is the work of grace that is wrought in the heart; he that casts water upon it to extinguish and put it out is the devil; but in that thou seest the fire, notwithstanding, burn higher and better, thou shalt also see the reason of that." So he led him about to the back side of the wall, where he saw a man with a vessel of oil in his hand, of which he did also continually cast (but secretly) into the fire.

Then said Christian, "What means this?" The Interpreter said, "This is Christ, who continually, with the oil of his grace, maintains the work already begun in the heart, by the means of which, notwithstanding what the devil can do, the souls of his people prove gracious still. And in that thou sawest that the man stood behind the wall to maintain the fire, this is to teach thee that it is hard for the tempted to see how this work of grace is maintained in the soul.—JOHN BUNYAN.

NECESSITY OF CHRISTIAN PERSEVERANCE.

No grace, no, not even the most sparkling and shining grace, can bring a man to heaven of itself without perseverance; not faith, which is the champion of grace, if it be faint and fail; nor love, which is the nurse of grace, if it decline and wax cold; nor humility, which is the adorner and beautifier of grace, if it continue not to the end; not obedience, not repentance, not patience, no, nor any other grace, except they have their perfect work. It is not enough to begin well except we end well. Manasseh and Paul began ill, but ended well; Judas and Demas began well, but ended ill. — THOMAS BROOKS.

GOD UNCHANGEABLE.

God asks no rest and requires no slumber, but holds straight on without weariness; wearing out the ages, himself unworn; changing all things, himself without variableness or shadow of turning. God is like the sun at noon, that casts down straight rays, and so throws down the shadows upon the ground underneath each tree; but he never, like the sun, goes westward toward his setting, turning all shadows from under the trees, and slanting them upon the ground. God stands in eternal fullness, like a sun that knows neither morning, nor evening, nor night, but only noon, and noon always.—H. W. BEECHER.

ENDURING TO THE END.

THINK of Christ's appointed work, the greatest that ever was to be done on the earth; so great as to be a counteraction to all the sins of all the saved! and at an awful cost of endurance. What toils, what grievances, what terrors (as to his humanity) attends his mighty task! But if he had been "wearied," and left but one thing undone! If he had shrunk and failed, what sensation in heaven—hell—earth! Let his followers advert to that when tempted to shrink from service, and to say it is too much. When this repugnance arises, go and look at him! Even imagine as if any given Christian service had been to be performed in his presence—under his inspection, would you then be weary? He is a grand, transcendent example to show that a good work must be gone through with; to constitute it such, the conclusion is indispensable: "He that endureth to the end shall be saved;" "He that looketh back is not fit for the kingdom of God."—JOHN FOSTER.

THE HOLY JERUSALEM.

Jerusalem, my happy home,
    Name ever dear to me,
When shall my labors have an end,
    In joy, and peace, and thee?

When shall these eyes thy heaven-built walls
    And pearly gates behold?
Thy bulwarks with salvation strong,
    And streets of shining gold?

There happier bowers than Eden's bloom,
    Nor sin nor sorrow know;
Bless'd seats! through rude and stormy scenes
    I onward press to you.

Why should I shrink from pain and woe,
    Or feel at death dismay?
I've Canaan's goodly land in view,
    And realms of endless day.

Apostles, martyrs, prophets there
    Around my Savior stand;
And soon my friends in Christ below
    Will join the glorious band.

Jerusalem, my happy home!
    My soul still pants for thee;
Then shall my labors have an end
    When I thy joys shall see.

LOOKING WESTWARD.

"I LOVE the western sky," said one who was afflicted in spirit; "it seems to carry my thoughts away to another country and a brighter morrow."

There is often something so unearthly about the sky at sunset; those golden rays, darting from behind the purple clouds, how full they seem of hope and promise! and on stormy evenings, when the "sun sets weeping," and gives prospect of a dreary day to come, I love to think of those distant countries where every day he shines as yesterday in cloudless splendor; and the thought of those distant countries leads me onward to "the land which is very far off," where this earthly sun will have ceased to rise and set, and where the glory of the Lord will be the light in which we shall live, and move, and have our being.—*Anon.*

TESTIMONY OF AN AGED CHRISTIAN.

I LEAVE it as my testimony (writes Isabella Graham, in the sixtieth year of her age) that God has been a father to the fatherless, a husband to the widow, the stranger's shield, and orphan's stay. Even to hoar years and old age he has carried me, and *not one good word has failed* of all that he has promised. "He has done all things well;" and at this day I am richer and happier than ever I was in my life. Not that I am yet made free from sin; that is still my burden; want of love and gratitude, indolence in commanded duty, self-will, and nestling in the creature. But my heart's wish and earnest desire is conformity. The bent of my will is for God, and, if my heart deceive me not, my God is the centre of my best affections. This God is my God. He will guide me even unto death, through death, and be my portion through eternity.

MILTON ON HIS BLINDNESS.

When I consider how my light is spent
Ere half my days, in this dark world and wide,
And that one talent which is death to hide,
Lodg'd with me useless, though my soul more bent
To serve therewith my Master, and present
My true account, lest he return and chide:
"Doth God exact day-labor, light denied?"
I fondly ask. But Patience, to prevent
That murmur, soon replies, "God doth need
Neither man's work nor his own gifts; who best
Bear his mild yoke, they serve him best: his state
Is kingly; thousands at his bidding speed,
And post o'er land and ocean without rest;
They also serve who only stand and wait."—Milton.

THE NIGHT-WATCH.

Watch ye, therefore; for ye know not when the master of the house cometh, at even, or at midnight, or at the cock-crowing, or in the morning; lest coming suddenly he find you sleeping. And what I say unto you I say unto all, Watch.—Mark xiii., 35-37.

THE Church must fulfill her night-watch. Whether long or short, perilous or easy, she must fulfill it. It is WATCHING to which she is specially called; and sadly will she belie her profession, as well as disobey her Lord, if she WATCHES not. She need not think to substitute other duties for this, as more needful, more important, or more in character. She dare not say, "I love, I believe, I pray, I praise, why should I also WATCH? Will not these do instead of watching, or is not watching included in these?" Her Lord has bidden her WATCH, and no other duty, no other grace, can be a substitute or excuse for this.

She is to believe; but that is not all—she is also to WATCH. She is to rejoice; but that is not all—she is also to WATCH. She is to love; but that is not all—she is also to WATCH. She is to wait; but that is not all—she is also to WATCH. She is to long; but that is not all—she is also to WATCH. This is to be her special attitude, and nothing can compensate for it. By this she is to be known in all ages as the watching one. By this the world is to be made to feel the difference between itself and her. By this she is specially to show how truly she feels herself to be a stranger here.

Men ask her, "Why stand ye gazing up into heaven?" Her reply is, "I am watching." Men taunt her, and say, "Why this unrestfulness?" Her reply is, "I am watching." Men think it strange that she runs not with them to the same excess of riot (1 Peter iv., 4). She tells them, "I am watching." They ask her to come forth and join their gayety, to come forth and sing their songs, to come forth and taste their pleasures, that thus they may teach her to forget her sorrows. She refuses, saying, "I dare not; I am watching." The scoffer mocks her, and says, "Where is the promise of his coming?" She heeds not, but continues watching, and clasps her hope more firmly.—H. Bonar.

STRENGTH SUFFICIENT FOR THE DAY.

Oh, ask not thou, "How shall I bear
  The burden of to-morrow?"
Sufficient for to-day its care,
  Its evil, and its sorrow;
God imparteth by the way
  Strength sufficient for the day.—*Anon.*

THE FINISHING OF THE TEMPLE.

SUPPOSE, then, the period arrived when the scaffolding is struck down and the rubbish moved away; that is, suppose this earth, which was the stage for its erection, now moved from beneath it, and the wicked, the refuse of mankind, cast far away out of sight. Conceive that you see nothing but the building. Lo! it stands high in view, for the admiration of the surrounding universe. "Walk about Zion, and go round about her; tell the towers thereof; mark ye well her bulwarks; consider her palaces, that ye may tell it to the generation following." What is her foundation? The Rock of Ages! Who is her inhabitant? Her inhabitant is God! Not a flaw nor a blemish is to be seen; every stone is in its proper place, and all contributing to the beauty of the whole! No want of symmetry in the general outline plan, nothing imperfect in the execution of each part. Behold, it stands an eternal monument to the glory of God—of his power, and wisdom, and grace! It is all bright and glorious, wherever you take your view of it; radiating in every part with the beamings of divine glory! Her light is like unto a stone most precious, even like a jasper! It is a temple of souls! Every stone is a living soul—blood-bought spirit! Every one is a chosen warrior, who has fought his battle in his days, and has conquered! They have come out of great tribulation to be stones for this building. Affliction gave them their polish, and the cement which unites them is love.—H. MARTYN.

MY TONGUE SHALL SPEAK OF THY PRAISE.

THE middle, we may observe, and the safest, and the fairest, and the most conspicuous places in cities are usually deputed for the erection of statues and monuments dedicated to the memory of worthy men, who have nobly deserved of their country. In like manner should we, in the heart and centre of our soul, in the best and highest apartments thereof, in the places most exposed to ordinary observation, and most secure from the invasions of worldly care, erect lively representations and lasting memorials unto the divine bounty; constantly attending to which we may be disposed to gratitude. Not one blessing, not the least favorable passage of providence, ought to perish with us, though long since passed, and removed out of the sphere of present sense. If a grateful affection lies in our hearts, it will respire through our mouths, and discover itself in the motion of our lips. Neither shall we content ourselves in lonesome tunes and private soliloquies to whisper out the divine praises, but shall loudly excite and provoke others to a melodious consonancy with us; we shall—we, the sweet singers of Israel—cite and invoke heaven and earth, the celestial choir of angels, the several estates and generations of men, the numberless company of all the creatures, to assist and join in concert with us in celebrating the worthy deeds, and magnifying the glorious name of our most mighty Creator, of our most bountiful Benefactor.—J. BARROW.

EVENING OFTEN PLEASANTER THAN MORNING.

OFTENTIMES we look forward with forebodings to THE TIME OF OLD AGE, forgetful that at eventide it shall be light. To many saints, old age is the choicest season of their lives. A balmier air fans the mariner's cheek as he nears the shores of immortality, fewer waves ruffle his sea, quiet reigns —deep, still, and solemn. From the altar of age the flashes of the fire of youth are gone, but the more real flame of earnest feeling remains. The pilgrims have reached the land Beulah, that happy country whose days are as the days of heaven upon earth. Angels visit it, celestial gales blow over it, flowers of Paradise grow in it, and the air is filled with seraphic music. Some dwell here for years, and others come to it but a few hours before their departure, but it is an Eden upon earth. We may well long for the time when we shall recline in its shady groves, and be satisfied with hope until the time of fruition comes. The setting sun seems larger than when aloft in the sky, and a splendor of glory tinges all the clouds which surround his going down. Pain breaks not the calm of the sweet twilight of age, for strength made perfect in weakness bears up with patience under it all. Ripe fruits of choice experience are gathered as the rare repast of life's evening, and the soul prepares itself for rest. The Lord's people shall also enjoy light in THE HOUR OF DEATH. Unbelief laments; the shadows fall, the night is coming, existence is ending. Ah! no, cries faith, the night is far spent, the true day is at hand. Light is come—the light of immortality, the light of a Father's countenance. Gather up thy feet in the bed; see the waiting band of spirits! Angels waft thee away. Farewell, beloved one; thou art gone; thou wavest thine hand. Ah! now it is light. The pearly gates are open, the golden streets shine in the jasper light. We cover our eyes, but thou beholdest the unseen. Adieu, brother; thou hast light at eventide, such as we have not yet.—CHARLES SPURGEON.

TAKING REST.

And he cometh the third time, and saith unto them, Sleep on now, and take your rest: it is enough, the hour is come; behold, the Son of man is betrayed into the hands of sinners. Rise up, let us go; lo, he that betrayeth me is at hand.—Mark xiv., 41, 42.

Now, the broad general lesson which we gain from this is not hard to read. It is that a Christian is to be forever rousing himself to recognize the duties which lie before him NOW. In Christ the motto is ever this: "Let us be going." Let me speak to the conscience of some one. Perhaps yours is a very remorseful past—a foolish, frivolous, disgraceful, frittered past. Well, Christ says, "My servant, be sad, but no languor; there is work to be done for me yet. Rise up! be going!" Oh, my brethren, Christ takes your wretched remnants of life, the feeble pulses of a heart which has spent its best hours, not for him, but for self and for enjoyment, and, in his strange love, he condescends to accept them.

Wake to the opportunities that yet remain. Ten years of life—five years—one year—say you have only that. Will you sleep that away because you have already slept too long? Eternity is crying out to you louder and louder as you near its brink, "Arise! be going." Count your resources; learn what you are not fit for, and give up wishing for it; learn what you can do, and do it with the energy of a man. That is the great lesson of this passage.

Christ impressed two things on his apostles' minds: 1. THE DUTY OF CHRISTIAN EARNESTNESS—"Rise!" 2. THE DUTY OF CHRISTIAN ENERGY—"Let us be going."

Christ roused them to earnestness when he said "Rise!" A short, sharp, rousing call. They were to start up and wake to the realities of their position. The guards were on them; their Master was about to be led away to doom. That was an awakening which would make men spring to their feet in earnest. Brethren, goodness and earnestness are nearly the same thing. In the language in which the Bible was written there was one word which expressed them both; what we translate a good man, in Greek is literally "earnest." The Greeks felt that to be earnest was nearly identical with being good. But, however, there is a day in life when a man must be earnest, but it does not follow that he will be good. "Behold, the Bridegroom cometh; go ye out to meet him." That is a sound that will thunder through the most fast-locked slumber, and rouse men whom sermons can not rouse. But that will not make them holy. Earnestness of LIFE, brethren, that is goodness. Wake in death you MUST, for it is an earnest thing to die. Shall it be this, I pray you? Shall it be the voice of death which first says "Arise!" at the very moment when it says "Sleep on forever?" Shall it be the bridal train sweeping by, and the shutting of the doors, and the discovery that the lamp is gone out? Shall THAT be the first time you know that it is an earnest thing to live? Let us feel that we have been DOING; learn what time is—sliding from you, and not stopping when you stop; learn what sin is; learn what "*never*" is. Awake, thou that sleepest.—F. W. ROBERTSON.

GOD OUR PORTION.

As the scattered rays of light are all included in the focus, as the fountain contains the streams, as the object reflected is prior to and nobler than the different reflections of it, so all finite and created good is contained in him who is the supreme good; all earthly excellence is but the partial emanation, the more or less bright reflection of the Great Original. To have a portion, therefore, in God, is to possess that which includes in itself all created good. The man who is in possession of some great masterpiece in painting or sculpture need not envy others who have only casts or copies of it. The original plate or stereotype is more valuable than any impressions or engravings thrown off from it; and he who owns the former, owns that which includes, is capable of producing all the latter. Surveying the wonders of creation, or even with the Word of inspiration in his hand, the Christian can say, "Glorious though these things be, to me belongs that which is more glorious far. The streams are precious, but I have a Fountain; the vesture is beautiful, but the Weaver is mine; the portrait in its every lineament is lovely, but that Great Original, whose beauty it but feebly depicts, is mine—my own. God is my portion, the Lord is mine inheritance. To me belongs all actual and all possible good, all created and uncreated beauty, all that eye hath seen or imagination conceived; and more than that, for eye hath not seen, nor ear heard, nor hath it entered into the heart of man to conceive what God hath prepared for them that love him. All things and beings, all that life reveals or death conceals, every thing within the boundless possibilities of creating wisdom and power, is mine, for God, the Creator and Fountain of all, is mine."—JOHN CAIRD.

LIVING BY FAITH.

My faith looks up to Thee,
Thou Lamb of Calvary,
   Savior divine!
Now hear me while I pray;
Take all my guilt away;
O let me from this day
   Be wholly Thine!

May Thy rich grace impart
Strength to my fainting heart,
   My zeal inspire!
As Thou hast died for me,
O may my love to Thee
Pure, warm, and changeless be,
   A living fire!

While life's dark maze I tread,
And griefs around me spread,
   Be Thou my Guide!
Bid darkness turn to day,
Wipe sorrow's tear away,
Nor let me ever stray
   From Thee aside.

When ends life's transient dream,
When death's cold sullen stream

Shall o'er me roll;
Bless'd Savior! then in love
Fear and distrust remove;
O bear me safe above,
A ransomed soul.—Ray Palmer.

THE BITTER WITH THE SWEET.

There was once a slave called Æsop. . . . . A courtier, to whom the king had praised Æsop for his obedience, answered, "Well may he love thee, for thou loadest him with all he can desire; but try him with some painful thing, and then thou wilt see what his love is worth." Now in the king's garden there grew a nauseous lemon, the stench of which was such that few could bear to approach it. The king told Æsop to go and cut one of the lemons, and eat every bit of it. Æsop accordingly cut the fruit, the largest he could find, and ate it every bit. The wily courtier said to him, "How can you bear to swallow such a nauseous fruit?" He answered, "My dear master has done nothing but load me with benefits every day of my life, and shall I not, for his sake, eat one bitter fruit without complaint, or asking the reason why?"—*Anon.*

MOTIVES TO PATIENCE.

LET us consider the motives that should persuade us to be patient as Christians. Far as patience includes meekness *under wrongs of our fellow-men,* we must forgive, or we may not hope ourselves before God to be forgiven. Christ laid the axe where no earthly reformer would have dared to place it, at the root of revengefulness. The Christian law of morals gropes in the heart of every petitioner oft as he prays, and it bids him pray without ceasing. We are warned again that in yielding to impatience and anger we cease to possess our own souls; and, as is darkly intimated, Satan takes hold of the deserted rudder and wields the ungoverned helm, and drives before him the infuriated and imbruted man. Cain, had he but curbed his impatient envy, need not have bequeathed his name and warning to all times as the first murderer and fratricide; and Christ told us that he who hates his brother in his heart is already, in the germ and essence, a murderer; the first act of Cain's sin is begun within HIM.

Far, again, as patience includes submission *to the divine appointments,* let us remark that our trials are lessened by serene meekness and resignation.

God lightens and removes them more early, and they do not so deeply wound and empoison the soul. But he who frets and fights against God, in the language of ancient prophecy, like a bullock unaccustomed to the yoke, drives the deeper into his own flesh the goad against which he vainly kicks.

We are to remember, too, the necessity of this grace to success and influence with our fellow-men. It is the patient perseverance in well-doing that builds up consistency, and influence, and weight of character. We are, again, all to remember our own unworthiness before God, and our liability to pay ten thousand talents, for which infinite and endless torments would be no sufficient amends, ere, in our fretfulness, we chide man harshly, or murmur bitterly against our God and his providence. Nor is it unfitting that we remember how much of mercy and kindness there is in God's allotments; and how, by the general presence of affliction, God has provided in every sphere, the most obscure and secluded even, a scene where he may be glorified, and where the power of his religion and grace may be illustrated; and how, out of such trials meekly borne, he weaves the confessor's wreath and the martyr's crown, and makes the blood of his slain servants the seed of his Church, whilst the wrath of man is forced to praise him, and the remainder of wrath is restrained.

Are we tempted to impatience and anger with some erring and injurious fellow-mortal? Let us test the old Puritan dilemma in such a case. The offender is a Christian or a child of hell. If already, or yet to become the first, we shall in heaven not remember with pleasure revengeful and retaliatory wrongs against one of our brethren and of Christ's people. If an enemy of God and an heir of his wrath, he is soon to endure more than man can inflict, and the bar to which he is rushing is one at which strict justice and unforgetting memory preside. Let us dread snatching into our hands the sceptre of him who has said "Vengeance is *mine*," and then pronouncing rash and false judgment, rooting up the wheat with the tares, and making sad the heart of the righteous, whom God has not made sad. The question of the Judge of all the earth to the over-fretted patriarch has much of dread significance: "Wilt thou also DISANNUL MY JUDGMENT? Wilt thou condemn me that thou mayest be righteous?" (Job xl., 8). Much of our impatience is a virtual disannulling of God's decisions, and a distinct intimation that his forbearance is wanting in righteousness.—WILLIAM R. WILLIAMS.

GOD THE ONLY DEPENDENCE OF THE SOUL.

You are tried alone; alone you pass into the desert; alone you must bear and conquer in the agony; alone you must be sifted by the world; there are moments known only to a man's own self, when he sits by the poisoned springs of existence, "yearning for a morrow which shall free him from the strife." . . . . Let life be a life of faith; do not go timorously about, inquiring what others think, what others believe, and what others say. . . . . God is near you. Throw yourself fearlessly upon him. Trembling mortal, there is an unknown might within your soul which will wake when you command it. . . . . Every son of man who would attain the true end of his being must be baptized with fire.— F. W. Robertson.

"YE SHALL REAP IF YE FAINT NOT."

In every trial of every kind, for every one of us, is it not the same? The answer may come sooner or later; the well of joy for which the heart yearns may be opened early in the pilgrimage or not till near the mountain top. But surely, unfailingly, we are drawing near the answer to all our prayers.— *Anon.*

GLORY OF THE CROSS.

THE Cross of Christ is an object of such incomparable brightness that it spreads a glory round it to all the nations of the earth, all the corners of the universe, all the generations of time, and all the ages of eternity. The greatest actions or events that ever happened on earth filled with their splendor and influence but a moment of time and a point of space; the splendor of this great object fills immensity and eternity. If we take a right view of its glory, we shall see it contemplated with attention, spreading influence, and attracting looks from times past, present, and to come; heaven, earth, and hell, angels, saints, devils. We shall see it to be both the object of the deepest admiration of the creatures and the perfect approbation of the infinite Creator; we shall see the best part of mankind, the Church of God, for four thousand years looking forward to it before it happened; new generations yet unborn rising up to admire and honor it in continual succession, till time shall be no more; innumerable multitudes of angels and saints looking back to it with holy transports to the remotest ages of eternity. Other glories decay by length of time; if the splendor of this object change, it will be only by increasing. The visible sun will spend his beams in process of time, and, as it were, grow dim with age; this object hath a rich stock of beams, which eternity can not exhaust. If saints and angels grow in knowledge, the splendor of this object will be increasing; 'tis unbelief that intercepts its beams; unbelief takes place only on earth; there is no such thing in heaven or in hell. It will be a great part of future blessedness to remember the object that purchased it, and of future punishment to remember the object that offered deliverance from it; it will add to the beams of love in heaven, and make the flames of hell burn more fiercely; its beams will not only adorn the regions of light, but pierce the regions of darkness; it will be the desire of the saints in light, and the great eyesore of the prince of darkness and his subjects.—J. MACLAURIN.

A HUMBLE HOME.

ARE you not surprised to find how independent of money. peace of conscience is, and how much happiness can be condensed into the humblest home? A cottage will not hold the bulky furniture and sumptuous accommodations of a mansion; but, if God be there, a cottage will hold as much happiness as might stock a palace.—JAMES HAMILTON.

TAKING UP THE CROSS.

Jesus, I my cross have taken,
  All to leave and follow Thee;
Destitute, despised, forsaken,
  Thou from hence my all shalt be:
Perish every fond ambition,
  All I've sought, or hoped, or known;
Yet how rich is my condition!
  God and heaven are still my own!

Let the world despise and leave me,
  They have left my Savior too;
Human hearts and looks deceive me;
  Thou art not, like them, untrue;
And, whilst Thou shalt smile upon me
  God of wisdom, love, and might,
Foes may hate, and friends may shun me;
  Show Thy face, and all is bright!

Go, then, earthly fame and treasure!
  Come disaster, scorn, and pain!
In Thy service pain is pleasure,
  With Thy favor loss is gain!
I have called Thee Abba, Father!
  I have stayed my heart on Thee!
Storms may howl, and clouds may gather,
  All must work for good to me.

Man may trouble and distress me,
   'Twill but drive me to Thy breast;
Life with trials hard may press me,
   Heaven will bring me sweeter rest;
O, 'tis not in grief to harm me,
   While Thy love is left to me!
O, 'twere not in joy to charm me,
   Were that joy unmixed with Thee!

Take, my soul, thy full salvation;
   Rise o'er sin, and fear, and care;
Joy to find, in every station,
   Something still to do or bear:
Think what Spirit dwells within thee!
   What a Father's smile is thine!
What a Savior died to win thee!
   Child of heaven, shouldst thou repine?

Haste then on from grace to glory,
   Armed by faith, and winged by prayer;
Heaven's eternal day's before thee,
   God's own hand shall guide thee there!
Soon shall close thy earthly mission,
   Swift shall pass thy pilgrim days;
Hope soon change to glad fruition,
   Faith to sight, and prayer to praise!

                   HENRY FRANCIS LYTE.

UPHELD BY THE DIVINE HAND.

THE almighty Architect stretches out the north, and its whole starry train, over the empty space; he hangs the earth and all the ethereal globes upon nothing, yet are their foundations laid so sure that they can never be moved at any time.

No unfit representation to the sincere Christian of his final perseverance; but such as points out the cause that effects it, and constitutes the pledge which ascertains it. His nature is all enfeebled; he is not able of himself to think a good thought; he has no visible safeguard, nor any sufficiency of his own, and yet whole legions of formidable enemies are combined to compass his ruin. The world lays unnumbered snares for his feet; the devil is incessantly urging the siege by a multitude of fiery darts or wily temptations; the flesh, like a perfidious inmate, under color of friendship and a specious pretense of pleasure, is always forward to betray his integrity; but, amid all these threatening circumstances of personal weakness and imminent danger, an invisible aid is his defense.

"I will uphold thee," says the blessed God, "with the right hand of my righteousness." Oh, comfortable truth! The arm which fixes the stars in their courses, and guides the planets in theirs, is stretched out to preserve the heirs of salvation.

"My sheep are mine; and they shall never perish, neither shall any pluck THEM OUT OF MY HAND" (John x., 27, 28). What words are these! And did they come from him who hath all power in heaven and earth? And were they spoken to every unfeigned though feeble follower of the great Shepherd? Then Omnipotence itself must be vanquished before they can be destroyed, either by the seductions of frauds or the assaults of violence.

If you ask, therefore, "What security we have of enduring to the end, and continuing faithful unto death?" The very same that established the heavens, and settles the ordinances of the universe. Can these be thrown into confusion? Then may the true believer draw back unto perdition. Can the sun be dislodged from his sphere, and rush lawlessly through the sky? Then, and then only, can the faith of God's elect be overthrown finally. Be of good courage, then. O my soul, rely on those divine succors which are so solemnly stipulated, so faithfully promised. Though thy grace be languid as the glimmering spark, though the overflowings of corruption threaten it with total extinction, yet, since the great Jehovah has undertaken to cherish the dim principle, many waters can not quench it, nor the floods drown it. Nay, though it were feeble as the smoking flax, Almighty goodness stands engaged to augment the heat, to raise the fire, and feed the flame, till it beam forth a lamp of immortal glory in the heavens.—JAMES HERVEY.

ENDURING UNTO THE END.

THE philosopher being asked, in his old age, why he did not give over his practice and take his ease, answered, "When a man is to run a race of forty furlongs, would you have him sit down at the nine and thirtieth, and so lose the prize?" We do not keep a good fire all day, and let it go out in the evening, when it is coldest, but then rather lay on more fuel, that we may go warm to bed. Thus he that slakes the heat of zeal in his age will go cold to bed, and in a worse case to his grave. To continue in giving glory to Christ is no less requisite than to begin; though the beginning be more than half, yet the end is more than all. The God of all perfection looks that our ULTIMUM VITÆ should be his OPTIMUM GLORIÆ; that our last works should be our best works; that we should persevere in goodness to the end.—SPENCER.

ALL FROM CHRIST.

IF ever thou look for sound comfort on earth and salvation in heaven, unglue thyself from the world and the vanities of it; put thyself upon thy Lord and Savior Jesus Christ; leave not till thou findest thyself firmly united to him, so as thou art become a limb of that Body whereof he is head, a spouse of that husband, a branch of that stem, a stone laid upon that foundation. Look not, therefore, for any blessing out of him; and in, and by, and from him look for all blessings. Let him be thy life, and wish not to live longer than thou art quickened by him. Find him thy wisdom, righteousness, sanctification, redemption; thy riches, thy strength, thy glory. Apply unto thyself all that thy Savior is or hath done. Wouldst thou have the graces of God's Spirit? fetch them from his anointing. Wouldst thou have power against spiritual enemies? fetch it from his sovereignty. Wouldst thou have redemption? fetch it from his passion. Wouldst thou have absolution? fetch it from his perfect innocence; freedom from the curse? fetch it from his cross; satisfaction? fetch it from his sacrifice; cleansing from sin? fetch it from his blood; mortification? fetch it from his grave; newness of life? fetch it from his resurrection; right to heaven? fetch it from his purchase; audience to all thy suits? fetch it from his intercession. Wouldst thou have salvation? fetch it from his session at the right hand of Majesty. Wouldst thou have all? fetch it from him who is one Lord, one God, and Father of all; who is above all, through all, and in all."—Joseph Hall.

MAGNETISM OF FAITH.

I HAVE observed at sea, and it is often noticed by mariners, that in the beginning of bad weather, before the storm was fairly set in and fixed in its course, the needle in the compass-box was considerably affected, and there was unusual oscillation, probably through the changing or disturbance of the atmosphere's electric forces. But, after the gale was fairly formed or at its height, the needle became true to its polarity. In like manner is it with a mind under trial that has been once thoroughly magnetized by the grace of God, so as to have the law of divine polarity impressed upon it, making it to turn always to the Pole-star of Bethlehem, the great magnet of the regenerated soul. Though ordinarily true to his pole, it is seldom or never that the Christian can at once repress the flutter and agitation of nature, control or understand its deviations, collect his energies, and repose calmly on God. It is seldom that faith, taken by surprise, does at once steady the soul, and lift a man clear above hostile infirmities and fears. Although it be true that, when once magnetized by the love of God, the soul does always point upward by strong attraction, as the compass-needle, to the north, yet, like that same needle, suddenly acted upon by a disturbing force, you must give it time to recover its balance, and, its oscillations done, to fasten upon the central point of rest.

We have known God's dear children sometimes, when calamities came suddenly in prospect, when huge billows seemed ready to go over them, and a black cloud of sorrows was about to burst upon their heads, at first trembling and anxious, swinging a little with trepidation to this side and that of the central point of rest; but, as the trial became more distinctly defined, the cloud's lightning began to flash, and its big drops to fall, the palpitating heart would be still, the vibrations of the will would cease, faith gather strength, and the eye of the soul be upturned and fastened on a faithful God, and its hand grasp firmly the promises which neither death, nor life, nor angels, nor principalities, nor powers, nor things to come, nor height, nor depth, nor any other creature, can even loosen.—H. T. CHEEVER.

FIDELITY TO THE FAITH.

St. Paul "kept the faith" at Antioch even when the infuriated crowd attempted to drown his voice with their clamors, and "interrupted him, contradicting and blaspheming." He "kept the faith" at Iconium, when the "envious Jews stirred up the people to stone him." He "kept the faith" at Lystra, when the fate of Stephen became almost his, and he was dragged, wounded and bleeding, outside the ramparts of the town, and left there to languish, and, for aught they cared, to die. He "kept the faith" against his erring brother Peter, and "withstood him to the face, because he was to be blamed." He "kept the faith" when shamefully treated at Philippi, and made the dungeon echo back the praises of his God. He "kept the faith" at Thessalonica, when "lewd fellows of the baser sort accused him falsely of sedition." He "kept the faith" at Athens, when to the world's sages he preached of him whom they ignorantly worshiped as "the Unknown God." He "kept the faith" at Corinth, when compelled to abandon that hardened and obdurate city, and to shake off the dust from his garment as a testimony against it. He "kept the faith" at Ephesus, when he pointed his hearers, not to Diana, but to Jesus Christ as their only Savior. He "kept the faith" at Jerusalem, when stoned by the enraged and agitated mob, when stretched upon the torturing rack, when bound with iron fetters. He "kept the faith" in Cæsarea, before the trembling, conscience-stricken Felix, when he "reasoned of righteousness, temperance, and judgment to come." He "kept the faith" before Agrippa, and by his earnestness compelled the king to say, "Almost thou persuadest me to be a Christian." And even in the closing hours of life, when the last storm was gathering over his head, when lying in the dark and dismal Roman cell, he wrote these triumphant words: "I am now ready to be offered, and the time of my departure is at hand. I have fought a good fight, I have finished my course, I have kept the faith. Henceforth there is laid up for me a crown of righteousness, which the Lord, the righteous Judge, shall give me at that day."—J. R. MACDUFF.

BUILD ON THE ROCK.

BUILD your nest upon no tree here, for you see God hath sold the forest to Death; and every tree whereupon we would rest is ready to be cut down, to the end we may flee, and mount up, and build upon the Rock.—SAMUEL RUTHERFORD.

CLOUD OF MERCY.

How vast the range of blessing your prayers may take! Who can tell the history or trace the wanderings of yon cloud, that sails in light and glory across the sky, or indicate from what source its bosom was filled with vapors it is to shed back upon the earth? Perhaps, though now wandering over the tilled field and the peopled village, its stores were drawn from some shaded fountain in the deep forest, where the eye of man has scarce even penetrated. In silent obscurity that fountain yielded its pittance, and did its work of preparing to bless the far-off lands that shall yet be glad for it. And even thus it is with the descending Spirit. Little do we know often of the secret origin of the dews of blessings that descend on the churches of God. In the recesses of some lowly cottage, in the depths of some humble heart, may be going on the work of pious intercession, in answer to which the grace of heaven descends on us and our children, on the labors of the wondering and joyful pastor, and on the hearts of the far heathen, until the wilderness and the solitary place are glad for them.—W. R. WILLIAMS.

THE ADVENT.

Joy to the world! the Lord is come:
  Let earth receive her King;
Let every heart prepare Him room,
  And heaven and nature sing.

Joy to the earth! the Savior reigns;
  Let men their songs employ;
While fields and floods, rocks, hills, and plains,
  Repeat the sounding joy.

No more let sins and sorrows grow,
  Nor thorns infest the ground:
He comes to make his blessings flow
  Far as the curse is found.

He rules the world with truth and grace,
  And makes the nations prove
The glories of His righteousness,
  And wonders of His love.—Isaac Watts.

LIFE OF FAITH.

Have you ever thought of the life of a child? Why, the life of a child is a perfect life of faith. That little child — what can that little child do? Why, that little child can not find its way to the street end and back again. It would be lost if you trusted it alone. That little child could not find the next meal. If you left that little child it would die of want. That little child could not furnish a shelter for its own head to-night, and yet has that little child any fear about it? Has that little child any sort of alarm about it? Not at all! How comes it that the child's life is the happy life it is? Because, instinctively and beautifully, it is a life of faith. That child could not buy the next loaf, but it has a firm belief that "father" can. That child could not provide for itself the garments for to-morrow, but it has an unbounded belief in "father's" power to do it, and "mother's" power to do it. That child could not do it for itself one day, but it never costs that child a moment's concern. Its life is a life of perfect faith in its parents.—S. COLEY.

CHRIST A FOUNTAIN.

"IF any man thirst, let him come unto me and drink." What man would dare to say of merely physical things, "If any man lacks knowledge, let him come to me?" Neither Humboldt, nor Liebig, nor Agassiz would dare to say this even of the departments in which they are pre-eminent, how much less of the whole range of learning! Yet Christ, disdaining physical things, appeals at once to the soul, with all its yearnings, its depths of despair, its claspings—like a mother feeling at midnight for the child whom death has taken—its infinite outreachings, its longings for love, and peace, and joy, which nothing can satisfy this side of the bosom of God, and says, "If any man thirsts, let him come unto me and drink." He stands over against whatever want there is in the human bosom, whatever hunger there is in the moral faculties, whatever need there is in the imagination, and says, "He that cometh unto me shall never hunger, and he that believeth on me shall never thirst."—H. W. BEECHER.

GOD A FRIEND.

A HEATHEN sage said to one of his friends, "Do not complain of thy misfortunes as long as Cæsar is thy friend!" What shall we say to those whom the Prince of the kings of the earth calls his sons and his brethren? "I will never leave thee nor forsake thee!" Ought not these words to cast all fear and care forever to the ground? He who possesses him, to whom all things belong, possesses all things. —F. W. KRUMMACHER.

CHRIST IN THE CHRISTIAN.

THIS communion is the motive and source, the secret and the reward, the talisman and the glory of our life toward God. Come, then, Lord Jesus, into our souls, and possess them, and pervade them with thyself! We would feel that Christ liveth in us beyond the contingency of removal. You know that Phidias so wrought his own name into the shield of the statue of Minerva that it could not be removed without destroying his masterpiece. Christ in his children engraves not merely his name, but as the Way, the Truth, and the Life, he interpenetrates their hearts, and dwells there in such essential, vital presence that his dislodgment would destroy the life and beauty of his people, and leave them withered and loathsome members in their wasting and decay. Here, then, is the source and guaranty of our life toward God: the constant indwelling of Jesus, who is the incarnation, not of the nature alone, but of the truth of God.

This is what gave Peter his consuming zeal at Pentecost; Paul his rapture, when whether in the body or out of the body he could not tell; and John his divine illumination to see that multitude which no man could number; martyrs their calmness and courage amid the crackling of fagots and the curling of flames; missionaries their hope and trust amid the death-damps of the Bassas and the horrors of Oung-pen-la; Christians love, and longing to toil and suffer for Jesus, and grace and joy to die in his service like Paul, with the triumph leaping from his quivering lips, "I have fought a good fight, I have finished my course, I have kept the faith; henceforth there is laid up for me a crown of righteousness," taken up eighteen centuries after by Payson on his dying-bed, "The battle's fought! the battle's fought! The victory is won! The victory is won forever!" O brethren, brethren, there is no God-ward living, no living in the Church, no spiritual, no evangelical living, no God-approved working, no brave and no glorious dying without communion with God, through an indwelling Christ as the divine embodiment of all spiritual truth, and as the divine source and authority of all spiritual life. May we feel the uplifting of this divine force in us. By the mystery of the new birth may we all be yielded up again to this inspiration of God, lost by our sinning, but recovered by our believing, and continued by our receiving and appropriating the truth of God through unceasing faith in his Son Jesus Christ.—A. H. BURLINGHAM.

IGNORANCE OF THE FUTURE.

None, indeed, can open the "seven-sealed book," or look forward over the dim and shadowy field stretching out illimitably before him. The astronomer discourses on the rate at which a sunbeam travels, and explains how the flashing lightning may be dispersed and its terrible swoop evaded. He even indicates those spheres where storms never gather and thunders never roll; but he can not solve the anxious problem of our future, nor help us by his great wisdom to avoid its manifold evils, because they come unforewarned. Nor will the lives of those gone before avail us, seeing no lives are marked by the same vicissitudes, or checkered by the same light and shades, the same joy and sorrow. In the eloquent words of a foreign divine, "We can become familiar with a landscape, we know where to find the waterfall, and the shady ledge where the violets grow in spring, and the sassafras gives forth its odors, but we can never become familiar with our life-landscape; we can never tell where we shall come upon the shady dell, or where the fountains will gush and the birds sing. That is with God." And his name be praised that it is so; for a definite prescience thereof would, in most instances, cloud the whole course of life, poison every stream of enjoyment, and render existence a curse of no ordinary magnitude.—EDWIN DAVIES.

FIDELITY IN PERSECUTION.

TRUE men are calm and faithful in the greatest trials and before the fiercest foes. Josephus records a case in point, the speech of Eleazar before the tyrant Antiochus. Said the intrepid martyr: "Old age has not so impaired my mind or enfeebled my body but, when religion and duty call upon me, I feel a youthful and vigorous soul. Does this declaration awaken your resentment? Prepare your instruments of torture, provoke the flames of the furnace to a fiercer rage; nothing shall induce me to save these silver locks by a violation of the ordinances of my country and of my God. Thou holy law! from whom I derive my knowledge, I will never desert so excellent a master. Thou prime virtue, temperance! I will never abjure thee. August and sacred priesthood! I will never disgrace thee. I will bear it to my ancestors a pure and unsullied soul, as free from stain as I stand in this place devoid of fear, amid the parade of your threatening engines and implements of martyrdom."— E. L. MAGOON.

SIMPLICITY OF FAITH.

ALL men are born with faith. Faith is as natural to a man as grief, or love, or anger. One of the earliest flowers that spring up in the soul, it smiles on a mother from her infant's cradle; and, living on through the rudest storms, it never dies till the hour of death. On the face of a child which has been left for a little time with strangers, and may be caressed with their kisses, and courted with their smiles, and fondled, and dandled in their arms, I have seen a cloud gathering and growing darker, till at length it burst in cries of terrors and showers of tears. The mother returns; and when the babe holds out its little arms to her, I see in these arms the arms of faith; and when, like a believer restored to the bosom of his God, it is nestling in a mother's embrace, and the cloud passes from its brow, and its tears are changed into smiles, and its terror into calm serenity, we behold the principle of faith in play.

This is one of its earliest, and—so far as nature is concerned—one of its most beautiful developments. So natural is it for us to confide, and trust, and believe, that a child believes whatever it is told until experience shakes its confidence in human veracity. Its eye is caught by the beauty of some flower, or it gazes up with wonder on the starry heavens; with that inquisitiveness which in childhood, active as a bee, is ever on the wing, it is curious to know who made them, and would believe you if you said you made them yourself. Such is the faith which nature gives it in a father that it never doubts his word. It believes all he says, and is content to believe where it is not able to comprehend. For this, as well as other reasons, our Savior presented in a child the living model of a Christian. He left Abraham, the father of the faithful, to his repose in heaven; he left Samuel undisturbed to enjoy the quiet rest of his grave; he allowed Moses and Elias, after their brief visit, to return to the skies, and wing their way back to glory. For a pattern of faith, he took a boy from his mother's side, and setting him up, in his gentle, blushing, shrinking modesty, before the great assembly, he said, "Whosoever shall not receive the kingdom of God as a little child, shall not enter therein."— THOMAS GUTHRIE.

You will excuse me if I ask you to look out for the sunlight the Lord sends into your days.—HOPE CAMPBELL.

THE SYMPATHY OF JESUS.

It is in this entire and perfect sympathy with all humanity that the heart of Jesus differs from every other heart that is found among the sons of men. And it is this, oh! it is this which is the chief blessedness of having such a Savior. If you are poor, you can only get a miserable sympathy from the rich; with the best intentions, they can not understand you. Their sympathy is awkward. If you are in pain, it is only a factitious and constrained sympathy you get from those in health—feelings forced, adopted kindly, but imperfect still. They sit, when the regular condolence is done, beside you, conversing on topics with each other that jar upon your ear.

They sympathize ? Miserable comforters are they all. If you are miserable, and tell out your grief, you have the shame of feeling that you were not understood, that you have bared your inner self to a rude gaze. If you are in doubt, you can not tell your doubts to religious people; no, not even to the ministers of Christ, for they have no place for doubts in their largest system. They ask, "What right have you to doubt?" They suspect your character. They shake the head, and whisper it about gravely that you read strange books—that you are verging on infidelity. If you are depressed with guilt, to whom shall you tell out your tale of shame? The confessional, with its innumerable evils, and yet indisputably soothing power, is passed away; but there is nothing to supply its place. You can not speak to your brother man, for you injure him by doing so, or else weaken yourself. You can not tell it to society, for society judges in the gross by general rules, and can not take into account the delicate differences of transgression. It banishes the frail penitent, and does homage to the daring, hard transgressor. Then it is that, repulsed on all sides and lonely, we turn to him whose mighty heart understands and feels all. "Lord, to whom shall we go? Thou hast the words of eternal life."—F. W. Robertson.

LOOK UP.

Hast thou no dwelling of thy own, no possession, and little for present supply?

Look up to him that passed through here in that very same way, and cleave the closer to him; so much the more eye him as thy riches and portion, and thou needest not envy kings in their best days; and whatsoever be thy estate, how soon shall it be past.—Robert Leighton.

SIGHT OF JESUS.

To see Jesus clearly with an eye of faith is to see the deep opening a way from Egypt to freedom's shore; is to see the waters gush full and sparkling from the desert rock; is to see the serpent gleaming on its pole over a dying camp; is to see the life-boat coming when our bark is thumping on the bank or ground on rocks by foaming breakers; it is to see a pardon when the noose is round our neck and our foot is on the drop. No sight in the wide world like Jesus Christ, with forgiveness on his lips, and a crown in his blessed hand! This is worth laboring for, praying for, living for, suffering for, dying for. You remember how the prophet's servant climbed the steps of Carmel. Three years, and never cloud had dappled the burning sky; three long years, and never a dew-drop had glistened on the grass or wet the lips of a dying flower; but the cloud came at last. No bigger than a man's hand it rose from the sea; it spread; and as he saw the first lightning's flash and heard the first thunder's roll, how did he forget all his toils, and would have climbed the hill, not seven, but seventy times seven times, to hail that welcome sight!

It is so with sinners so soon as their eyes are gladdened with a believing sight of Christ; when they have got Christ, and with him peace.—THOMAS GUTHRIE.

THE WELSH PEASANT.

It is told of a poor peasant on the Welsh mountains that, month after month, year after year, through a long period of declining life, he was used every morning, as soon as he awoke, to open his casement window toward the east, and look out to see if Jesus Christ was coming. He was no calculator, or he need not look so long; he was a student of prophecy, or he would not have looked at all; he was ready, or he would not have been in so much haste; he was willing, or he would rather have looked another way; he loved, or it would not have been the first thought of the morning. His Master did not come, but a messenger did, to fetch the ready one home; the same preparation sufficed for both; the longing soul was satisfied with either.

Often, when in the morning the child of God awakes, wearily and encumbered with the flesh, perhaps from troubled dreams, perhaps with troubled thoughts, his Father's secret comes presently across him; he looks up, if not out, to feel, if not to see, the glories of that last morning when the trumpet shall sound, and the dead shall arise indestructible; no weary limbs to bear the spirit down; no feverish dreams to haunt the visions; no dark forecasting of the day's events, or returning memory of the griefs of yesterday.—CAROLINE FRY.

SIMPLY TRUSTING.

I KNOW not the way I am going,
    But well do I know my Guide;
With a child-like trust I give my hand
    To the mighty Friend by my side.
The only thing that I say to Him,
    As he takes it, is "Hold it fast;
Suffer me not to lose my way,
    And bring me home at last."

As when some weary wanderer,
    Alone in an unknown land,
Tells the guide his destined place of rest,
    And leaves all the rest in his hand:
'Tis home, 'tis home that we wish to reach,
    He who guides us may choose the way;
Little we heed which path we take
    If nearer home each day.—*Anon.*

THE DISCOURAGEMENTS OF LIFE.

And they journeyed from Mount Hor by the way of the Red Sea, to compass the land of Edom; and the soul of the people was much discouraged because of the way.—Numbers xxi., 4.

WE doubt not that there will be seasons, even in the happiest Christian pilgrimage, when the soul will be discouraged, and even "much discouraged, because of the way." When difficulties, which we thought had passed over, will reappear; when temptations, which we thought had been forever vanquished, will again rise up against us; when sins, which we trusted we had forsaken, will once more mar our path; and these things will lead us to feel a deep sensation of despondency; we shall be tempted to think that God can not pardon delinquencies so frequent and unprovoked, and that we shall certainly perish on the journey, and never arrive at that journey's blissful end. Let us be careful that such feelings lead us not into temptation; that they do not close our eyes and our hearts against the infinity of God's mercy in Christ Jesus; that they do not teach us to forget that "the blood of Jesus Christ cleanseth us from all sin;" yea, all, "however deep, however oft-repeated, if it be but faithfully and earnestly sought through the power of the Holy Ghost, and

if, through the same promised aid, the sin be truly repented of, and steadily and perseveringly forsaken." Perhaps you may find it difficult to think so, but remember that your thoughts are, blessed be God, not the limits of his mercy, for has he not himself declared that "he is able to do abundantly above all that we can ask or think?" Be not, therefore, "discouraged because of the way;" look to him who was "the author," to be also "the finisher of your faith," and you shall yet, under his divine and blessed guidance, reach the haven where you would be.
—Henry Blunt.

ANGEL OF PATIENCE.

Angel of Patience! sent to calm
Our feverish brows with cooling palm;
To lay the storms of hope and fear,
And reconcile life's smile and tear;
The throbs of wounded pride to still,
And make our own our Father's will.
Oh! thou who mournest on thy way,
With longings for the coming day;
He walks with thee, that angel kind,
And gently whispers, "Be resigned."
Bear up, bear on, the end shall tell
The dear Lord ordereth all things well.
J. G. Whittier.

JOINT HEIRS WITH CHRIST.

And if children, then heirs; heirs of God, and joint heirs with Christ: if so be that we suffer with him, that we may be also glorified together.—Romans viii., 17.

OBSERVE how he enhances the gift by little and little. For, since it is a possible case to be children, and yet not become heirs—for it is not all children that are heirs—he adds this besides, that we are heirs. But the Jews, besides their not having the same adoption as we, were also cast out from the inheritance; for "he will miserably destroy those wicked men, and will let out the vineyard to other husbandmen." And before this he said that "many shall come from the east and from the west, and shall sit down with Abraham, but the children of the kingdom shall be cast out." But even here he does not pause, but sets down something even greater than this. What may this be, then? That we are *heirs of God;* and so he adds, "Heirs of God." And, what is still more, that we are not simply heirs, but also *joint heirs with Christ.*

Observe how ambitious he is of bringing us near to the Master. For, since it is not all children that are heirs, he shows that we are both children and heirs; next, as it is not all heirs that are heirs to any great amount, he shows that we have this point with us too, as we are heirs of God. Again, since it were possible to be God's heir, but in no sense joint heirs with the Only-Begotten, he shows that we have this also.

And consider his wisdom. For, after throwing the distasteful part into a narrow compass, when he was saying what was to become of such as " live after the flesh," for instance, that "they shall die," when he comes to the more soothing part, he leadeth forth his discourse into a large room, and so expands it on the recompense of rewards, and in pointing out that the gifts, too, are manifold and great; for if the being a child were a grace unspeakable, just think how great a thing it is to be heir too! But if this be great, much more is it to be JOINT HEIR.

Then, to show that the gift is not of grace only, and to give, at the same time, a credibility to what he says, he proceeds, "If so be that we suffer with him, that we may be also glorified together." If, he would say, we be sharers with him in what is painful, much more shall it be so in what is good. For he who bestowed such blessings upon those who had wrought no good, how, when he seeth them laboring and suffering so much, shall he do else than give them greater requital!

Having, then, shown that the thing was matter of

return, to make men give credit to what was said, and prevent any from doubting, he shows farther that it has the virtue of a gift. The one he showed, that what was said might gain credit even with those that doubted, and that the receivers of it might not feel ashamed, as being evermore receiving salvation for naught; and the other, that you might see that God outdoeth the toils by his recompenses. And the one he hath shown in the words, "If we suffer with him, that we may be also glorified together;" but the other in what follows respecting the greatness of the reward.

THE GLORY OF OUR INHERITANCE.

For we shall receive again our bodies incorruptible, and be glorified together, and reign together with Christ. How great this is we shall see from hence —or, rather, there is no means of making us see it clearly now. But, to start from our present blessings, and to get from them at least some kind of scanty notice of it, I will endeavor, so far as I may be able, to put before you what I have been speaking of.

Tell me, then, if, when you were grown old, and were living in poverty, and any one were to promise suddenly to make you young, and to bring you to the very prime of life, and to render you very strong and pre-eminently beautiful, and were to give you the kingdom of the whole earth for a thousand years, a kingdom in a state of the deepest peace, what is there that you would not choose to do and to suffer to gain this promise? See, then, Christ promises not this, but much more than this. For the distance between old age and youth is not to be compared with the difference of corruption and incorruption, nor that of a kingdom and poverty to that of the future glory and the present, but the difference is that of dreams and a reality.

Or, rather, I have yet said nothing to the purpose, since there is no language capable of setting before you the greatness of the difference between things to come and things present. And as for time, there is no place for the idea of difference, for what mode is there for a man to compare with our present state a life that hath no end? And as for the peace, it is as far removed from any present peace as peace is different from war; and for the incorruption, it is as much better as a clear pearl is than a clod of clay. Or, rather, say as great a thing as one may, nothing can put it before you; for were I even to compare the beauty of our bodies to the light of the sunbeam, or the brightest lightning, I shall not yet be saying aught that is worthy of their brilliancy. At present, if any one were to lead thee into a palace, and in the presence of all were to give thee an opportunity of conversing with the king, and make thee sit at his table and join in his fare, thou wouldst call thyself the happiest of men. But when you are going up to heaven, and stand by the King of the universe himself, and vie with angels in brightness, and enjoy even that unutterable glory, do you hesitate? And suppose one must need give up property, or put off even life itself, one ought to leap and exult, and mount on wings of pleasure. But you, that may get an office as a place to pillage from (for call a thing of this sort gain I can not), put all you have to hazard. But when the kingdom of heaven is set before you, that office which hath none to supersede you in it, and God bids you take, not a part of a corner of the earth, but the whole heaven entirely, are you hesitating, and reluctant, and gaping after money, and forgetful that if the parts of that heaven which we see are so fair and beautiful, how greatly so must the upper heaven be, and the heaven of heaven?

But since we have as yet no means of seeing this with our bodily eyes, ascend in thy thought, and, standing above this heaven, look up unto that heaven beyond this, into that height without a bound, into that light surcharged with awe, into the crowds of angels, into the endless ranks of archangels, into the rest of the incorporeal powers. What language is to set before us that blessedness, brightness, glory? Alas! my soul. For weeping comes upon me and great groaning as I reflect what good things we have fallen from, what blessedness we are estranged from. For estranged we are; speak not, then, of hell to me now, for more grievous than any hell is the fall from this glory, worse than punishments unnumbered the estrangement from that lot. But still we are gaping after this present world, and we take not thought of the devil's cunning, who by little things bereaves us of those great ones, and gives us clay that he may snatch from us gold, or, rather, that he may snatch heaven from us, and showeth us a shadow that he may dispossess us of the reality, and put phantoms before us in dreams (for such is the wealth of this world), that at daybreak he might prove us the poorest of men. Laying these things to heart, late though it be, let us fly from this craft, and pass to the side of things to come.—CHRYSOSTOM.

> "Arise, my soul, on wings sublime,
> Above the vanities of time;
> Let faith now pierce the veil, and see
> The glories of eternity.
> Born by a new celestial birth,
> Why should I grovel here on earth?
> Why grasp at vain and fleeting toys,
> So near to heaven's eternal joys?"

ACCESS TO GOD.

However early in the morning you seek the gate of access, you find it already open; and however deep the midnight moment when you find yourself in the sudden arms of death, the winged prayer can bring an instant Savior near. And this wherever you are. It needs not that you ascend some special Pisgah or Moriah. It needs not that you should enter some awful shrine, or put off your shoes on some holy ground. Could a memento be reared on every spot from which an acceptable prayer has passed away, and on which a prompt answer has come down, we should find *Jehovah-Shammah,* "the Lord hath been here," inscribed on many a cottage hearth and many a dungeon floor. We should find it not only in Jerusalem's proud Temple and David's cedar galleries, but in the fisherman's cottage by the brink of Gennesaret, and in the upper chamber where Pentecost began. And whether it be the field where Isaac went to meditate, or the rocky knoll where Jacob lay down to sleep, or the brook where Israel wrestled, or the den where Daniel gazed on the hungry lions and the lions gazed on him, or the hillsides where the man of sorrows prayed all night, we should still discern the prints of the ladder's feet let down from heaven—the landing-place of mercies, because the starting-point of prayer. And all this whatsoever you are. It needs no saint, no proficient in piety, no adept in eloquent language, no dignity of earthly rank. It needs but a simple Hannah or a lisping Samuel. It needs but a blind beggar or a loathsome lazar. It needs but a penitent publican or a dying thief. And it needs no sharp ordeal, no costly passport, no painful expiation, to bring you to the mercy-seat; or, rather, I should say, it needs the costliest of all; but the blood of atonement—the Savior's merit—the name of Jesus, priceless as they are, cost the sinner nothing. They are freely put at his disposal, and instantly and constantly he may use them. This access to God in every place, at every moment, without any price or personal merit, is it not a privilege?—JAMES HAMILTON.

Thou art with me, O my Father,
  In the changing scenes of life,
In loneliness of spirit,
  And in weariness of strife.

My sufferings, my comfortings,
  Alternate at thy will;
I trust Thee, O my Father,
  I trust Thee, and am still.

H

THE TRIAL OF OUR FAITH.

THE first and great end of God's permitting the temptations which bring heaviness on his children is the trial of their faith, which is tried by these even as gold by the fire. Now we know gold tried in the fire is purified thereby, is separated from its dross. And so is faith in the fire of temptation; the more it is tried, the more it is purified. Yea, and not only purified, but also strengthened, confirmed, increased abundantly by so many more proofs of the wisdom and power, the love and faithfulness of God. This, then, to increase our faith, is one gracious end of God's permitting those manifold temptations.

They serve to try, to purify, to confirm, and increase that living hope also, whereunto "the God and Father of our Lord Jesus Christ hath begotten us again of his abundant mercy." Indeed, our hope can not but increase in the same proportions with our faith. On this foundation it stands. Believing in his name, living by faith in the Son of God, we hope for, we have confident expectation of the glory which shall be revealed; and, consequently, whatever strengthens our faith, increases our hope also. At the same time, it increases our joy in the Lord, which can not but attend a hope full of immortality.

In this view the apostle exhorts believers to "rejoice that ye are partakers of the sufferings of Christ." On this very account "happy are you; for the spirit of glory and of God resteth upon you." And hereby ye are enabled, even in the midst of sufferings, to "rejoice with joy unspeakable and full of glory." They rejoice the more, because the trials which increase their faith and hope increase their love also; both their gratitude to God for all his mercies, and their good will to all mankind. Accordingly, the more deeply sensible they are of the loving-kindness of God their Savior, the more is their heart inflamed with love to him who first loved us. The clearer and stronger evidence they have of the glory that shall be revealed, the more do they love him who hath purchased it for them, and given them the earnest thereof in their hearts; and this, the increase of their love, is another end of the temptations permitted to come upon them.

Yet another end of temptations is advance in holiness, holiness of heart, and holiness of conversation; the latter naturally resulting from the former, for a good tree will bring forth good fruit; and all inward holiness is the immediate fruit of the faith that worketh by love. By this the blessed Spirit purifies the heart from pride, self-will, passions, from love of the world, from foolish and hurtful desires, from vile and vain affections. Besides that, sanctified afflictions have (through the grace of God) an immediate and direct tendency to holiness. Through the operation of his Spirit, they humble more and more, and abase the soul before God. They calm and weaken our turbulent spirit, tame the fierceness of our nature, soften our obstinacy and self-will, crucify us to the world, and bring us to expect all our strength from, and to seek all our happiness in God.

And all these terminate in that great end—that our faith, hope, love, and holiness may be found (if it doth not yet appear) unto praise from God himself, and honor from men and angels, and glory assigned by the great Judge to all that have endured to the end. And this will be assigned in that awful day to every man according to his works, according to the work which God had wrought in his heart, and the outward works which he has wrought for God, and likewise according to what he had suffered; so that all these trials are unspeakable gain. So many ways do these "light afflictions, which are but for a moment, work out for us a far more exceeding and eternal weight of glory."

Add to this the advantage which others may receive by seeing our behavior under affliction. We find by experience example frequently makes a deeper impression upon us than precept. And what examples have a stronger influence, not only on those who are partakers of the like precious faith, but even on them who have not known God, than that of a soul calm and serene in the midst of storms; sorrowful, yet always rejoicing; meekly accepting whatever is the will of God, however grievous it may be to nature; saying, in sickness and pain, "The cup which my Father hath given me, shall I not drink it?" in loss or want, "The Lord gave; the Lord hath taken away: blessed be his holy name!"

I am to conclude with some inferences. And, first, how wide is the difference between darkness of soul and heaviness? which, nevertheless, are so generally confounded with each other even by experienced Christians! Darkness, or the wilderness state, implies a total loss of joy in the Holy Ghost; heaviness does not; in the midst of this we may rejoice with joy unspeakable. They that are in darkness have lost the peace of God; they that are in heaviness have not; so far from it that at the very time peace as well as grace may be multiplied unto them. In the former, the love of God is waxed cold, if it be not utterly extinguished; in the latter, it retains its full force, or, rather, increases daily. In those, faith itself, if not totally lost, is, however, grievously decayed. Their evidence and conviction of things not seen, particularly of the pardoning love of God, is not so clear or strong as in time past, and their trust in him is proportionably weakened. These, though they see him not, yet have a clear, unshaken confidence in God, and an abiding evidence of that love, whereby all their sins are blotted out. So that, as long as we can distinguish faith from unbelief, hope from despair, peace from war, the love of God from the love of the world, we may infallibly distinguish heaviness from darkness.

We may learn, therefore, that there may be need of heaviness, but there can be no need of darkness. There may be need of our being in heaviness FOR A SEASON, in order to the ends above recited; at least in this sense, as it is a natural result of those manifold temptations which are needful to try and increase our faith, to confirm and enlarge our hope, to purify our hearts from all unholy tempers, and to perfect us in love. And, by consequence, they are needful, in order to brighten our crown, and add to our eternal weight of glory. But we can not say that darkness is needful in order to any of these ends. It is no way conducive to them; the loss of faith, hope, love, is surely neither conducive to holiness, nor to the increase of that reward in heaven which will be in proportion to our holiness on earth.

From the apostle's manner of speaking, we may

gather that even heaviness is not *always* needful. Now for a season, if need be; so it is not needful for ALL PERSONS, nor for any person at all times. God is able—he has both power and wisdom to work when he pleases the same work of grace in any soul by other means, and, in some instances, he does so. He causes those whom it pleaseth him to go on from strength to strength even till they PERFECT HO-LINESS IN HIS FEAR with scarce any heaviness at all, as having an absolute power over the heart of man, and moving all the springs of it at his pleasure. But these cases are rare. God generally sees good to try "acceptable men in the furnace of affliction," so that manifold temptations and heaviness, more or less, are usually the portion of his dearest children.

We ought, therefore, to watch and pray, and use our utmost endeavors to avoid falling into darkness. But we need not be solicitous how to avoid, so much as how to improve by heaviness. Our great care should be so to behave ourselves under it, so to wait upon the Lord therein, that it may fully answer all the design of his love in permitting it to come upon us, that it may be a mean of increasing our faith, of confirming our hope, of perfecting us in all holiness. Whenever it comes, let us have an eye to these gracious ends, for which it is permitted, and use all diligence, that we may not "make void the council of God against ourselves." Let us earnestly work together with him, by the grace which he is continually giving us, in "purifying ourselves from all pollution both of flesh and spirit," and daily "growing in the grace of our Lord Jesus Christ," till we are received into his everlasting kingdom.—JOHN WESLEY.

CONTENTMENT.

WERE it not that God supports me, and by his Omnipotent goodness often totally suspends all sense of worldly things, I could not sustain the weight many days, perhaps hours. But even in this low ebb of fortune I am not without some kind interval. . . . . Upon the best observation I could ever make, I am induced to believe that it is much easier to be contented without riches than with them. It is so natural for a rich man to make his gold his god; for, whatever a person loves most, that thing, be it what it will, he will certainly make his god. It is so difficult not to trust in it, not to depend on it for support and happiness, that I do not know one rich man in the world with whom I would exchange conditions. —THE MOTHER OF THE WESLEYS.

LETTER TO AN AGED PERSON.

MUCH HONORED SIR,—Grace, mercy, and peace be to you. I beseech you, sir, by the salvation of your precious soul, and the mercies of God, make good and sure work of your salvation, and try upon what ground-stone you have builded. Worthy and dear sir, if ye be upon sinking sand, a storm of death and a blast will loose Christ and you, and wash you off the rock! Oh! for the Lord's sake, look narrowly to the work. Read over your life with the light of God's daylight and sun. It is good to look to your compass and all you have need of ere you take shipping, for no wind can blow you back again. Remember, when the race is ended, and the flag either won or lost, and you are in the utmost circle and border of time, and put your foot within the march of eternity, all your good things of this short nightdream shall seem to you like the ashes of a blaze of thorns or straw, and your poor soul shall be crying, "Lodging, lodging, for God's sake!" Then shall your soul be more glad at one of your Lord's lovely smiles than if you had the charters of three worlds for all eternity. Let pleasures and gain, will and desires of this world, be put over in God's hands as arrested goods that you can not claim. Now, when you are drinking the grounds of your cup, and are upon the utmost ends of the last link of time, and old age, like death's long shadow, is casting a covering upon your days, it is no time to court this vain life, and to set love and heart upon it. It is near after supper; seek rest and ease for your soul in God through Christ. Come in, come in to Christ, and see what you want, and find it in him. He is the short cut, as we used to say, and the nearest way to an outgate of all your burdens. I dare avouch, you shall be dearly welcome to him. Angels' pens, angels' tongues, nay, as many worlds of angels as there are drops of water in all the seas, and fountains, and rivers of the earth, can not paint him out to you. I think his sweetness, since I was a prisoner, has swelled upon me to the greatness of two heavens. Oh for a soul as wide as the utmost circle of the highest heaven, that containeth all, to contain his love!—SAMUEL RUTHERFORD.

OUR TRIALS.

TRIALS are medicines which our gracious and wise Physician prescribes because we NEED them, and he proportions the frequency and the weight of them to what the case requires. Let us trust in his skill, and thank him for his prescriptions.—JOHN NEWTON.

"CASTING ALL YOUR CARE UPON HIM."

Lord, it belongs not to my care,
    Whether I die or live;
To love and serve Thee is my share,
    And shall be while I live.
If life be long, I will be glad,
    That I may long obey;
If short, yet how can I be sad
    To soar to endless day?

Christ leads me through no darker rooms
    Than he went through before;
He that unto Christ's kingdom comes,
    Must enter by His door.
Come, Lord, when grace has made me meet
    Thy blessed face to see;
For if Thy work on earth be sweet,
    What will Thy glory be.

Then shall I end my sad complaints,
    My weary, sinful days;
And join with the triumphal hosts
    That sing Jehovah's praise.
My knowledge of that life is small,
    The eye of faith is dim;
But 'tis enough that Christ knows all,
    And I shall be with him.

                  RICHARD BAXTER.

COMFORT IN TRIBULATION.

There is an island in a distant sea from whose shores the fishermen sail in tiny crafts to procure the treasures of the deep. During their absence thick mists often descend and cover highland, cliff, and beacon with so thick a veil that these hardy mariners are left without a mark by which to steer their laden barks. But in these dull hours they are not left to wander unguided on the pathless sea. When the time for their return arrives, the women of the islet—mothers, wives, sisters, and daughters—descend to the shores and raise the voice of song. Borne on the quiet air, their voices soon fall sweetly on the ears of the loved ones at sea. Guided by the well-known sounds, they steer their boats in safety to the shore.

And thus to thee, oh Christian, comes the voice of love from the celestial shore, as thou wanderest, a bewildered child of tribulation, on the misty sea of life. Hearken! "Be of good cheer!" is the cry that greets thee. It comes from Jesus, who has overcome this world, which is the scene and source of your trials. His conquest of your adversary is the pledge of your victory. Therefore, "Be of good cheer."—*Anon.*

SILENCE OF GOD.

It sometimes seems as if God cared for nothing. The wicked are at ease. The good are vexed incessantly. The world is full of misery and confusion. The darling of the flock is always made the sacrifice. Some child, in the very midst of its glee, becomes suddenly silent—as a music-box, its spring giving way, stops in the midst of its strain, and never plays out the melody. The mother staggers and wanders through day and night, as if these were mingled into one, and that shot through with preternatural influence of woe. But think not that God's silence is coldness or indifference. When Christ stood by the dead, the silence of tears interpreted his sympathy more wonderfully than even that voice which afterward called back the footsteps of the brother from the grave, and planted them in life again. God's stillness is full of brooding. Not one tear shall be shed by you that does not hang heavier at his heart than any world upon his hand.—H. W. BEECHER.

It was when the doors were shut that He who came to succor and to save stood in the midst of his disciples.

WE ARE ON OUR WAY TO GOD.

From Egypt lately come,
   Where death and darkness reign,
We seek our new, our better home,
   Where we our rest shall gain.
      Hallelujah!
We are on our way to God!

To Canaan's sacred bound
   We haste with songs of joy,
Where peace and liberty are found,
   And sweets that never cloy.
      Hallelujah!
We are on our way to God!

There sin and sorrow cease,
   And every conflict's o'er;
There we shall dwell in endless peace,
   And never hunger more.
      Hallelujah!
We are on our way to God!

There in celestial strains
   Enraptured myriads sing;
There love in every bosom reigns,
   For God himself is King.
      Hallelujah!
We are on our way to God!

We soon shall join the throng,
  Their pleasure we shall share,
And sing the everlasting song
  With all the ransomed there.
    Hallelujah!
We are on our way to God!

How sweet the prospect is!
  It cheers the pilgrim's breast;
We're journeying through the wilderness,
  But soon shall gain our rest!
    Hallelujah!
We are on our way to God!—THOMAS KELLY.

THROUGH DARKNESS TO LIGHT.

As we pass beneath the hills which have been shaken by earthquake and torn by convulsions, we find that periods of perfect repose succeed those of destruction. The pools of calm water lie clear beneath their fallen rocks, the water-lilies gleam, and the reeds whisper among their shadows; the village rises again over the forgotten graves, and its church-tower, white through the storm twilight, proclaims a renewed appeal to his protection in whose hand are "all the corners of the earth, and the strength of the hills is his also." . . . . It is just where "the mountains falling cometh to naught, and the rock is removed out of his place," that, in the process of years, the fairest meadows bloom between the fragments, the clearest rivulets murmur from their crevices among the flowers; and the clustered cottages, each sheltered beneath some strength of mossy stone, now to be removed no more, and, with their pastured flocks around them, safe from the eagle's swoop and the wolf's ravine, have written upon their fronts, in simple words, the mountaineer's faith in the ancient promise, "Neither shalt thou be afraid of destruction when it cometh, for thou shalt be in league with the stones of the field, and the beasts of the field shall be at peace with thee."—JOHN RUSKIN.

BUILDING.

IF the architect of a house had one plan, and the contractor had another, what conflicts would there be! How many walls would have to come down, how many doors and windows would need to be altered before the two could harmonize! Of the building of life, God is the Architect, and man the contractor. God has one plan, and man has another. Is it strange that there are clashings and collisions?—H. W. BEECHER.

NIGHT OF SORROW—MORNING OF JOY.

"*Weeping may endure for a night, but joy cometh in the morning.*"

TRIALS are ill to bear. To be reduced from affluence to poverty; to lie on a bed of languor; to pass sleepless nights of pain; to be exposed to evil tongues; to sit amid the ruins of fortune; to lay loved ones in a lonesome grave—such things are not joyous, but grievous. Winter, no doubt, is not the pleasant season that summer brings, with her songs, and flowers, and long, bright sunny days. Bitter medicines, no doubt, are not savory meat; yet he who believes that all things shall work together for good will be ready to thank God for physic as well as food; and for the winter frost that kills the weeds and breaks up the soil, as for the dewy nights and sunny days that ripen the fields of corn. May God give us such a faith! With nature weak, and grace imperfect—when there is no lifting of the cloud, and trials are severe and long protracted—oh! though it may be easy for an onlooker to preach patience, it is not easy for a sufferer to practice it. In such circumstances, how prone we are to take the case out of God's hands, and, getting discontented with his discipline, how ready are we to cry, "How long,

O Lord, how long? if it be possible, let this cup pass from me;" or, "Take away this, and give me any one else to drink." Yet let me have a firm faith in God's truth and love; let me be confident that he will do what he has said, and perform all that he has promised, and I shall discover mercy's bow bent on fortune's blackest cloud, and, under the most trying providences, shall enjoy in my heart, and exhibit to others in my temper, the blessed difference between a sufferer that mourns and a spirit that murmurs. "Call upon me in the day of trouble." "Weeping may endure for a night, but joy cometh in the morning."—THOMAS GUTHRIE.

LIGHT AND DARK.

GOD doth checker his providences white and black, as the pillar of cloud had its light side and dark. Look on the light side of thy estate: who looks on the dark side of a landscape? Suppose thou art cast in a lawsuit—there is the dark side; yet thou hast some land left—there is the light side. Thou hast sickness in thy body—there is the dark side; but grace in thy soul—there is the light side. Thou hast a child taken away—there is the dark side; thy husband lives—there is the light side. God's providences in this life are various, represented by those speckled horses among the myrtle-trees which were red and white (Zechariah i., 8); mercies and afflictions are interwoven; God doth speckle his work. "Oh," saith one, "I want such a comfort;" but weigh all thy mercies in a balance, and that will make thee content. Look on the light side of your condition, and then all your discontent will easily be dispersed; do not pore upon your losses, but ponder upon your mercies. What! wouldst thou have no cross at all? Why should one man think to have all good things, when he himself is good but in part? Wouldst thou have no evil about thee? Thou art not fully sanctified in this life; how, then, thinkest thou to be fully satisfied? Never look for perfection of contentment till there be perfection of grace.—RICHARD WATSON.

LOOK WITHIN.

They that would be loved must render themselves lovable. They that would have friends must show themselves friendly. Do you complain of others? Ask yourselves what you have done to make them happy. Do you complain that the consolations of God are small with you? Look within, and inquire whether there is not some secret thing there which ought not to be, for "there is no peace, saith my God, to the wicked."—*Anon.*

LIGHT THROUGH TEARS.

You say that your sun has gone done while it is yet day, and that your path looks bleak and dreary in the gathering twilight. I know it, my friend; I know that the brightness has vanished from your life, and that from henceforth you must endure hardness even unto the end.

But take courage; advance in perfect faith. Mercies you do not dream of now will be strewn around your footsteps. Powers which till now have lain as sleeping shadows within you will awake to life; powers of faith, of hope, of love, and of that perfect patience which will enable you to lift your streaming eyes to heaven and say, "Lord, I am thine; do with me what thou wilt; strip me of all earthly coverings, only save my soul alive." Then let the shades of evening fall; let your path be dark and desolate; but in the surrounding stillness you will hear voices from the everlasting hills, and the sound as of the waving of angels' wings around you. One also mightier than the angels will make his presence felt, and as you place your trembling hand in his and cry, "Lord, guide me, for I can not see," there will descend a stream of light upon your darkening path, and peace so perfect that with songs of praise and of thanksgiving you will pursue your way, willing to wait, willing to endure, willing to do all things for his dear sake who is leading you through the valley of the shadow of death to the fountains of living waters, to the land of everlasting joy.—*Anon.*

HEARING AND DOING.

WHEN life is going smoothly on—when its surface is calm, its course easy and prosperous—when nothing further seems to be called for than a respect for religion and religious observances, and that it should be made to contribute to a Sunday or festival attendance on divine service, the want of an inward and vital principle of godliness is not so apparent. But in seasons of deep and heartfelt sorrow; in the hour of distress and bitter disappointment, or in the unguarded moments of turbulent passion, of resentment, and hatred, at such times a RELIGIOUS principle is especially required for guidance and restraint; yet how seldom, in such cases, does a religious feeling supply the proper motive for action—seldom that, under such circumstances, men are found prepared to meet their trials as members of Christ's body, or as his followers and disciples. Every one must feel that it is a real, not a nominal Christian profession on which they must depend in the time of trial, in the hour of death, and at the day of judgment. The works of faith, the labors of love, therefore, which belong to us as members of Christ, must be carried on without delay, from the morning of life to its close; not reserved for the languor of disease and the infirmities of age, but in the freshest years of life—the days of its health and strength, its energy of mind and body. Not in the pain and weakness of a sick-bed, or the distraction of a death-bed scene, but in the calm hours of a composed spirit and a collected mind. In fact, we must ALWAYS be ready.—E. B. RAMSAY.

AFFLICTION.

MANY and precious are the benefits arising from affliction. It tends to wean us from this world and enable us rightly to appreciate its fading enjoyments. When our path is strewed with roses, when nothing but brightness and fragrance float around us, how apt we are to be enamored with our present condition, and to forget the crown of glory at THE END of the Christian race, and to forget Jesus, and everlasting ages! But affliction, with a warning voice, rouses us from the sweet delusion, warns our hearts to "arise and depart" from these inferior delights, because this is "not our rest"—true and lasting joys are not here to be found. The sweeping tempest and the beating surge teach the mariner to prize the haven, where undisturbed repose awaits his arrival. In like manner, disappointments, vexations, anxieties, and crosses teach us to long for those happy mansions where "all tears will be wiped away, and there shall be no more death, neither sorrow, nor crying, neither shall there be any more pain, for the former things are done away" (Revelation xxi., 40). —*Anon.*

ABIDE WITH US.

ABIDE with me! Fast falls the eventide,
The darkness deepens. Lord, with me abide!
When other helpers fail, and comforts flee,
Help of the helpless, O bide with me!

Swift to its close ebbs out life's little day;
Earth's joys grow dim, its glories pass away;
Change and decay in all around I see;
O Thou who changest not, abide with me!

I need Thy presence every passing hour;
What but Thy grace can foil the tempter's power?
Who like Thyself my guide and stay can be?
On to the close, O Lord, abide with me!

HENRY FRANCIS LYTE.

A PARABLE.

"If any be afflicted, let him pray."

HILLEL walked, on a moonlight night, with his disciple Sadi, in the garden of Olivet.

Sadi said, "See that man there in the light of the moon; what is he doing?"

Hillel replied, "It is Zadoc; he sits on the grave of his son, and weeps."

"Can not Zadoc, then," said the youth, "moderate his mourning? The people call him the just and wise."

"Shall he not on that account feel pain?" said Hillel.

"But," said Sadi, "What advantage, then, has the wise over the simple?"

The teacher replied, "Behold, the briny tear of his eye falls to the ground, but his countenance is direct to heaven."—F. W. KRUMMACHER.

THE GOSPEL NOT GLOOMY.

THE Gospel gloomy! It is an anthem from the harps of heaven; the music of the River of Life washing its shores on high, and pouring in cascades upon the earth. Not so cheerful was the song of the morning stars, nor shout of the sons of God so joyful. Gushing from the fountains of eternal harmony, it was first heard on earth in a low tone of solemn gladness, uttered in Eden by the Lord God himself. This gave the key-note of the Gospel song. Patriarchs caught it up, and taught it to the generations following. It breathed from the harp of the psalmists, and rang like a clarion from tower and mountain top as prophets proclaimed the year of jubilee. Fresh notes from heaven have enriched the harmony, as the Lord of hosts and his angels have revealed new promises, and called on the suffering children of Zion to be joyful in their King. From bondage and exile, from dens and caves, from bloody fields, and fiery stakes, and peaceful death-beds have they answered in tones which have cheered the disconsolate, and made oppressors shake upon their thrones; while sun, and moon, and all the stars of light, stormy wind fulfilling his word, the roaring sea and the fullness thereof, mountains and hills, fruitful fields, and all the trees of the wood, have rejoiced before the Lord, and the coming of his Anointed, for the redemption of his people, and the glory of his holy name.—W. J. HOGE.

THE DUE TIME.

"*Humble yourselves, therefore, under the mighty hand of God, that he may exalt you in due time.*"—1 Peter v., 6.

In due time—not thy fancied time, but his own wisely-appointed time. Thou thinkest, now I am sinking; if he help not now, it will be too late. Yet he sees it otherwise; he can let thee sink still lower, and yet bring thee up again. He doth but stay till the most fit time. Thou canst not see it now, but thou shalt see it, that his chosen time is absolutely best. "God waiteth to be gracious" (Isaiah xxx., 18). Doth he wait, and wilt not thou? Oh, the firm belief of his wisdom, power, and goodness, what difficulty will it not surmount? So, then, be humble under his hand; submit not only thy goods, thy health, thy life, but thy soul. Seek and wait for pardon. Lay thyself low before him, and speak and say, "Lord, I am justly under the sentence of death; if I fall under it, thou art righteous, and I here acknowledge it; but there is deliverance in Christ; thither I would have recourse." And what, though most or all of our life should pass without much sensible taste even of spiritual comforts, a poor all it is! Let us not over-esteem this moment, and so think too much of our better or worse condition in it, either in temporals or spirituals; provided we can humbly wait for free grace, and depend on the word of promise, we are safe. It is "but weeping for a night, and joy comes in the morning"—that clearer morning of eternity to which no evening succeeds. —ROBERT LEIGHTON.

WE GLORY IN TRIBULATIONS ALSO.

WHEN I can read my title clear
    To mansions in the skies,
I'll bid farewell to every fear,
    And wipe my weeping eyes.

Should earth against my soul engage,
    And hellish darts be hurled,
Then I can smile at Satan's rage,
    And face a frowning world.

Let cares like a wild deluge come,
    And storms of sorrow fall,
So I but safely reach my home,
    My God, my heaven, my All.

There shall I bathe my weary soul
    In seas of heavenly rest,
And not a wave of trouble roll
    Across my peaceful breast.—ISAAC WATTS.

USES OF AFFLICTION.

What an interpreter of Scripture is affliction! How many stars in its heaven shine out brightly in the night of sorrow and pain which were unperceived or overlooked in the garish day of our prosperity! What an enlarger of Scripture is any other outer or inner event which stirs the depths of our hearts, which touches us near to the core and centre of our lives!

Trouble of spirit, condemnation of conscience, sudden danger, strong temptation — when any of these overtake us, what veils do they take away, that we may see what hitherto we saw not; what new domains of God's Word do they bring within our spiritual ken! How do promises, which once fell flat upon our ears, become precious now; psalms become our own . . . . which were before aloof from us! How do we see things now with the eye which before we knew only by the hearing of the ear; which before men had told us, but now we ourselves have found! So that on these accounts also the Scripture is fitted to be our companion, and to do us good all the years of our life.—Richard Chenevix Trench.

LOOK ON JESUS, NOT ON THE WAVES.

But when Peter saw that the wind was boisterous, he was afraid; and beginning to sink, he cried, saying, Lord, save me.—Matthew xiv., 30.

"It was," says the evangelist, "when he saw the wind boisterous that he began to sink." He had, therefore, withdrawn his steadfast gaze from his divine Master, and was faithlessly looking around upon the dark clouds, and the still darker waters. How does every word of this instructive narrative agree with the believer's experience, and come home to the believer's heart! When is it that the Christian fails? When is it that the Christian desponds? When is it that the Christian begins to sink? Not in the hour, however great the trial or afflicting the dispensation, that the eye of faith is steadfastly fixed upon his Savior. This is not the hour when the Christian sinks. It is when he forgets and disobeys that most important command, "Look unto me, and be ye saved;" when his path is overcast, and trouble and temptation so thickly surround him that his thoughts are led to fasten themselves upon these outward difficulties or inward trials, and thus to be withdrawn from the Fountain of strength and succor. Christian friends, this is a temptation against which we can not too earnestly or too constantly be upon our guard, for it is one of the most common and most successful with which our spiritual enemy assails us. Let nothing induce you to turn the eye of faith, even for a passing hour, from the Savior of sinners. While you look to him, you are safe; danger begins the moment that you cease to do so. Once turn aside because the cloud is dark or the wind is boisterous; give the reins to a desponding imagination; follow out the delusive reasonings of a deceitful or a doubting heart, and the inevitable effect will be that every moment so spent will the more widely separate you from him who alone can be your refuge and your support. Your strength, your only strength, consists in cleaving daily, and hourly, to your Redeemer, and drawing from his unsearchable riches and his inexhaustible fullness a sufficiency for all your poverty and for all your need.—HENRY BLUNT.

Look not mournfully into the past—
It comes not back again;
Wisely improve the present—it is thine.
Go forth to meet the shadowy future
Without fear and with a manly heart.
H. W. LONGFELLOW.

GOD A ROCK.

WHAT are the reasons for which our God is compared to a rock? First, then, a rock is steadfast; its stability, as contrasted with the flowing waters of the sea or the shifting sands of the desert, is the first thing that strikes us; and with regard to God,

"Firm as a rock Thy promise stands;"

"With him is no variableness, neither shadow of turning." Next, a rock is often chosen as a site of a stronghold, from the security it gives. Men build their castles upon a rock for purpose of defense. The wise man built his house upon the rock for safety in the storm: "The Lord is my rock and my fortress." Again, in Palestine we find that the rock often contained a cave or cleft, used as a hiding-place: "Enter into the rock, and hide thee in the dust." In such a cleft Moses was hidden: "I will put thee in a cleft of the rock, and will cover thee with my hand while I pass by" (Exodus xxxiii., 22). A rock became also a shelter in a common sense: "The shadow of a great rock in a weary land;" "Lead me to the rock that is higher than I." And the rock that gave security was also a source of refreshment; for "He opened the rock, and the waters gushed out," so that "they drank of that spiritual rock that followed them, and that rock was Christ."—ANDREW CAMERON.

THE TREMBLING CHRISTIAN.

IT is the duty of good people to labor after a holy security and serenity of mind, and to use the means appointed for the obtaining it. Give not way to the disquieting suggestions of Satan, and to those tormenting doubts and fears that arise in your own souls. Study to be quiet; chide yourself for your distrusts; charge yourselves to believe and to hope in God, that you may yet praise him. You are in the dark concerning yourselves. Do as Paul's mariners did: cast anchor, and wish for the day.

Poor, trembling Christian! thou art tossed with tempests, and not comforted. Try to lay thee down in peace and sleep; compose thyself into a sedate and even frame. In the name of him whom winds and seas obey, command down thy tumultuous thoughts, and say, "Peace, be still." Lay that aching, trembling head of thine where the beloved disciple laid his, in the bosom of the Lord Jesus; or, if thou hast yet attained such boldness of access to him, lay that aching, trembling head of thine at the feet of the Lord Jesus by an entire submission to him, saying, "If I perish, I will perish here." Put it into his hand by an entire confidence in him; submit it to his disposal who knows how to speak to the heart. And if thou art not yet entered into this present rest that remaineth for the people of God, yet look upon it to be a land of promise; and, therefore, though it tarry, wait for it, for the vision is for an appointed time, and at the end it shall speak, and shall not lie. "Light is sown for the righteous," and what is sown shall come up again at last in a harvest of joy.—M. HENRY.

THE RIPER FRUITS OF FAITH.

THE certainty that God will work all for good; the seeing the dawn of morning from the hour of midnight; the being able to detect the folds of the wing under the black shell of the chrysalis; the seeing no single probable doorway to escape the difficulty, and yet to make no effort, but to feel sure that God will extricate; to see Isaac bound on the altar, and yet to believe that from him will spring a multitude—are signs of a living faith which few possess, while the reward is boundless.perfect peace.—*Anon.*

THE BIBLE IS A HISTORY OF COMPENSATION.

The prophecies of the new covenant were uttered in seasons of depression—at the fall of Adam, the separation of Abraham, the bondage of Israel, the giving of the law by Moses, and the captivity of Babylon. Cloud and rainbow appear together. There is wisdom in the saying of Feltham, that the whole creation is kept in order by discord, and that vicissitude maintains the world. Many evils bring many blessings. Manna drops in the wilderness; corn grows in Canaan. Rarely two afflictions or two trials console or trouble us at the same time. Human life is the prophet's declaration drawn out into examples. "God stayeth his rough wind in the day of his east wind."

And one curious and beautiful feature of the divine scheme of compensation is seen in its changing our sorrows into instruments and channels of joy and comfort. The curtained chamber of sickness sows the barren field with flowers. A sick man seated in his garden, or tottering down a green lane for a few minutes, might suppose himself transported into the morning and sunlight of creation:

> The common air, the earth, the skies,
> To him are opening Paradise.

Plato relates that Socrates, on the day of his death, being in the company of his disciples, began to rub his leg, which had been galled by the chain, and mentioned the pleasurable sensation in the released member. The Greek prison represents the world; the philosopher, the Christian; the fetters, the calamities of life. When one of these is loosened, the soul experiences a feeling of delight. It is the leg of Socrates unchained. The iron enters into the soul, and afterward the wound is healed. St. Paul told the Corinthians that when he came to Macedonia his flesh had no rest; without were fighting, within were fears; but God comforted him by "the coming of Titus." So it is ever.

The future of a man is his recompense. Something is promised which he desired, or something is withdrawn of which he complained. Hope is the compendium of compensation. The Esquimau, who numbers among his pleasures a plank of a tree cast by the ocean currents on his desolate shores, sees in the moon plains overshadowed by majestic forests; the Indian of the Orinoko expects to find in the same luminary green and boundless savannas, where people are never stung by musquitoes. Thus the chain of compensation encircles the world.—R. A. WILLMOTT.

THE OLD MAN'S BIBLE.

My Bible own, my Bible old,
   Give back my faithful friend;
I've read it oft, I've read it long,
   I'll keep it to the end.

You call it spoiled, and worthless deem,
   Because it is so old;
But this to me doth make it dear,
   Beyond all gems and gold.

This is the page o'er which I wept
   When first my sins I knew,
And here's the promise and the fount
   Whence all my hopes I drew.

'Twas here were writ our household names,
   My children's natal day;
And here is marked the doleful time
   When death took them away.

'Tis not in gilt and purple dress
   The volume's price is known;
The heart and mem'ry have a wealth
   In what we call OUR OWN.

My head is gray, my eye is dim,
   I can not court the new;
Give back the old, the worn, the tried,
   The wonted and the true.—WILLIAM ADAMS.

SUBMITTING TO WHAT?

THE late Ephraim Peabody, about twenty years ago, was attacked with bleeding at the lungs, and was obliged to resign his pastoral duties at Cincinnati. His only child was laid in a New England grave; his young wife had temporarily lost the use of her eyes; his home was broken up, and his prospects were very dark. They had sold their furniture, and went to board in a country tavern in the town of Dayton.

One day, as he came in from a walk, his wife said to him, "I have been thinking of our situation here, and have determined to be submissive and patient."

"Ah!" said he, "that is a good resolution; let us see what we have to submit to. I will make a list of our trials. First, we have a home—we will submit to that; second, we have the comforts of life—we will submit to that; third, we have each other; fourth, we have a multitude of friends; fifth, we have a God to take care of us."

"Ah!" said she, "I pray stop, and I will say no more about submission."

Crosses are ladders to heaven.

KEEP THE HEART ALIVE.

The longer I live, the more expedient I find it to endeavor more and more to extend my sympathies and affections. The natural tendency of advancing years is to narrow and contract these feelings. I do not mean that I wish to form a new and sworn friendship every day, to increase my circle of intimates; these are very different affairs. But I find it conduces to my mental health and happiness to find out all I can which is amiable and lovable in those I come in contact with, and to make the most of it. It may fall very far short of what I was once wont to dream of; it may not supply the place of what I have known, felt, and tasted, but it is better than nothing. It seems to keep the feelings and affections in exercise; it keeps the heart alive in its humanity; and, till we shall be all spiritual, this is alike our duty and our interest.—BERNARD BARTON.

 Fullness to such a burden is,
  That go on pilgrimage;
 Here little, and hereafter bliss,
  Is best from age to age.
       JOHN BUNYAN.

BEST AS IT IS.

"*If thou hadst been here, my brother had not died.*" These little words plainly showed that these afflicted sisters both believed that, had they been permitted to order the course of events, the result would have been far happier. If something had happened which has not happened, the event might have been less wretched. Oh how often do reflections similar to this barb the arrow of affliction with a poignancy which nothing else can give! These are the thoughts which in our wretchedness make us doubly wretched: "If we had taken such a course, if we had acted in some other manner, how different would have been the issue!" There can be nothing more unwise, perhaps few things more unholy, than reasoning thus. In dwelling upon secondary causes, we overlook the first great cause of all — the God of heaven and earth, who alone ordereth all things, and doeth all things well. Has the Lord no share in the decision? Did he not direct our present disappointment? Was he not present when our friend was taken from us? Duties are ours, events are God's.—HENRY BLUNT.

LIFE'S CHANGES.

Our life is hastening along. One scene presents itself, and then vanishes; a second follows, and disappears in like manner. Now we are well; anon sickness seizes us. At this moment every thing is prosperous and comfortable; the next all is dark and miserable. From reflecting upon these changes, however, we may learn two important lessons—the one solemn, the other encouraging. It is a solemn consideration that, amidst all the fluctuations of life, we are still making rapid advances toward eternity. Every wave, whether placid or turbulent, wafts us nearer to that awful shore. Like a ship which continues to make its way, whatever the passengers on board may be doing, we are perpetually hurried forward, whatever may be our employments. But as this is a solemn thought, so is it encouraging to contrast the uncertainty of all things here below with the unchangeableness of our gracious and Almighty Lord. This is our safety, that there is one who hath said, "Because I live, ye shall live also;" and that there is an unfailing fountain of love and mercy in him to remedy all the evils of time, and crown us with every blessing.—LIFE OF BISHOP WILSON, OF CALCUTTA.

DEPENDENCE UPON GOD.

"CASTING all your care upon him, for he careth for you." . . . . What a calm, what a peace in the midst of a storm does this gracious habit of godly dependence give to a man! Suppose to-morrow that you were expecting something very important to take place, and a heavy burden of care is the natural consequence of so grave an expectation. You are calm and composed, your mind is at peace. You have done your best to meet the emergency, and, as a Christian, as a man of God, you cast all your care on him, knowing assuredly that he careth for you.

And there is really a to-morrow of importance to every one of us. We shall have to unloose the bands of mortality. We shall have to take off our outer garments, and, bidding good-night to all about our strange and narrow bed, we shall have to lie down for the last time on earth, and let death put out our light. Oh! what a happy thing it will be for faith, the handmaid of the Lord, to sound in our ear for the last time, "Casting all your care upon him;" and for us to reply, "Yes! yes! he careth for us!" and then to fall asleep.—J. HULLETT.

SANCTIFICATION A WORK OF TIME.

My daughter, do not imagine that the work of sanctification will be an easy one. Cherry-trees bear fruit soon after they are planted, but that fruit is small and perishable; while the palm, the prince of trees, requires a hundred years before it is mature enough to bring forth dates. A lukewarm degree of piety may be acquired in a year, but the perfection to which we aspire, oh my dear daughter, must be the growth of long and weary years.— JACQUELINE PASCAL.

MEMORIES OF THE WAY.

"Thou shalt remember all the way which the Lord thy God hath led thee." ALL THE WAY — it is necessary that all the way should be remembered—the hill of difficulty as well as the valley of humiliation; the time of prosperity as well as the time of pain. Necessary for our advantage that we may understand our position, learn the lessons of providence and grace; necessary that we may construct a narrative, for every event in our history is connected and mutually interpreted; necessary that we may trace the outworkings of Jehovah's plan in the successive achievements of our lives. And if by the memory of joy you are impressed with God's beneficence, kept in cheerful piety, and saved from the foul sin of repining; and if by the memory of sorrow you are moulded into a gentler type, taught a softer sympathy, and receive a heavenward impulse, and anticipate a blessed reunion; if by the memory of sin you are reminded of your frailty and rebuked of your pride, stimulated to repentance and urged to trust in God, then it will be no irksomeness, but a heaven-sent and precious blessing that you have thus remembered the way that the Lord hath led thee in the wilderness.—WILLIAM M. PUNSHON.

MEMORIAL OF GRATITUDE.

A VERY poor and aged man, busied in planting and grafting an apple-tree, was rudely interrupted by this interrogation: "Why do you plant trees, who can not hope to eat the fruit of them?" He raised himself up, and, leaning upon his spade, replied, "Some one planted trees for me before I was born, and I have eaten the fruit. I now plant for others, that the memorial of my gratitude may exist when I am dead and gone."—*Anon.*

"NOT MY WILL, BUT THINE."

Thy way, not mine, O Lord,
    However dark it be!
Lead me by Thine own hand,
    Choose out the path for me.

Smooth let it be or rough,
    It will be still the best;
Winding or straight, it leads
    Right onward to Thy rest.

I dare not choose my lot;
    I would not if I might;
Choose Thou for me, my God;
    So shall I walk aright.

The kingdom that I seek
    Is Thine; so let the way
That leads to it be Thine,
    Else I must surely stray.

Take Thou my cup, and it
    With joy or sorrow fill,
As best to Thee may seem;
    Choose Thou my good and ill;

Choose Thou for me my friends,
    My sickness or my health;
Choose Thou my cares for me,
    My poverty or wealth.

Not mine, not mine the choice,
    In things or great or small;
Be Thou my Guide, my Strength,
    My Wisdom, and my All.
HORATIUS BONAR.

LEAD, KINDLY LIGHT.

LEAD, kindly Light, amid th' encircling gloom,
    Lead Thou me on;
The night is dark, and I am far from home;
    Lead Thou me on;
Keep Thou my feet; I do not ask to see
The distant scene—one step enough for me.

I was not ever thus, nor prayed that Thou
    Shouldst lead me on;
I loved to choose and see my path; but now
    Lead Thou me on.
I loved the garish day, and, spite of fears,
Pride ruled my will. Remember not past years.

So long Thy power has bless'd me, sure it still
    Will lead me on
O'er moor and fen, o'er crag and torrent, till
    The night is gone,
And with the moon those angel faces smile
Which I have loved long since, and lost a while.
JOHN HENRY NEWMAN.

THE VISION OF GOD AND A KNOWLEDGE OF HEAVENLY MYSTERIES.

One thing have I desired of the Lord, that will I seek after; that I may dwell in the house of the Lord all the days of my life, to behold the beauty of the Lord, and to inquire in his temple.—Psalm xxvii., 4.

Dost thou ask what he desires? Peradventure it is a land flowing with milk and honey, in a carnal sense, although this is to be spiritually sought after and desired; or, peradventure, the subjugation of his enemies, or the death of his personal foes, or the power and wealth of this world. For he is on fire with love; much he sigheth, and gloweth, and panteth. Let us see what he desires: "One thing have I desired of the Lord, that will I seek after." What is it he doth seek after? "That I may dwell," saith he, "in the house of the Lord all the days of my life." And suppose thou dost dwell in the house of the Lord, what will be the source of thy joy there? "That I may behold," saith he, "the fair beauty of the Lord."

My brethren, why is it that you cry out, why is it that you exult, why is it that you love, but because the spark of this affection is there? What long you for, I pray you? Can it be seen with the eyes? Can it be touched? Is it some beauty which delights the eyes? Were not the martyrs ardently loved? and when we commemorate them, do not we burn with love? What love we in them, brethren? Their limbs torn by wild beasts? What more loathsome if you ask the eyes of the flesh! What more beautiful if thou ask the eyes of the heart! What would be thy feelings at the sight of some beautiful youth who was a thief? How would thine eyes be shocked? Would the eyes of the flesh be shocked? If thou ask them, nothing more exquisitely adjusted, more gracefully proportioned than that person. The symmetry of the limbs, and the comeliness of the complexion, allure the eyes; yet when thou hearest that he is a thief, thy mind revolts from him. On the other hand, thou seest an old man, bent double, staying himself upon a staff, moving himself with extreme difficulty, furrowed all over with wrinkles; what seest thou to delight thine eyes? Thou art told that he is a righteous man: thou lovest him; thou embracest him.

Such are the rewards promised to us, my brethren. Let such be the object of your affections; such the kingdom for which you sigh; such the country for which you long, if you would attain to that with which our Lord did come — that is, to grace and truth. But if they be bodily rewards which thou hast coveted at God's hand, thou art still under the law, and the law, for that very reason, thou wilt not fulfill. For when thou perceivest those temporal things poured forth in abundance upon men who offend God, thy footsteps falter, and thou sayest to thyself, "Behold, I worship God; every day I run to church; my knees are worn with prayers, and yet I am always sick. Men commit murders, they are guilty of extortion, they overflow and abound, every thing goes on well with them." Were, then, such as these the things thou didst seek at God's hand? Certain it is thou didst belong to grace. If the grace God gave thee is *grace* because *gratuitous*, because he freely gave, then do thou freely love. Do not love God for a reward; let himself be thy reward. Let thy soul say, "ONE thing have I desired of the Lord, that will I seek after; that I may dwell in the house of the Lord all the days of my life, that I may behold the fair beauty of the Lord." Fear not to be cloyed and surfeited. Such will be that beauty that it will be always present with thee, and yet thou wilt never be satiated; or, rather, thou wilt be always satiated and never satiated. For if I should say thou wilt not be satiated, this would imply hunger; and if thou wilt be satiated, I am afraid lest I convey the idea of surfeit. Where there shall be neither surfeit nor yet hunger, I know not what word to use. But God hath it to make good to those who find no word wherewith to express it, yet believe that they shall receive it.—AUGUSTINE.

HEAVEN OUR HOME.

A MAN should be bound for home, as it were, as you see all creatures be. Let a stone be removed from home, from the centre, let it be put out of its place, it will never be quiet till it be put home again. Let a bird be far from the nest and it grows toward night, she will home even upon the wings of the wind. Let every poor beast and every creature, though the entertainment be but slender at home, yet if you let it slip loose, it will home as fast as it can. Every thing tends to its place; there is its safety, there is its rest, there it is preserved, there it is quiet. Now, since it is so with every creature, why should it not be so with us? Why should we not be for our home? This, my brethren, is not our home; here is not our rest. There is our home where our chief friends be, where our Father God is, where our husband Christ is, where our chief kindred and acquaintance be, all the prophets, and apostles, and martyrs of God departed are—that is our home, and thither should we go.—RICHARD SIBBES.

THE ABUNDANT ENTRANCE.

For so an entrance shall be ministered unto you abundantly into the everlasting kingdom of our Lord and Savior Jesus Christ.—2 Peter i., 11.

IT is because God made the entrance into the everlasting kingdom that it is so broad and free. If man had made it, it would have been not only narrow and difficult, but a failure outright. And, indeed, man has attempted to make these human gateways into the everlasting kingdom, and he has persuaded himself that they are very fair and successful, and all sorts of complex rules have been laid down to secure the passage through, but no man ever yet found his way into the everlasting kingdom of Jesus over these legal thresholds. God's way is *free salvation* to all who will take it by trusting his Son. The Gospel is thus marvelously simple—so simple that thousands overlook it. There is no crook or corner in it; the smallest child can comprehend it as well as the loftiest philosopher. It is just this, "Believe on the Lord Jesus." There is no one atom more needed—this is the whole Gospel. Man may learn many interesting and profitable particulars besides, but this is the saving truth; this makes the saint; this secures peace and joy eternal.

Now it is because of this divine simplicity of salvation that the apostle can use the word "abundantly" in the text — "an entrance ministered unto you abundantly." We see the same word in the epistle to Titus (iii., 5, 6), "The Holy Spirit which he shed on us *abundantly* through Jesus Christ." It is elsewhere translated "richly," and refers to the *profusion* of the supply. There is enough and to spare. No demand upon us need find us straitened. If sin rises up and says, "I'm the monster that shall destroy you," we reply, "Christ has robbed you of your fangs, and we defy you." If Satan suggest his doubts, we can refer him to the Master, who has undertaken to transact all our business with Satan. Past remissness, present care, infirmity, trial — we can make one bundle of them all, and commit them to the arm that is ready to receive all our burden. It is an *abundant* entrance, and so any dwelling upon any extreme unworthiness, although all very true, is quite away from the point. God knew that unworthiness before I did, and knows it now far better than I do, and he made the entrance abundant so as to let in the full breadth of my unworthiness. It is utterly vain for me to hunt up an objection when God has provided against every objection for my soul. When it is grace, and that grace *infinite*, that has made the provision, how foolish it is to be objecting any personal deficiency, and suggesting any doubts and difficulties on that score! An acceptance of the grace utterly annihilates all the objections, and leaves the doubts nothing to stand on. Now, although God has made this entrance into his kingdom so gloriously broad that not a sinner need talk of inability, nor a saint fret himself into melancholy, yet we find sinners all over saying, "I can't," and saints all over making themselves very uncomfortable. In regard to the sinners who say "I can't," let me simply say you'd come nearer the truth if you say "I won't." You can't read the Bible and say "I can't." "Whosoever will, let him come and take the water of life freely," doesn't sound very suggestive of inability. But the text is not addressed to sinners, but to saints, and to God's people I now commend it. I speak to the melancholy ones who have made God's abundant entrance so narrow that it is always pinching them. The text says, "So the entrance shall be ministered (or furnished) unto you abundantly." What does that "so" refer to? To the acquisition and growth of the seven graces in addition to faith, to wit, virtue, knowledge, temperance, patience, godliness, brotherly kindness, and charity. In other words, growth in the elements of the Christian life will widen the entrance to us individually, making us more and more aware of the exceeding fullness of our salvation. The use of the same verb (and an uncommon one) in the Greek is striking, "Giving all diligence, *furnish* with your faith virtue," etc. . . . . "for so an entrance shall be *furnished* you abundantly." If you'll diligently add to your graces, God will add to your peace and joy. Here, then, we have reached the great lesson of the text. May the Holy Spirit write it deeply on our hearts!—HOWARD CROSBY.

DEATH WELCOME.

DEATH comes at Christ's command to call the believer to himself; and, grim and ghastly though be the look of the messenger, surely that may well be welcome in the sweetness of the message he brings. Death comes to set the spirit free; and, rude though be the hand that knocks off the fetters, and painful though be the process of liberation, what need the prisoner care for that when it is to freedom, life, and honor he is about to be emancipated? Death strikes the hour of the soul's everlasting espousals; and, though the sound may be harsh, what matters that? To common ears it may seem a death-knell; to the ear of faith it is a bridal peal.—JOHN CAIRD.

THE ROD.

VISITING a friend one day, Gotthold found him seated with his family at table, and observed that the children all received a due portion of food, and were required to eat it in a quiet and orderly way; but that beside the father's plate there was also lying upon the table a rod, to warn them against improprieties of conduct and manners. He thereupon observed to his friend: "You treat your children as our heavenly Father treats his. He, too, prepares a table before them, and gives them all sorts of good things, spiritual and temporal, to enjoy, and yet the rod, which is another name for the cross, must likewise be at hand, that we may not become froward, but walk in holy fear and filial obedience. Of this truth God has given us almost a similar emblem in the sacred Scriptures; for the ark of the Old Testament contained not only the golden pot with the manna, but also Aaron's rod, which blossomed, to intimate the authority he exercises over his family, and teach us that, although he feeds the members with the hidden manna of his sweet grace, he also purposes to use the rod if he shall see cause, and to do both the one and the other for our welfare and salvation. The same hand prepares the table and wields the rod. From one and the same heart flow both comfort and cross. God continues our loving and gracious Father when he chastens and corrects no less than when he refreshes and comforts us. A good man once pertinently said that it was a doubtful matter whether bread or chastisement was best for children, because, while bread was necessary for them to live, chastisement was necessary for their living well. Even so must we, too, confess that the dear cross is as needful to us as life itself, and far more needful and salutary than all the blessings and honors of the world. In heaven, the glorified spirits, who now fully understand its mystery, and enjoy in the everlasting rest the sweet fruit which grows upon the thorny brier, will thank the all-wise and gracious God especially for his holy cross and fatherly correction, without which they would never have reached the seat of bliss and glory. Let us also learn this lesson, and say from the heart, 'It is good for me that I have been afflicted, that I might learn thy statutes.' Whether we like it or not, the Lord our God will not change his ways. Whosoever wishes to be a child must take bread and sorrow together from his hand. No guest at his table need think it strange to see the rod upon it, and be obliged to eat his heavenly Father's bread moistened with tears. Here in this world it can not be otherwise; but when we shall one day sit at his table in heaven, every rod shall be cast into the fire. Oh, my Father! I am becoming accustomed by degrees to thy ways, and have no objection to the rules of thy domestic government. Daily do I strive to learn not only to relish the bread, but also to kiss the rod."—CHRISTIAN SCRIVER.

LOVE OF GOD.

HISTORY's noblest deed and record of love is in the self-devotion of one generous heathen, Pylades, who forfeited his life to save his friend. But "God commendeth his love to us in that, while we were yet sinners, Christ died for us." "You have not yet seen," says a great writer and profound thinker, "the greatest gift of all—the heart of God, the love of his heart, the heart of his love. And will he, in very deed, show us that? Yes; unveil that cross and see. It was his only mode of showing us his heart. It is infinite love laboring to reveal itself, agonizing to utter the fullness of infinite love; apart from that act, a boundless ocean of love concealed in the heart of God. But now it has found an ocean channel. Beyond this he can not go. Once and forever the proof has been given — 'God is love.' "—J. R. MACDUFF.

"*REST ONLY IN GOD.*"

My spirit longeth for Thee,
   Within my troubled breast,
Although I be unworthy
   Of so divine a Guest.

Of so divine a Guest
   Unworthy though I be,
Yet has my heart no rest
   Unless it come from Thee.

Unless it come from Thee,
   In vain I look around;
In all that I can see
   No rest is to be found.

No rest is to be found
   But in Thy blessed love;
Oh let my wish be crowned,
   And send it from above!

JOHN BYROM.

IN pain, sickness, trouble, methinks I hear God say, "Take this medicine, exactly suited to the case, prepared and weighed by my own hand, and consisting of the choicest drugs which heaven affords."

SIN FORGIVEN IN OLD AGE.

Though your sins be as scarlet, they shall be as white as snow.—Isaiah i., 18.

Oh ye that lean wearily on your staff, the support of your old age, have ye not sins still clinging to your garments? Are your lives as white as the snowy hair that crowns your head? Do you not still feel that transgression besmears the skirts of your robe and mars its spotlessness? How often are you now plunged into the ditch till your own clothes do abhor you? Cast your eyes over the sixty, the seventy, the eighty years during which God hath spared your lives, and can ye for a moment think it possible that ye can number up your innumerable transgressions, or compute the weight of the crimes which you have committed? Oh ye stars of heaven! the astronomer may measure your distance and tell your height, but, oh ye sins of mankind! ye surpass all thought. Oh ye lofty mountains, the home of the tempest, the birthplace of the storm! man may climb your summits and stand wonderingly upon your snows, but, ye hills of sin! ye tower higher than our thoughts; ye chasms of transgressions! ye are deeper than our imagination dares to dive. Do you accuse me of slandering hu-

man nature? It is because you know it not. If
God had once manifested your heart to yourself,
you would bear me witness that, so far from exag-
gerating, my poor words fail to describe the desperateness of our evil. Oh! if we could each of us
look into our hearts to-day—if our eyes could be
turned within so as to see the iniquity that is graven
as with the point of the diamond upon our stony
hearts, we should then say to the minister, that however he may depict the desperateness of guilt, yet
can he not by any means surpass it. How great,
then, beloved, must be the ransom of Christ when
he saved us from all these sins! The men for
whom Jesus died, however great their sin, when
they believe, are justified from all their transgressions. Though they may have indulged in every
vice and every lust which Satan could suggest and
which human nature could perform, yet, once believing, all their guilt is washed away. Year after
year may have coated them with blackness till their
sin hath become of double dye; but in one moment
of faith, one triumphant moment of confidence in
Christ, the great redemption takes away the guilt
of numerous years. Nay, more; if it were possible
for all the sins that men had done, in thought, or
word, or deed, since worlds were made or time began, to meet on one poor head, the great redemp-

tion is all-sufficient to take all these sins away, and wash the sinner whiter than the driven snow.—SPURGEON.

RELIGIOUS DEPRESSION.

THERE are hours in which physical derangement darkens the windows of the soul; days in which shattered nerves make life simply endurance; months and years in which intellectual difficulties, pressing for solution, shut out God. Then faith must be replaced by hope. "What I do thou knowest not now, but thou shalt know hereafter." Clouds and darkness are round about him; but righteousness and truth are the habitation of his throne. "My soul, hope thou in God, for I shall yet praise him, who is the health of my countenance and my God."

David's hope was IN God.

The mistake we make is to look for a source of comfort in ourselves; self-contemplation, instead of gazing upon God. In other words, we look for comfort precisely where comfort can never be.

For, first, it is impossible to derive consolation from our feelings, because of their mutability; to-day we are well, and our spiritual experience, partaking of these circumstances, is bright; but to-mor-

LIGHT AT EVENING TIME. 165

row some outward circumstances change—the sun does not shine, or the wind is chill, and we are low, gloomy, and sad. Then, if our hopes were unreasonably elevated, they will now be unreasonably depressed; and so our experience becomes flux and reflux, ebb and flow, like the sea, that emblem of instability.

Next, it is impossible to get comforts from our own acts; for, though acts are the test of character, yet in a low state no man can judge justly of his own acts. They assume a darkness of hue which is reflected on them by the eye that contemplates them. It would be well for all men to remember that sinners can not judge of sin, least of all can we estimate our own sin.

Besides, we lose time in remorse. I have sinned. Well, by the grace of God, I must endeavor to do better for the future. But if I mourn for it overmuch all to-day, refusing to be comforted, to-morrow I shall have to mourn the wasted to-day, and that, again, will be the subject of another fit of remorse.

In the wilderness, had the children of Israel, instead of gazing on the serpent, looked down on their own wounds, to watch the process of the granulation of the flesh, and see how deep the wound was, and whether it was healing slowly or fast, cure would have been impossible; their only chance was to look off the wounds. Just so, when giving up this hopeless and sickening work of self-inspection, and turning from ourselves in Christian self-oblivion, we gaze on God, then first the chance of consolation dawns.

He is not affected by our mutability; our changes do not alter him. When we are restless, he remains serene and calm; when we are low, selfish, mean, or dispirited, he is still the unalterable *I AM*—"the same yesterday, to-day, and forever, in whom is no variableness, neither shadow of turning." What God is in himself—not what we may chance to feel him in this or that moment to be—that is our hope. "My soul, hope thou IN GOD."—F. W. ROBERTSON.

THE BELIEVER'S DEATH.

Though a believer may have his darkness, doubts, and fears, and many conflicts of soul while on his dying bed, yet usually these are all over and gone before his last moments come. From the gracious promises of God to be with his people even unto death, and from the observations I have made through the course of my life, I am of opinion that generally the people of God die comfortably, their spiritual enemies being made to be as still as a stone while they pass through Jordan.—JOHN GILL.

SUFFERING A HIGHER PATH THAN DOING.

SAUL had anxiously inquired, "What wouldst thou have me to do?" Our Lord sends his minister to tell him, not what great things he shall do, but what far greater things he shall suffer.

Sufferings are, after all, the great achievements of the Christian. Where one man is permitted to effect mighty things for his Lord by carrying the words of the everlasting Gospel over the burning sands of Africa, or the frozen mountains of the north, thousands and tens of thousands are called to the high privilege of the Philippians of old, "not only to believe, but also to suffer for his name's sake." To sit on his right hand and on his left are not now to be given, but to drink of his cup of trial, and to be baptized with his baptism of affliction, are still among the choicest blessings which he bestows upon his people. Be not, then, disappointed, if, with every desire to do great things for your divine Master, you are denied the power or the opportunity. If, as it has been beautifully said, "They also serve who only stand and wait," how much more do they serve who are called upon to endure and to suffer! Yes; in the chamber of sickness, upon the bed of pain, you may as greatly glorify your Redeemer as amid the trials of the mission or the tortures of the stake; and often does it please your heavenly Father that while you are meditating what great things you shall do for Christ, he is preparing the great things you shall suffer.

THE ABIDING CITY.

For here we have no continuing city.—Hebrews xiii., 14.

WE'VE no abiding city here:
   This may distress the worldling's mind,
But should not cost the soul a tear,
   Who hopes a better rest to find.

We've no abiding city here:
   Sad truth! were this to be our home;
But let this thought our spirits cheer—
   We seek a city yet to come.

We've no abiding city here:
   Then let us live as pilgrims do;
Let not the world our rest appear,
   But let us haste from all below.

We've no abiding city here:
   We seek a city out of sight;
Zion its name, the Lord is there,
   It shines with everlasting light.

Zion! Jehovah is her strength;
  Secure she smiles at all her foes;
And weary travelers at length
  Within her sacred walls repose.

Oh sweet abode of peace and love,
  Where pilgrims freed from toil are bless'd!
Had I the pinions of the dove,
  I'd fly to Thee, and be at rest.

THOMAS KELLY.

LOOKING TO CHRIST.

THERE is no holiness if thou, Lord, withdraw thy presence; no wisdom profiteth if thy Spirit cease to direct; no strength availeth without thy support; no chastity is safe without thy protection; no watchfulness effectual when thy holy vigilance is not our guard; for no sooner are we left to ourselves than the waves of corruption rush upon us, and we sink and perish; but if thou reach forth thy omnipotent hand, we walk upon the sea and live. In our own nature we are unsettled as the sand upon the mountain, but in thee we have the stability of the throne in heaven. We are cold and insensible as darkness and death, but are kindled with light and life by the holy fire of thy love.—THOMAS À KEMPIS.

SOME NOBLE LIVES.

A LIFE OF FAITH.

We are called Christians, and our name connects us with Christ. For our Christian life is one of faith. We are distinguished from the rest of men by believing Christ. We are marked by our faith. The object of that faith is the Lord Jesus, the Son of God. He was disclosed to us in the Word. The Holy Spirit fixed our attention on him, showed us our need of him as Savior, and in his own way led us to trust in him and be his. This distinguishes us from all who are living to themselves or to the devil. They may assign different reasons for their course of conduct when you take them to task. You inquire why they are not religious, which they are likely to interpret in reference to their acts, such as going to the church and receiving the communion. They will tell you, perhaps, they do not like the church, or the minister, or the pew, or the worshipers—any thing but the simple fact that they do not wish for the inward power of religion. They do not desire to be what Christ would have them to be. Just as there are persons who do not choose to be under the oversight of a minister, to be missed from church, or to be warned or cautioned, and who invent other reasons for their conduct, so there are unbelievers in Christ who offer reasons for their ways altogether wide of the truth. They are averse to the fellowship, to the law, to the authority of him whom we preach as a Savior from sin, but they will not say so in words. On the other hand, a godly life is a life of faith, beginning and running on through faith. The story of Benjamin West, the greatest artist America has yet produced, may well illustrate this truth. When a boy of seven, he was sitting by the cradle of an elder sister's infant, when the child smiled in its sleep. Charmed with its beauty, the boy got paper and made a portrait of it; the kiss that acknowledged his effort inspired him to follow the bent of his taste. There were no models, no teachers. The simple Quaker people, of whom he was one, were on principle opposed to his art, though they gave way afterward, and through extraordinary difficulties he prosecuted his career, in Philadelphia, Rome, and London, till he was President of the Royal Academy, and the painter of "Death on the Pale Horse." From the first to the last, the one prevailing taste urged him on. It was his life. So it is with the believer, from the time when the Redeemer wins his regard, attracts his confidence, and becomes the object of his faith.

And how does Christ attract the soul? As he

attracted Paul's. Let the apostle tell it himself, "Who loved me and gave himself for me." The manifested love of Christ wins the confidence of the heart. And what is the character of that love? It is free; unbought; unsolicited; saving; self-denying; it is love unto death, measured by the height of heaven, whence Christ came down, by the depth of sorrow and humiliation to which he descended— "Who loved me and gave himself for me." Measure it! Nay, it is immeasurable; infinite; everlasting. And it has, if possible, another charm. It is individual love. David was a true patriot, but in the nature of things every Hebrew could not be a Jonathan to him. But to the Redeemer of men every believer is as a brother, loved with an individualizing love—"Who loved me and gave himself for me." When we look on the clear, starry sky, we are perplexed by the multitude of lights, and we can only single out and identify the brighter among them. But the astronomer will fix his glass on one far away in the silent depths, and watch it in its movements as if there was not another twinkling sister in all the sky. And so through all the ages, and all the millions of chosen saints —stars-to-be in heaven forever—the eye of the Redeemer, all-seeing, fixes its gaze on each as truly as if there were not another, and settles the plan of his life as if it were the sole object of his care.

A LIFE "IN THE FLESH."

Some one may pronounce such a life as I have described transcendental and impossible except in heaven. But it is a life "in the flesh;" not in the bad sense, as opposed to life in the spirit, but in the good sense, as opposed to life in glory. Paul says the life which he lived "in the flesh" he lived "by the faith of the Son of God."

Being a life in the flesh, it is subject to all the conditions of earthly life. Faith in Christ will not exempt from the pain that racks the body, nor from the sorrow that harrows the mind. It will not avert the temptation to evil, though it will help to resist it, and it will not ward off weariness, though it enables us to hold out when any other power would fail. It will not secure us against errors and mistakes, though it makes us sorry for them, and sets us to repair them; and it will not avert death, though it makes us more than conquerors over it. The earth is redeemed, but the thorns and the thistles still remain. The curse is lifted off the Lord's people, though they still toil uncertainly, and with labor and pain. But the thorns and thistles have been converted into benefits, and the toil and anxiety turned into lesson-books in which God's children acquire the knowledge of sin, of themselves, and of God. How shall they know how evil and bitter transgression is if they feel not its temporal consequences? These are shut out of heaven. Where shall they learn such graces as patience, submission, and contentment under privations if not on earth? Heaven has nothing to evoke or exercise these graces. Paul, therefore, who lives the life of faith, has his share of "tribulation," but he glories in it. He endures sufferings, but he rejoices in them. I can not but think that the Hebrew children, if they had any eyes for the fires, or for any thing but their Companion, might have looked with some pardonable exultation on the flames that raged impotent around them. And so do the godly, when faith is in full vigor within, feel their advantage over the trials of this present time, as a general on the battle-field when he takes and turns upon his foes their own guns. "For our light affliction, which is but for a moment, worketh for us a far more exceeding and eternal weight of glory."

A LIFE OF SELF-DENYING EFFORT.

But, as it is "a life in the flesh," the life of the godly must be a life of self-denial. There are appetites within us calling for indulgence. They must be held in check. There are tastes seeking gratification. They must be held in their place. There are passions ready to leap forth upon their respective objects; and, like appetites and tastes, they must be kept under the all-dominating sway of conscience. That conscience has authority from God. We may deny it the power, but, like a rightful sovereign dethroned, it has authority to utter its commands, though passions, like rebellious subjects, may be too powerful to be forced to obedience. Its court is set up by our Creator, and it makes and issues its decrees. We may refuse it executive power. It will, however, proceed to register its judgments; and the finally impenitent shall read them, if not here, in the light of the great white throne, and it may be through eternity. We must see that conscience be at once enlightened by the Word that its sentences be just, and that it be obeyed.

This implies diligence in keeping the heart; watchfulness against temptations; resistance to evil; and endurance in the struggle—all which are against our natural love of ease. But they are necessary. Many things impair the health though they are not fatal; and a godly man would have the utmost vigor with which to serve God. He must sleep like the soldier who lies down with his weapons beside him on the battle-field to guard against a surprise.

"Soldier, rest, but not for thee
　　Spreads the world its downy pillow;
On the rock thy couch must be,
　　While around thee chafes the billow.
Thine must be a watchful sleep,
　　Wearier than another's waking;
Such a charge as thou dost keep
　　Brooks no moment of forsaking."

A LIFE OF DEPENDENCE.

And on this account also is a godly life a life of dependence. A good man does not get a store of grace at his conversion to serve him all his life. He gets it daily, hourly. The children of God get the manna as they require it, that they may learn dependence on God. To live "from hand to mouth," as the proverb has it, in things temporal, is far from being prudent, but it is the only wise way in things spiritual. And this dependence is complete. We get holiness from the same saving grace that brings us forgiveness. An incident of the crucifixion is left on record, doubtless, to teach us this. A soldier pierced the Savior's side with his spear, and "forthwith came thereout blood and water." Both came from the wounded side. The atonement that brings pardon is attended by the water that purifies. "Both elements flow from the same heart of love, pierced by the spear of justice, and are poured out with the same design and for the same persons."

A TRULY NOBLE LIFE.

But let no one be repelled by the general aspect of this godly life; for, after all, it employs the noblest and best feelings of which our nature is capable. It is a life of the loftiest style attainable by man. It carries us farthest away from the mean and the sordid. Look at its exercises. Hope smooths the brow, lightens the eye, and nerves the arm.

> "Auspicious Hope! in whose sweet garden grow
> Wreaths for each toil, a charm for every woe."

Hume was no sentimentalist; he saw that "a propensity to hope and joy is real riches; to fear and sorrow, real poverty." Hope is the medicine of the miserable.

> "True hope is swift, and flies with swallows' wings,
> Kings it makes gods, and meaner creatures kings."

So many have said of hope—their common earthly hope—of which, as Leighton says, they dare only say "*dum spiro spero*" (while I breathe I hope), but the children of God can say "*dum expiro spero*" (while I die I hope). Hope, joy, gratitude, love, these are the feelings this life brings into play.

They are the highest we can exercise. If our hearts are to be opened and expanded; if despondency is to be commanded away; if selfishness is to die out within us, these are the very feelings to be employed for the purpose. Nor is there any thing tumultuous in their movements, for peace is diffused over all—such peace as filled the holy soul of Jesus Christ when making it his meat and drink to do his Father's will. Hence gentleness, goodness, meekness come into play, to complete the harmony of the character, and to render the child of God Christlike. Is there any thing mean or sordid about these feelings? We pity the desponding; we shun the coarse and rude; we despise the selfish and the envious; we fear the vindictive and the malicious; we shrink from the heartless and unloving; but we cling to the joyous and hopeful, the generous and grateful. We admire the unselfish; we are drawn to the meek, patient, and gentle; we love the loving. We can not have any goodness in ourselves without feeling the power and owning the worth of these qualities; but these are just the qualities in which this life consists. You may have thought, dear readers, that if you set yourselves to be godly people, you must become machines rather than men, dull, depressed drudges, working out your slave's-task of duty without one element of what your heart feels to be "life," until you get into heaven, and become, through what change I know not, capable of enjoying what your nature here counts misery. It is a hateful lie. Every thing that belongs to real life is in the godly here, and if it were not in them here, what room is there for its production hereafter? Does death regenerate? Does the stroke that lays low the body alter the nature of the soul? No. Death can but set the seal of changelessness on the character it finds in us. If we be living a life on earth "by the faith of the Son of God," death can but draw aside the curtain of flesh, and let the light from his immediate glory fall on our naked souls, to make clear and perfect that image of himself which only showed in broken lines while he appeared dimly to our hardly unbelieving hearts. In the warmth and security of heaven, the elements of our life, that were like stunted shrubs growing in uncongenial soil, expand into the perfection of their nature; but these elements must be in us here, or they shall never be matured hereafter.—JOHN HALL.

GRACE teaches us, in the midst of life's greatest comforts, to be willing to die, and in the midst of its greatest crosses to be willing to live.—MATTHEW HENRY.

FEELINGS CHANGEFUL.

The variableness of Christian moods is often a matter of great and unnecessary suffering; but Christian life does not follow the changes of feeling. Our feelings are but the torch, and our life is the man that carries it. The wind that flares the flame does not make the man waver. The flame may sway hither and thither, but he holds his course straight on. Thus oftentimes it is that our Christian hopes are carried as one carries a lighted candle through the windy street, that seems never to be so nearly blown out as when we step through the open door, and in a moment are safe within. Our wind-blown feelings rise and fall through all our life, and the draught of death threatens quite to extinguish them; but one moment more, and they shall rise and forever shine serenely in the unstormed air of heaven.—H. W. Beecher.

WAITING TIMES.

Waiting times are times when God is pleased to give his people some sweet tastes of his love, and to lift up the light of his countenance upon them.—Thomas Brooks.

THE RETURNING WANDERER.

WEARY of wandering from my God,
  And now made willing to return,
I hear, and bow me to the rod;
  For Him, not without hope, I mourn;
I have an Advocate above,
A friend before the throne of Love.

O Jesu, full of pardoning grace,
  More full of grace than I of sin,
Yet once again I seek Thy face;
  Open Thine arms and take me in,
And freely my backslidings heal,
And love the faithless sinner still.

Thou know'st the way to bring me back,
  My fallen spirit to restore;
O, for Thy truth and mercy's sake,
  Forgive, and bid me sin no more!
The ruins of my soul repair,
And make my heart an house of prayer.

The stone to flesh again convert,
  The veil of sin once more remove;
Drop Thy warm blood upon my heart,
  And melt it with Thy dying love:
This rebel heart by love subdue,
And make it soft, and make it new.

Give to mine eyes refreshing tears,
　And kindle my relentings now;
Fill all my soul with filial fears,
　To the sweet yoke my spirits bow;
Bend by Thy grace—oh bend, or break
The iron sinew in my neck.

Ah! give me, Lord, the tender heart,
　That trembles at th' approach of sin;
A godly fear of sin impart,
　Implant, and root it deep within;
That I may dread Thy gracious power,
And never dare offend Thee more.
CHARLES WESLEY.

THE SAINT'S DELIGHT IN GOD.

IN what transports have holy souls been upon the view and contemplation of his sovereign power and dominion; his wise and righteous government; his large and flowing goodness, that extends in common to all the works of his hands! Labor to imitate the ingenuous and loyal affection of this kind, whereof you find many expressions in the sacred volume. For what hath been master of delight to saints of old ought surely still as much to be accounted so. To give instances:

You sometimes find them in a most complacential adoration of his wonderful wisdom and counsels. Oh the depth of the riches both of the wisdom and knowledge of God! How unsearchable are his judgments, and his ways past finding out! (Rom. xi., 33.) And again: To God only wise, be glory, through Jesus Christ, forever, Amen (Rom. xvi., 27). To the king eternal, immortal, invisible, the only wise God, be honor and glory forever (1 Tim. i., 17), etc. To the only wise God our Savior be glory and majesty, dominion and power, now and ever (Jude 25, etc.). Elsewhere we have them in transports admiring his holiness. Who is like unto thee, O Lord, among the gods! Who is like thee, glorious in holiness! (Exod. xv., 11.) There is none holy as the Lord; for there is none besides thee, neither is there any rock like our God (1 Sam. ii., 2). And this is recommended and enjoined to his holy ones as the special matter of their joy and praise: Rejoice in the Lord, ye righteous, and give thanks at the remembrance of his holiness (Psalm xcvii., 12). At other times we have their magnificent celebrations of his glorious power, and that by way of triumph over the paganish gods: Our God is in the heavens: he hath done whatsoever he pleased (Psalm cxv., 3). Their idols are silver and gold, etc. Be thou exalted, O God, in thine own strength (Psalm xxi., 13). We will sing and praise thy power. Forsake me not until I have showed thy strength unto this generation, and thy power to every one that is to come (Psalm lxxi., 18). This is given out as the song of Moses and the Lamb: Who shall not fear thee, O Lord, and glorify thy name? Great and marvelous are thy works, Lord God Almighty, etc. And how do they magnify his mercy and goodness, both toward his own people and his creatures in general (Psalm xxxi., 19). Oh how great is thy goodness which thou hast laid up for them that fear thee; which thou hast wrought for them that trust in thee before the children of men! Rejoice in the Lord, O ye righteous, for praise is comely for the upright; praise the Lord with harp; sing unto him with the psaltery (Psalm xxxiii., 1, etc.). The earth is full of the goodness of the Lord. I will extol thee, my God, oh King; I will bless thy name for ever and ever (Psalm cxlv., 1, etc.). Men shall speak of the might of thy terrible acts; they shall abundantly utter the memory of thy great goodness, and shall sing of thy righteousness. The Lord is gracious and full of compassion, slow to anger, and of great mercy. The Lord is good to all, and his tender mercies are over all his works. To insert all that might be mentioned to this purpose were to transcribe a great part of the Bible. And in what raptures do we often find them in the contemplation of his faithfulness and truth; his justice and righteousness; his eternity; the boundlessness of his presence; the greatness of his works; the extensiveness of his dominion; the perpetuity of his kingdom; the exactness of his government. Who is a strong God like unto thee, and to thy faithfulness round about thee? (Psalm lxix.) Thy mercy, O Lord, is in the heavens, and thy faithfulness reaches unto the clouds (Psalm xxxvi.). Before the mountains were brought forth, or ever thou hadst formed the earth or the world, from everlasting to everlasting thou art God (Psalm xc., 2). But will God indeed dwell on the earth? Behold, the heaven and heaven of heavens can not contain thee (1 Kings viii.). The works of the Lord are great, sought out of them that have pleasure therein. His work is honorable and glorious (Psalm cxi., etc.). All thy works shall praise thee, O Lord, and thy saints shall bless thee; they shall speak of the glory of thy kingdom, and talk of thy power, to make known to the sons of men his mighty acts, and the glorious majesty of his kingdom (Psalm cxlv.). Thy kingdom is an everlasting kingdom, and thy dominion endureth throughout all generations.

And his glory in the general (which results from his several excellences in conjunction), how loftily is it often celebrated with the expression of the most loyal desires, that it may be every where renowned, and of greatest complacency, in as far as it is apprehended so to be. The glory of the Lord shall endure forever. They shall sing in the ways of the Lord, for great is the glory of the Lord. Be thou exalted above the heavens: let thy glory be above all the earth (**Psalm civ., 31**; **cxxxviii., 5**; **lvii., 7, 11**). Let them praise the name of the Lord, for his name alone is excellent; his glory is above the earth and the heavens (**Psalm cxlviii., 13**). When you read such passages as these (whether they be elegies or commendations of him, or doxologies and direct attributions of glory to him), you are to bethink yourselves with what temper of heart these things were uttered; with how raised and exalted a spirit; what high delight and pleasure was conceived in glorifying God, or in beholding him glorious. How large and unbounded a heart, and how full of his praise, doth still every where discover itself in such strains; when all nations, when all creatures—when every thing that hath breath—when heaven and earth are invited together to join in the concert and bear a part in his praises!—JOHN HOWE.

THE SICKNESS AND DEATH OF ELISHA.
2 Kings xiii., 14.

ELIJAH was spared the common doom of mortality, and was taken to heaven in a chariot and horses of fire, without dying. But Elisha, who had honored God so much longer, goes the way of all the earth. Why was this difference? Even so, Father; for so it seemed good in thy sight. But he does not die of natural infirmity; neither does he die suddenly—he had fallen sick. This mode of dissolution was less desirable with regard to comfort, but it was more favorable to usefulness. It afforded him opportunity for glorifying God, and instructing and impressing his attendants. And "the chamber where the good man meets his fate" has often been to others, as well as to the dying individual himself, the house of God, and the gate of heaven.—WILLIAM JAY.

POVERTY IN OLD AGE.

WHEN Mr. Wilberforce had lost his fortune and was in reduced circumstances—his confidence was still in God—he said, "He will not suffer me to be disgraced in my old age. What gives me support in all things is the thought of their being his appointment. I doubt not that the same God who has in mercy ordered so many events for so long a course of time, will never fail to overrule all things both for my family and myself." And on recovering from a temporary illness, "I can scarce understand," he said, "why my life is spared so long except it be to show that a man can be as happy without a fortune as with one;" and then soon after, when his only surviving daughter died, he writes, "I have often heard that sailors on a voyage will drink 'Friends a-stern' till they are half way over, then 'Friends a-head.' With me it has been 'Friends a-head' this long time."

THE BELIEVER'S SUFFICIENCY.

"Thus saith the Lord that created thee, O Jacob, and he that formed thee, O Israel, Fear not. I have redeemed thee; I have called thee by THY NAME."

What a beautiful thought that is! Just get the meaning and beauty out of it. How many thousands of believers, thousands and thousands of believers, have there been in the world from the beginning of its history until now—thousands in the patriarchal ages who looked through the glass, and who saw dimly the streak of the morning in the distance, and even with that streak of light were glad —thousands in the prophetical times who discovered it in the brightness of a nearer vision—thousands who basked in its full-orbed lustre when Christ came into the world—thousands upon thousands since that time who have washed their robes and made them white in the blood of the Lamb— thousands who are now upon the earth working out their salvation with fear and trembling—thousands upon thousands that shall come into the Church in the time of its millennial glory, when the gates of it shall not be shut day nor night, because the porter shall have no chance of shutting them, the people crowd in so fast. Now get all that mass of believers, past, present, and future, a company that no man can number, and to each of them God comes in this promise, and says, "I have called thee by thy name; I know all about thee"—that is, I have not a merely vague, indefinite knowledge of thee. As an individual believer, I know thy name; I could single thee out of millions; I could tell the world all thy solicitudes, and all thy apprehensions, and all thy hopes, and all thy sorrows. "I have called thee by thy name." Oh, precious promise! Take it to your hearts. "I have called thee by thy name; thou art mine. When thou passest through the waters I will be with thee, and through the rivers"—deeper than the waters—they shall not overflow thee. "When thou walkest through the fire thou shalt not be burned, neither shall the flames kindle upon thee."—W. M. PUNSHON.

ENTERING INTO REST.

AND while the soul shall pass to God, to enter on the rest of glory, the mortal body has its rest no less, sleeping peacefully till the resurrection day. And when the green grass of another June waves over us; when the soft summer wind of another June sighs through the green leaves; when the sunshine of some more genial longest day shall brighten cheerfully the stone which shall bear our name and yours, what better can we wish than that, if we leave behind us those who may sometimes visit the quiet spot, they may be able to say, humbly and hopefully, "Surely here at last, and surely there in a better place, the weary heart and hand are still; yea, surely God hath given his beloved sleep?"—MADAME DE GASPARIN.

GRACE tried is better than grace, as it is more than grace—it is glory in its infancy.—SAMUEL RUTHERFORD.

THE TROUBLES OF LIFE.

SOMETIMES I compare the troubles which we have to undergo in the course of the year to a great bundle of fagots, far too great for us to lift; but God does not require us to carry the whole at once. He mercifully unties the bundle, and gives us first one stick, which we are to carry to-day, and then another, which we are to carry to-morrow, and so on. This we might easily manage if we would only take the burden appointed for us each day; but we choose to increase our troubles by carrying yesterday's stick over again to-day, and adding to-morrow's burden to our load before we are required to bear it.—JOHN NEWTON.

PATIENT WAITING.

"PATIENCE, poor soul! the Savior's feet were worn;
  The Savior's heart and hands were weary too;
His garments stained, and travel-worn, and old;
  His vision blinded with a pitying dew.
Love thou the paths of sorrow that he trod;
  Toil on, and wait in patience for thy rest;
Oh! city of our God, we soon shall see
  Thy glorious walls—home of the loved and bless'd."
                              Anon.

THROUGH DARKNESS TO LIGHT.

. . . . IT dwelt on her mind that for some deficiency in her Christian character this chastisement had been appointed. The language of her contrite prayer was, "Lord, what wilt thou have me to do?" And he told her; and she became a mother in Israel; a sleepless, untiring benevolence was the striking lineaments of her life. After the stroke of widowhood fell upon her, and she stood entirely alone, it seemed as if every vestige of selfishness was extinct, and that her whole existence was devoted to the good of others.—*Anon.*

PERSONAL GOODNESS.

IT is common enough to confound religion with a series of religious acts. A man's prayers are offered with regularity; his place in God's house is never vacant; his donation is never wanting when there is a call upon him; he goes regularly to "the communion." But these religious acts are only the stones in the river of his life, which flows through them and over them, but is not of them. Hard, distinct, and, in part, of another nature from his life, they are interruptions of the current of his being rather than a help to it or a part of it. Religion of the true and genuine kind, on the other hand, is the water of the river. It has entered into the man's being. It has penetrated his heart, and guided his affections. It has reached his will, and touched its springs. It has moulded his tastes, and bridled his appetites. It has helped to form his plans, and colored his being. His love to God has become as truly a part of his being as his love to wife or child. He is not doing religion—he is religious. "The Word and the sacraments," says Henry Smith, the Puritan, "are the two breasts from which our mother church nurses her children." But the dead child can not be nursed. It is the living that feed on the Word and sacraments. They only can say, "The life I live in the flesh I live by the faith of the Son of God." Then let us look at the "*religious*" (as the monk is called), who has given himself up to the service of God. His garments are only for worship. His work is to pray and praise. He is a dweller in the courts of God's house. He is devoted to "religion." Is all right with him? Not necessarily. His seclusion, that shuts him out from men, may not shut him up to God. He may be in "religion," but not in Christ. He may put on the monk's hood, and not put on the wedding garment. Religion is not only life — it is an INWARD life

There may be an unbroken profession of godliness as credible as that of Judas, in whose cloak of "covetousness" there was not a rent. The sheep's clothing may fit so exactly that not a suspicion shall be raised; but "the kingdom of God is within you," and if it be not there the forms of godliness are forms only.—JOHN HALL.

DIFFICULTIES SOLVED.

SOME one said to Copernicus, "If the world were constituted as you say, Venus would have phases like the moon; she has none, however. What have you to say to that?" Copernicus answered, "I have no reply to give, but God will be so good as that an answer to this difficulty will be found." In fact, GOD WAS SO GOOD that Galileo invented the telescope with which these phases of Venus were discovered; but Copernicus was dead. GOD will be so good that we shall see the prodigies of his power; but we shall then be living an eternal life, and shall only wonder at one thing—our own former difficulties, when we could depend upon the great God of heaven for their solution.—MADAME DE GASPARIN.

—BUT Patience was willing to wait.—J. BUNYAN.

SAVED BY GRACE.

MR. M‘LAREN and Mr. Gustart were both ministers of the Tolbooth Church, Edinburg. When Mr. M‘Laren was dying, Mr. Gustart paid him a visit, and put the question to him, "What are you doing, brother?" His answer was, "I'll tell you what I am doing, brother. I am gathering together all my prayers, all my sermons, all my good deeds, all my ill deeds, and I am going to swim to glory on the plank of FREE GRACE."—J. WHITECROSS.

WORDS OF CHEER.

DROOPING art thou in the service
   Of thy loved and loving Lord?
Do thy hands, thy feet, oft falter?
   Listen to this cheering word:

To the faint God giveth power,
   To the weak increaseth strength;
And they that wait on him shall mount
   Up on eagles' wings at length.

They shall run and not be weary,
   They shall walk and shall not faint:
Such the promise of thy Father,
   "Weary, yet pursuing" saint.

TRIAL OF THE WORLDLY CHRISTIAN.

It is a painful work, that weeding work. "Every branch in me that beareth fruit, he purgeth it, that it may bring forth more fruit." The keen edge of God's pruning-knife cuts sheer through. No weak tenderness stops him whose love seeks goodness, not comfort, for his servants. A man's distractions are in his wealth, and perhaps fire or failure make him bankrupt. What he feels is God's sharp knife. Pleasures have dissipated his heart, and a stricken frame forbids his enjoying pleasure. Shattered nerves and broken health wear out the life of life. Or perhaps it comes in a sharper, sadder form—the shaft of death goes home; there is heard the wail of danger in his household; and then, when sickness has passed on to hopelessness, and hopelessness has passed on to death, the crushed man goes into the chamber of the dead, and there, when he shuts down the lid upon the coffin of his wife or the coffin of his child, his heart begins to tell him the meaning of all this. Thorns had been growing in his heart, and the sharp knife has been at work making room, but by an awful desolation, tearing up and cutting down, that the Life of God in the soul may not be choked.—F. W. Robertson.

FINISH THY WORK.

Finish thy work, the time is short—
  The sun is in the west,
The night is coming down—till then,
  Think not of rest.

Yes, finish all thy work, THEN rest;
  Till then, rest never:
The rest prepared for thee above
  Is rest forever.

Finish thy work, then wipe thy brow;
  Ungird thee from thy toil;
Take breath, and from each weary limb
  Shake off the soil.

Finish thy work, then sit thee down
  On some celestial hill,
And of its strength-reviving air
  Take thou thy fill.

Finish thy work, then go in peace;
  Life's battle fought and won,
Hear from the throne the Master's voice,
  "Well done! well done!"

Finish thy work, then take thy harp,
  Give praise to God above;
Sing a new song of endless joy
  And everlasting love.

Give thanks to Him who held thee up
  In all thy path below;
Who made thee faithful unto death,
  And crowns thee now!—*Anon.*

EVIL EFFECTS OF UNBELIEF.

Why are ye so fearful, and how is it that ye have no faith?—Mark iv., 40.

THE less faith, still the more fear. Fear is generated by unbelief, and unbelief strengthened by fear. As in nature there is an observable circular generation, vapors beget showers, and showers new vapors, so it is in things moral, and therefore all the skill in the world can never cure us of the disease of fear till God first cures us of our unbelief. Christ therefore took the right method to rid his disciples of their fear by rebuking their unbelief. The remains of this sin in God's own people are the cause and fountain of their fears.—JOHN FLAVEL.

HAPPY OLD AGE.

NOTHING so smooths out wrinkles from the brow as a sound Christian experience. When the heart is full of peace, the face is apt to be full of smiles. The countenance, as a faithful index of the soul, can not do otherwise than manifest the joy which reigns within. The best way to make a good face is to cultivate a good heart. It is one of the compensations for the decay of nature, that age can derive a serenity and lustre from the radiant spirit of piety which renders it so attractive as to forbid all thought of diminished power and every feeling of repulsion. "Every thing is beautiful in its time. If the glory of young men is their strength, the beauty of old men is the gray head." "The gray head is a crown of glory when it is found in the way of righteousness." All things young and tender draw by their sweetness and promise—innocence is associated with them, and there is a charm in original freshness for the hardest nature; hence, all men delight in young children and young animals; but equally, age which is ripened by large and healthful experiences, mellowed by happy and generous views of God and humanity, is an object of universal recognition and pleasure. The happy old man is never envied or hated, but always congratulated and loved. Having passed the rivalries and strifes of life, he usually receives the full measure of consideration which is his due.

I say the happy aged man is never envied; yet truly, if any man's state is to be coveted, it is his. "Better is the end of a thing than the beginning thereof." A journey safely ended, a work well finished, a battle fought and the victory won: surely to end a life with a good conscience, to arrive at advanced years with a character unimpeached, a faith undimmed, and a spirit unbroken—this is a consummation of all others most to be desired. We look at a child, and while we are drawn toward its simplicity, and are impressed with its promise, yet a cold shudder creeps over us as we think of the possibilities of evil which the little nature compresses within it. What an uncertain path it must tread! To how many dangers it must be exposed! So that, in the presence of the joy inspired by childhood, there obtrudes the terrible misgiving as to its future and ultimate safety. But no such doubts come when we look into the calm eyes of the veteran Christian, whose habits of goodness have become so fixed as to make his final salvation almost if not wholly a moral certainty. We would think it a great privilege to see angels who have been in heaven. Angels are all about us. These aged saints of God, who, if they have not already been there, are quite as sure to be as if their feet had already touched the pavements of gold, and the crowns of glory had already pressed their victorious brows. One of God's best gifts to his Church is, that he allows such to linger among his people in every community, whose names are household words, synonyms of piety, and whose presence is a holy fragrance in the congregation and in the home.

If there is a peculiar satisfaction in contemplating age purified and gladdened by piety, there is an equally intense pain in looking at an old person who is destitute of the comforts of religion. It is bad enough when such a one, however amiable and thoughtful, is indifferent to spiritual truth: to see an aged man, whose days are few, insensible to its claims, is a sad sight; but to see him not only insensible, but wicked and frivolous, is both painful and pitiable. There is something so far removed from good sense, as well as good religion, for a person under the weight of years to attempt to cheat himself and every body else by assuming, in the very shadow of the grave, a light and trifling manner, that one scarcely knows how to restrain contempt. Respect for gray hairs and a sorrow which overbalances all other feelings alone check and hold it back. How such hate to grow old! to what tricks do they resort to stave off the approach of decay! They try to light a fire on the outside which should be lighted within. Their experience is, in many things, very pleasant, but it is not the experience which worketh hope — the Christian hope. The flowers of the heart lie withered in a dead past, which can never return: no buds of promise, looking out toward the sunlight of the sky, swell in their souls. The past is gone, and there is no future of immortal life to beckon the heart away. The eye catches no lustre from the radiance of heaven, the brightness of the adorable Lamb, and now is dim indeed, both from infirmity and despondency. While the aged believer is like the mariner who, as he nears the end of his voyage to the Spice Islands, is already regaled with the sweet odors of the clime he seeks, the aged irreligious man is as one sailing toward the frozen seas, with whom the chilly breath is felt long before the seas are reached. The cheerlessness of an old man whose heart knows nothing of the warmth of divine love and Christian faith is indescribable. It is, however, a grateful thought, that through the hard crust of inveterate habits of impiety, grace can and does often penetrate. The aged sinner need not despair, for even his wilted heart may revive with all the freshness of a spiritual joy, which is the foretaste and pledge of eternal bliss.— H. B. RIDGAWAY.

I FIND it easier to go six miles to hear a sermon (said Philip Henry) than to spend one quarter of an hour in meditating and praying over it in secret after I come home.

"THE PATH OF THE JUST."

YES, the path of the just is as the shining light, shining more and more, brighter and brighter, unto the perfect day. It is imperfect now, and often stormy and cloudy; but through the storm and the sunshine the path runs on. The beings toiling in it are not such beings in appearance as you would think destined to thrones of glory; but they look rather like weather-beaten mariners, poor way-worn pilgrims, with garments worn and dusty; but they are to be all presented without spot or wrinkle, or any such thing, before the throne of God, in his likeness. They are to be all kings and priests. They are all to shine as the stars. Light, knowledge, sanctification in all things in the Christian life, all in the progress to glory, are gradual and partial now, entire and perfect hereafter. Now we know in part, there shall we know even as we are known; now we see as through a glass darkly, but then face to face. The process of growth and sanctification is going on now, mainly as a discipline of redemption from sin, deliverance from the carcass of the old man, purification from indwelling corruption; so that, at present, there is more positive experience of sin and of the conflict with it, than of holiness and grace in triumph. Yet the work is going on through all fluctuations; through providences afflictive often, and seemingly adverse; through temptations and the trial of faith working experience; and experience is gradually building up a hope that maketh not ashamed, and more and more the love of God is shed abroad, and all the affections gathered up to heaven.

The dross may be continually rising to the surface now, and a great part of God's very discipline with us is to bring it out. When you put a lump of gold into the crucible there is no dross visible *upon* it, but there may be a great deal *in* it. A skillful goldsmith will tell you at once, on exposing it to some of his tests, that there is much alloy in it. You put it into the crucible to bring out that alloy, and the consequence is that the dross speedily becomes more manifest than any thing else, which is the consequence of the very process of purification; and so God often detects and brings out the indwelling evils of his jewels; and the consequence of such a discipline for a season is just this, that, to themselves, the children of God seem to be nothing but dross, for dross and not pure gold is the most marked feature, and they seem to be doing any thing but growing in grace. And yet this is one of the very processes of growth. Mortification, self-abasement, and humiliation now, leading to glory hereafter; a toilsome and craggy way now, and sometimes winding through places like the shadow of Death, but nevertheless rising, and, on the whole, growing brighter and brighter toward the perfect day. The dross, indeed, is rising to the surface now, but by-and-by there shall be a clean, pure, beautiful reflection of the image of the Great Refiner.—GEORGE B. CHEEVER.

CAST ALL YOUR CARE UPON CHRIST.

"*Cast all thy care.*" "Nay," the rebel heart says, "there is some little of it I must bear myself; something that has reference to the heart's bitterness, that it alone knoweth; or to the heart's deep, dark sorrow, with which no stranger intermeddles, that I must bear myself." "Cast ALL thy care upon me, for I care for thee." What! distrustful still? Can you not take God at his word? Hark! he condescends to expostulate with you upon your unbelief. "Why sayest thou, O Jacob, and speakest, O Israel, my way is hid from the Lord?" How often have you said that in the time of your sorrow—you know you have—"my way is hid from the Lord, my judgment is passed over from my God. Hast thou not known, hast thou not heard that the everlasting God, the Lord, the creator of the ends of the earth, fainteth not, neither is weary? There is no searching of his understanding. He giveth power to the faint. He does not merely take his swoon away and leave him weakly, he makes him strong. He giveth power to the faint, and to them that have no might he increaseth strength." Are you still dissatisfied?

The God who knows human nature knows how much better a teacher's example is than precept, and so, sparkling upon the pages of his holy truth, he has left us many bright instances of his interposition on behalf of his saints. Abraham rises early in the morning, goes a three days' journey with the son of his love, intending all the while, with set and resolute purpose, to offer him in sacrifice to the God of heaven. Arrived at the place of their destination, all the ritual preparations are made: the altar is prepared; the willing victim, unresisting, is bound; the sacrificial knife is lifted; no escape, then, surely! But man's extremity is God's opportunity, and the ram is caught in the thicket by its horns, and God's grace is sufficient—none too much—but sufficient still.—W. M. Punshon.

Whatever our trials are, the strength of the conflict lies between faith and unbelief.

THE OLD MAN.

No desert without limits extends before the old man. He walks beside a river whose banks are seen to approach. A diminishing stream separates them each day less and less; and on the opposite bank stand wife and son, with arms outstretched to meet him.—MADAME DE GASPARIN.

CROSS-BEARING.

And he, bearing his cross, went forth.—John xix., 17.

LEARN, then, brethren, that your heavenly Father sometimes sees good in the treatment of his spiritual children, as here in the treatment of the Only-begotten Son, to let great trials and great weaknesses meet together; to lay on crosses at those very moments when we appear most unfit to bear them; to permit wave to follow wave in such quick and terrible succession that the eye of faith grows dim, and even the undying flame of a Christian's lamp is flickering in the socket. If such a season ever visits you, remember there is ONE to whom even this case is no new case — ONE upon whom his cross was laid when he was weak even to faintness, and yet of whom we are told that, without one repining, one reproachful word, "he went forth bearing his cross." He can not, then, although now in heaven, ever forget that hour on earth, and never does he see a weak and fainting sufferer, upon whom fresh trials are accumulating and fresh crosses laid, without calling to mind that heavy cross and that toilsome journey up Mount Calvary, or without stretching forth a hand to help and succor him. How merciful is it of our heavenly Father that there is not that sorrow in life—that peculiar state of trial—that bitterness of anguish from which the believer can look upward to the throne of grace without beholding one beside that throne to whom that sorrow, trial, bitterness are all experimentally well known!—HENRY BLUNT.

BEFORE THE CROSS.

SWEET the moments, rich in blessing,
  Which before the cross I spend;
Life, and health, and peace possessing,
  From the sinner's dying Friend.

Here I'll sit, with transport viewing
  Mercy's streams, in streams of blood;
Precious drops, my soul bedewing,
  Plead and claim my peace with God.

Truly blessed is the station,
  Low before his cross to lie,
While I see divine compassion
  Floating in His languid eye.

Here it is I find my Heaven,
  While upon the Lamb I gaze.
Love I much? I've much forgiven;
  I'm a miracle of grace.

Love and grief my heart dividing,
  With my tears His feet I'll bathe;
Constant still in faith abiding,
  Life deriving from His death.

May I still enjoy this feeling,
  In all need to Jesus go;
Prove His wounds each day more healing,
  And Himself more fully know.
THOMAS BATTY.

GOD HATH LED ME ALL THESE YEARS.

WHEN a Christian, towards the close of life, looks back upon his pilgrimage as a whole and in its parts, the only way in which he can describe it is that suggested by the words of Scripture, "GOD HATH LED ME all these years." I see it now so plainly: how there has been a hand over me, the hand of a real and living person, giving this, and withholding that, both alike for good; placing me perhaps where I would not, and then showing me that it had been well; not suffering me to forget, or else recalling me to recollection; denying me, or else taking away from me something on which my heart was too much set, and then giving me something else which, because less desired, was safer; chastening me when I fell away, and often by sharp and painful strokes bringing back to himself. Doubtless heaven will be full of such remembrances of earthly life, each remembrance ending in the ascription of praise. And can not earth anticipate these recollections, these ascriptions of praise? Yes, the youngest life has had some such experiences; middle life has them in abundance; oh how we forget God when we are in prosperity! When life smiles on us, how do we think scorn, as it were, of the pleasant land beyond; how do we provoke God by our murmurings; how do we dishonor him by setting our affection on things below!... When he slays us, we seek him, as it is written; when he hides his face, we humble ourselves; when he delivers us again, we sing his praise, but within a while we forget his works; we live carelessly; we scarcely pray; we cleave to the dust of this world; again the stroke falls; again we repent; again we amend; alas! again it is a short-lived effort:—and in many such backslidings, and a few such returns, life slips away; the call comes, and is the door still open?

My brethren, God is leading you, offering at least to lead you, all your life long; and oh the safety, the happiness—oh the deep peace of those who accept the offer! Every morning let your prayer be, LORD, LEAD ME..... If I stray, follow me into the desert and recall me. If I faint, carry me in thy bosom. When I walk at last through the valley of the shadow of death, be thou with me. Let thy goodness and mercy follow me all the days of my life, and then let me dwell in thy house forever.—C. J. VAUGHAN.

THE HOLY SPIRIT OUR GUIDE.

THE Holy Spirit of God is our guide. Who will displease his guide?—a sweet, comfortable guide, that leads us through the wilderness of this world. As the cloud before the Israelites by day, and the pillar of fire by night, so he conducts us to the heavenly Canaan. If we grieve our guide, we cause him to leave us to ourselves. The Israelites would not go a step farther than God by his angel went before them. It is in vain for us to make toward heaven without our blessed Guide; we can not do, nor speak, nor think any thing that is holy and good without him. Whatsoever is holy and pious, it grows not in our garden, in our nature, but it is planted by the Spirit.

There is nothing in the world so great and sweet a friend that will do us so much good as the Spirit if we give him entertainment. Indeed, he must rule; he will have the keys delivered him; we must submit to his government. And when he is in the heart, he will subdue by little and little all high thoughts, rebellious risings, and despairing fears. This shall be our happiness in heaven, when we shall be wholly spiritual, that *God shall be all in all.* We shall be perfectly obedient to the Spirit in our understandings, wills, and affections. The Spirit will then dwell largely in us, and will make the room where he dwelleth sweet, and lightsome, and free, subduing whatsoever is contrary, and bring fullness of peace, and joy, and comfort.

And, in the mean time, in what condition we are, we shall have suitable help from the Spirit. We are partly flesh and partly spirit. God is not all and in all; the flesh hath a part in us; we are often in afflictions and under clouds. Let us, therefore, prize our fellowship with the Spirit. For are we in darkness? he is a Spirit of light. Are we in deadness of spirit? he is a Spirit of life. Are we in a disconsolate estate? he is a Spirit of consolation.

Are we in perplexity, and know not what to do? he is a Spirit of wisdom. Are we troubled with corruptions? he is a sanctifying, a subduing, a mortifying Spirit. In what condition soever we are, he will never leave us till he has raised us from the grave, and taken full possession of body and soul in heaven. He will prove a comforter when neither friends, nor riches, nor any thing in the world can comfort us. How careful should we be to give contentment to this sweet Spirit of God!

No Christian is so happy as the watchful Christian—that is, careful of his duty, and to preserve his communion with the Holy Spirit of God, for by entertaining him, he is sure to have communion with the Father and the Son. It is the happiest condition in the world when the soul is the temple of the Holy Spirit—when the heart is as the holy of holies—where there be prayers and praises offered to God. The soul is, as it were, a holy ark, the memory like the pot of manna, preserving heavenly truths. It is a heavenly condition; a man prospers to heavenward when the Spirit of God is with him. You know Obed-Edom, when the ark was in his house, all thrived with him; so, while the Spirit and his motions are entertained by us, we shall be happy in life, happy in death, happy to eternity.—RICHARD SIBBES.

RETROSPECT AND PROSPECT.

MATURE age is a hill from which one may look in opposite directions—backward and forward. It is a kindly arrangement of Providence by which the aged are not only inclined to look backward to early life, but the scenes of childhood and youth are made unusually distinct. When the faculties are so much impaired or clouded that memory loses the impression of recent events, the scenes of early life are recalled and retained with wonderful freshness and vividness. Persons who could not retain in mind what they had seen or heard five minutes before, can repeat with accuracy whole pages of hymns, the odes of Horace, Cowper's poems, which they committed to memory when they were boys. That which is intrusted to memory in childhood is like the casting of plaster when it is fresh and liquid; it sets, and every line and edge is permanently preserved. If the young did but know it, what they are saying, and thinking, and reading, and doing is fresco-painting, the colors striking through the fresh mortar, and hardening into permanent forms by the progress of time. The review of life by the aged gives a peculiar pleasure. The little annoyances which were felt day by day in earlier life drop out of view. Children have their own griefs and trials. These are largely forgotten as time goes on, and the pleasant things of childhood remain like a bright picture before the dim eye of the aged. The first home, father and mother, the fireside and the barn, the brook and the meadow, school and vacation, the trees, the birds and the animals, the seasons, spring, summer, autumn, and winter, how clear and distinct they are! It is as if they were all back again, and this to relieve the burdens, cheer the loneliness, and comfort the infirmities of age. How much of thankfulness is diffused through the heart by these pleasant memories of early life! By means of them, age is often toned down into ineffable sweetness, so that not unfrequently old men and little children are the closest and happiest companions.

Some things there are in the review of every life which are to be regretted. Happy is he who recalls but few of them associated with remorse. This is the sharpness of that remorse—the acts by which it is excited can not be changed or obliterated. The unkind word, the undutiful act toward an affectionate parent! Would that this parent were now alive, to be soothed by our confession and augmented tenderness. But now the wrong which we did stands like an oak or a rock, against which we brace ourselves, and strain, only to become conscious of our inability to move it. Nothing crumbles—nothing can be removed from the honest past. It stands. As we look at it, what occasion have we to make use of the prayer which inspiration has made ready for us, "Remember not the sins of my youth, nor my transgressions; according to thy mercy, remember thou me for thy goodness' sake, O Lord!" (Psalm xxv., 7.) So much of imagination mingles with all anticipations of the young that one is apt to be deceived in regard to his probable character and conduct; the past is simple, real fact, and so much of defect and unworthiness are associated with it all, that an honest mind must feel its need of divine forgiveness, resting more and more implicitly on the abounding grace of Jesus Christ.

Threescore years and ten! In prospect how remote! in retrospect how brief! How long appears the journey when setting out! how short when it has been accomplished!

"Time in advance behind him hides his wings,
And seems to creep decrepit with his age.
Behold him when passed by: what then is seen
But his broad pinions, swifter than the wind."

Each day has two twilights, that of the morning and that of the evening. The latter darkens into night, the former brightens into day. "The way of the wicked is as darkness; they know not at what they stumble. But the path of the just is as the shining light, that shineth more and more unto the perfect day." Here is a phenomenon which can be explained only by the comforts and promises of the Gospel of Christ. Cicero wrote a treatise on old age which has come down into our hands. It contains much—we might say all of the wisdom of the world. The utmost which it pretends to teach is how to grow old, and be old, with somewhat of resignation and gracefulness. The Gospel of our Redeemer, bringing life and immortality to light, teaches man how to advance in life, and terminate life with cheerfulness, gladness, and joy. It continually presents, what nothing else ever did or can, the sure method by which one may always, even to the very last day of life, be confident *that the best part of existence is yet to come.* It supplies man with what is better than all memory, even with an unfailing object of hope. Bright and pleasant was life's morning. Gratitude is enkindled by recalling all that was so happy in childhood and youth. But faith assures us that our greatest happiness is not receding, but approaching. Thanks for the way in which God has led us thus far; but, turning to that which is before us, what is it? Gloom, fear, nothingness? Oh no. We have a sure word of the Lord, which reveals and promises what is perma-

P

nent, blessed, and divine. True life is before us, not behind us. Our best and happiest youth is yet to come. God has promised his adopted children perpetual rejuvenescence. "The outward man perisheth, but the inward man is *renewed* day by day." How often is this realized in the experience of Christian believers! When the eye has lost its lustre, and the ear its quickness—when the frame is bowed, and the silvered head droops, peace becomes like a river, and joy as the waves of the sea. "They that wait upon the Lord shall renew their strength; they shall mount up with wings as eagles; they shall run and not be weary; they shall walk and not faint."

Those far advanced in life are in danger of regarding themselves as useless in the world, because incapable of active service after the manner of younger life. Many are saddened by the mistaken thought that they are cumbering the ground. The contrary is true decidedly, emphatically, of the aged found in the way of righteousness. The simple, quiet, trustful continuance of such is a public benefit. The hoary head, with its glory of true Christian faith, is a testimony in honor of religion which can never be gainsaid or silenced. At no time is passive goodness so potent. It is, indeed, light at eventide. It is a proof of our faith when one who is bereft of all which the world esteems, like a tree stripped of its foliage, can in his old age look forward with comfort and cheerfulness to that better life which is promised by his divine and faithful **Redeemer**. Talk of the beauty of childhood!—it is of its own kind. But there is another beauty—old age, leaning happily on Christ, and looking forward, without fear, without gloom, without doubt, to that glory which is YET TO BE REVEALED.—WILLIAM ADAMS.

THE OCCUPATION FOR THE LAST HOURS OF LIFE.

I HAVE had large experience of both joy and sorrow. I have seen the nakedness and the emptiness, and I have seen the beauty and sweetness of life. What I have to say now, let me say to Jesus. What time and strength I used to spend in writing, let me now spend in praying for all men, for all sufferers, for all who are out of the way, for all whom I love; and their name is legion, for I love every body.

Yes, I love every body! That crowning joy has come to me at last. Christ is in my soul; he is mine; I am as conscious of it as that my husband and children are mine; and his Spirit flows forth from mine in the calm peace of a river, whose banks are green with grass, and glad with flowers. If I die, it will be to leave a wearied and worn body, and a sinful soul, to go joyfully to be with Christ, to weary and to sin no more. If I live, I shall find much blessed work to do for him. So, living or dying, I shall be the Lord's.

But I wish, oh! how earnestly, that, whether I go or stay, I could inspire some lives with the joy that is now mine. For many years I have been rich in faith—rich in an unfaltering confidence that I was beloved of my God and Savior. But something was wanting. I was ever groping for a mysterious grace, the want of which made me often sorrowful in the very midst of my most sacred joy—imperfect when I most longed for perfection. It was that PERSONAL LOVE TO CHRIST, of which my precious mother so often spoke to me, which she often urged me to seek upon my knees. If I had known then, as I now know, what this priceless treasure could be to a sinful human soul, I would have sold all that I had to buy the field wherein it lay hidden. But not till I was shut up to prayer and to the study of God's Word by the loss of earthly joys, sickness destroying the flavor of them all, did I begin to penetrate the mystery that is learned under the Cross. And, wondrous as it is, how simple is this mystery! To love Christ, and to know that I love him — this is all! — MRS. E. PRENTISS, "*Stepping Heavenward.*"

HAPPINESS OF THE LIFE TO COME.

WHAT are these things, the false glare and shadows whereof in this earth are pursued with such keen and furious impetuosity—riches, honors, pleasures? All these, in their justest, purest, and sublimest sense, are comprehended in this blessed life. It is *a treasure* that can neither fail nor be carried away by force or fraud. It is *an inheritance* uncorrupted and undefiled; *a crown* that fadeth not away; a never-failing stream of joy and delight. It is a marriage feast, and, of all others, the most joyous and most sumptuous; one that always satisfies, and never cloys the appetite. It is an eternal spring and an everlasting light; a day without an evening. It is a paradise, where the lilies are always white and in full bloom, the saffron blooming, the trees sweat out their balsams, and the tree of life in the midst thereof. It is a city where the houses are built of living pearls, the gates of precious stones, and the streets paved with the purest gold.

Yet all these are nothing but veils of the happiness to be revealed on that most blessed day; nay, the light itself, which we have mentioned among the rest, though it be the most beautiful ornament in this visible world, is at best but a shadow of that heavenly glory; and how small soever that portion of this inaccessible brightness may be, which, in the sacred Scriptures, shines upon us through these veils, it certainly very well deserves that we should often turn our eyes toward it, and view it with the closest attention.

Now the first thing that necessarily occurs in the constitution of happiness is a full and complete deliverance from every evil and every grievance, which we may as certainly expect to meet with in that heavenly life, as it is impossible to be attained while we sojourn here below. All tears shall be wiped away from our eyes, and every cause and occasion of tears forever removed from our sight. There there are no tumults, no wars, no poverty, no death, nor disease—there there is neither mourning, nor fear, nor sin, which is the source and fountain of all other evils—there is neither violence within doors nor without, nor any complaint in the streets of that blessed city—there no friend goes out nor enemy comes in.

Full vigor of body and mind, health, beauty, purity, and perfect tranquillity.

The most delightful society of angels, prophets, apostles, martyrs, and all the saints; among whom there are no reproaches, contentions, controversies, nor party spirit, because there are there none of the sources whence they can spring, nor any thing to encourage their growth; for there is there particularly no ignorance, no blind self-love, no vainglory, nor envy, which is quite excluded from those divine regions; but, on the contrary, perfect charity, whereby every one, together with his own felicity, enjoys that of his neighbors, and is happy in the one as well as the other. Hence there is among them a kind of infinite reflection and multiplication of happiness, like that of a spacious hall adorned with gold and precious stones, dignified with a full assembly of kings and potentates, and having its walls quite covered with the brightest looking-glasses.

But what infinitely exceeds, and quite eclipses all the rest, is that boundless ocean of happiness, which results from the beatific vision of the ever-blessed God, without which neither the tranquillity they enjoy, nor the society of saints, nor the possession of any particular finite good, nor, indeed, of all such taken together, can satisfy the soul, or make it completely happy.—ROBERT LEIGHTON.

EVERY man is, what he once was and always will be, a condemned sinner, notwithstanding any repentance or future obedience, without an interest in Christ.—T. ADAM.

THE OPENED GATES.

Oh sometimes, when adown the sky
  The fiery sunset lingers,
Heaven's gates swing inward noiselessly,
  Unlocked by unseen fingers.

And while they stand a moment half ajar,
  Gleams from the inner glory
Stream from the azure vault afar,
  And half reveal the story.—*Anon.*

NEARER HEAVEN.

Now is our salvation nearer than when we believed.—Romans xiii., 11.

One sweetly solemn thought
  Comes to me o'er and o'er—
I'm nearer home to-day
  Than I've ever been before.

Nearer my Father's house,
  Where the many mansions be;
Nearer the great white throne,
  Nearer the crystal sea.

Nearer the bound of life,
  Where we lay our burden down;
Nearer leaving the cross,
  Nearer gaining the crown.

But lying daily between,
  Winding down through the night,
Is the deep and unknown stream
  That leads at last to the light.

Jesus, perfect my trust,
  Strengthen the band of my faith;
Let me feel Thee near when I stand
  On the edge of the shore of death;

Feel Thee near when my feet
  Are slipping over the brink;
For it may be I'm nearer home,
  Nearer now than I think.

WANDERING THOUGHTS.

To expect deliverance from those wandering thoughts which are occasioned by evil spirits is to expect that the devil should die or fall asleep, or at least should no more go about as a roaring lion. To expect deliverance from those which are occasioned by other men is to expect either that men should cease from the earth, or that we should be absolutely secluded from them, and have no intercourse with them; or that, having eyes, we should not see, neither hear with our ears, but be as senseless as stocks or stones. And to pray for deliverance from those which are occasioned by the body is in effect to pray that we may leave the body. Otherwise it is praying for impossibilities and absurdities; praying that God would reconcile contradictions by continuing our union with a corruptible body without the natural necessary consequences of that union. It is as if we should pray to be angels and men, mortal and immortal at the same time. Nay, but when that which is immortal is come, mortality is done away.

Rather let us pray, both with the spirit and with the understanding, that "all these things may work together for our good;" that we may suffer all the infirmities of our nature, all the interruptions of men, all the assaults and suggestions of evil spirits, and in all be "more than conquerors." Let us pray that we may be delivered from all sin—that both root and branch may be destroyed; that we may be "cleansed from all pollution of flesh and spirit," from every evil temper, and word, and work; that we may "love the Lord our God with all our heart, with all our mind, with all our soul, and with all our strength;" that all the fruits of the Spirit may be found in us; not only love, joy, peace, but also "long suffering, gentleness, goodness, fidelity, meekness, temperance." Pray that all "these things may flourish and abound, may increase in you more and more, till an abundant entrance be ministered unto you into the everlasting kingdom of our Lord Jesus Christ."—JOHN WESLEY.

CLOUDS.

BE cheerful beneath the cloud. And if the cloud should come in the daytime, still be cheerful. The Israelites had the cloud in the day. I recollect once kneeling with familiar friendliness and love around the family altar of a dear friend, whom I loved as I believe I loved no other on this earth, and he prayed for me that I might know what it was to have the pillar of cloud when the day was too bright, and the pillar of fire when the night was too dark. We need that always, do we not? The pillar of cloud and pillar of fire are needed as much for us as for the Israelites of old. Did I mention to you what I thought as I saw that picture of the German painter some time ago? I could not make out what he meant by it. It was called "cloud-land," and it seemed nothing but cloud on cloud. But what do you think? As I looked, I saw that every cloud turned into an angel or an angel's wing, and the whole picture, that seemed at first only a mass of gloom, looked out upon me with hundreds of angels' eyes and hundreds of angels' wings. So with all clouds; if God comes nigh to us by them, look at them, and they turn into angels. They are not desirable in themselves, they are not pleasant; no chastisement, no affliction, no cloud is at present joyous, but grievous. We foolish men would walk always in the day-brightness; we do not want clouds; but the angels know their value, and God too, or he would never send them to us.—EDW. PAXTON HOOD.

JUST AS I AM.

Him that cometh to me I will in no wise cast out.—John vi., 37.

> Just as I am, without one plea
> But that Thy blood was shed for me,
> And that Thou bidd'st me come to Thee,
>   O Lamb of God, I come!
>
> Just as I am, and waiting not
> To rid my soul of one dark blot,
> To Thee, whose blood can cleanse each spot,
>   O Lamb of God, I come!
>
> Just as I am, though tossed about
> With many a conflict, many a doubt,
> Fightings and fears within, without,
>   O Lamb of God, I come!
>
> Just as I am, poor, wretched, blind,
> Sight, riches, healing of the mind,
> Yea, all I need, in Thee to find,
>   O Lamb of God, I come!

Just as I am, Thou wilt receive,
Wilt welcome, pardon, cleanse, relieve;
Because Thy promise I believe,
    O Lamb of God, I come!

Just as I am (Thy love unknown
Has broken every barrier down),
Now, to be Thine, yea, Thine alone,
    O Lamb of God, I come!

Just as I am, of that free love
The breadth, length, depth, and height to prove,
Here for a season, then above,
    O Lamb of God, I come!

CHARLOTTE ELLIOTT.

BLESSED WORK FOR OLD AGE.

. . . . But oh, it is not so; old age is a blessed time, when, looking back on the follies, sins, and mistakes of past life, too late indeed to remedy, but not too late to repent, we may "put off earthly garments one by one, and dress ourselves for heaven." Griefs that are heavy to the young are to the old calm and almost joyful, as tokens of the near and ever-nearing time when there shall be no more death, neither sorrow, nor crying, neither any more pain.

. . . . Even though walking in darkness for a while, the aged have the sure promise, "At eventide it shall be light."—*Anon.*

LIKE THE SWIFT SHIPS.

You may well conceive how swiftly the mariner flies from a threatening storm, or seeks the port where he will find his home. You have sometimes seen how the ship cuts through the billows, leaving a white furrow behind her, and causing the sea to boil around her. Such is life, says Job, "like the swift ships," when the sails are filled by the wind, and the vessel dashes on, dividing a passage through the crowded water. Swift are the ships, but swifter far is life. The wind of time bears me along. I can not stop its motion. I may direct it with the rudder of God's Holy Spirit. I may, it is true, take in some small sails of sin, which might hurry my days on faster than otherwise they would go; but, nevertheless, like a swift ship, my life must speed on its way until it reaches its haven. Where is that haven to be? Shall it be found in the land of bitterness and barrenness, that dreary region of the lost? Or shall it be that sweet haven of eternal peace, where not a troubling wave can ruffle the quiescent glory of my spirit? Wherever the haven is to be, that truth is the same, we are "like the swift ships."—CHARLES SPURGEON.

THE BIBLE.

A POOR old woman, being asked if she had a Bible, said, "What should I do without my Bible? It was the guide of my youth, and it is the staff of my age. It wounded me, and it healed me; it condemned me, and it acquitted me. It showed me I was a sinner, and it led me to the Savior; it has given me comfort through life, and I trust it will give me hope in death."

COMFORT FOR MOURNERS.

"A BRUISED reed will he not break." Perhaps the imagery may be derived from the practice of the ancient shepherds, who were wont to amuse themselves with the music of a pipe of reed or straw; and when it was bruised, they broke it, or threw it away as useless. But the bruised reed shall not be broken by this divine Shepherd of souls. The music of broken sighs and groans is, indeed, all that the broken reed can afford him; the notes are but low, melancholy, and jarring, and yet he will not break the instrument, but he will repair and tune it till it is fit to join in the concert of angels on high; and even now its humble strains are pleasing to his ears.
—SAMUEL DAVIES.

THE LESSONS OF SORROW.

THERE are many things which nothing but sorrow can teach us. Sorrow is the great teacher. Sorrow is the realizer. It is a strange and touching thing to hear the young speak truths which are not yet within the limits of their experience; to listen while they say that life is sorrowful, that friends are treacherous, that there is quiet in the grave. When we are boys we adopt the phrases that we hear. In a kind of prodigal excess of happiness, we say that the world is a dream, and life a nothing; that eternity lasts forever, and that all here is disappointment. But there comes a day of sharpness, when we find, to our surprise, that what we said had a meaning in it, and we are startled. That is the sentimentalism of youth passing into reality. In the lips of the young, such phrases are only sentimentalities. What we mean by sentimentalism is that state in which a man speaks things deep and true, not because he feels them strongly, but because he perceives that they are beautiful, and that it is touching and fine to say them—things which he fain WOULD feel, and fancies he DOES feel. Therefore, when all is well, when friends abound, and health is strong, and the comforts of life are around us, religion becomes faint and shadowy. Religious phraseology passes into cant; the gay, and light, and trifling use the same words as the holiest, till the earnest man, who FEELS what the world is sentimentalizing about, shuts up his heart, and either coins other phrases or else keeps silence. And then it is that, if God would rescue a man from that unreal world of names and mere knowledge, he does what he did with Job—he strips him of his flocks, and his herds, and his wealth; or else, what is the equivalent, of the power of enjoying them. The desire of his eyes falls from him at a stroke. Things become real then. Trials bring man face to face with God. God and he touch, and the flimsy veil of bright cloud that hung between him and the sky is blown away. He feels that he is standing outside the earth, with nothing between him and the Eternal Infinite. Oh! there is something in the sick-bed, and the aching heart, and the restlessness and the languor of shattered health, and the sorrow of affections withered, and the stream of life poisoned at its fountain, and the cold, lonely feeling of utter rawness of the heart which is felt when God strikes home in earnest, that forces a man to feel what is real and what is not.

This is the blessing of affliction to those who will lie still, and not struggle in a cowardly or a resentful war. It is God speaking to Job out of the whirlwind, and saying, "In the sunshine and the warmth you can not meet *me;* but in the hurricane and the darkness, when wave after wave has swept down and across the soul, you shall see my form, and hear my voice, and know that your Redeemer liveth."—F. W. ROBERTSON.

"NOT A FORGETUL HEARER."

AN old Scotch woman was sprinkling water upon some linen stretched upon the grass by the roadside for bleaching. Her minister chanced to pass by at the time, and, stopping, he inquired if she had been to church on the last Sabbath. She said she had. But, upon being asked for the text and subject of discourse, she could remember neither the one nor the other. "What good, then," asked the minister, "does it do you to go to church and hear the Gospel if you so soon forget the text and every word of the sermon?" Pausing a moment, the old woman, looking up, replied, "The water which I sprinkle on this linen is quickly dried up, and not one drop of it is left, yet the linen grows whiter and whiter; and if I can not remember either the text or the sermon, I hope that I grow better and better."—*Anon.*

HARDENING THE HEART.

ON a winter evening, when the frost is setting in with growing intensity, and when the sun is now far past the meridian, and gradually sinking in the western sky, there is a double reason why the ground grows every moment harder and more impenetrable to the plow. On the one hand, the frost of evening, with ever-increasing intensity, is indurating the stiffening clods. On the other hand, the genial rays, which alone can soften them, are every moment withdrawing and losing their enlivening power. Take heed that it be not so with you. As long as you are unconverted, you are under a double process of hardening. The frosts of an eternal night are settling down upon your souls, and the Sun of Righteousness, with westering wheel, is hastening to set upon you evermore. If, then, the plow of grace can not force its way into your ICEBOUND heart to-day, what likelihood is there that it will enter TO-MORROW?—R. M. MCCHEYNE.

'TIS little troubles that wear the heart out. It is easier to throw a bomb-shell a mile than a feather—let us seek, then, especial grace to bear them.

BE MERCIFUL TO ME, A SINNER.

When at Thy footstool, Lord, I bend,
   And plead with Thee for mercy there,
Think of the sinner's dying friend,
   And for His sake receive my prayer.

Oh think not of my shame and guilt,
   My thousand stains of deepest dye;
Think of the blood which Jesus spilt,
   And let that blood my pardon buy.

Think, Lord, how I am still Thy own,
   The trembling creature of Thy hand;
Think how my heart to sin is prone,
   And what temptations round me stand.

Oh think upon Thy holy Word,
   And every plighted promise there;
How prayer should evermore be heard,
   And how Thy glory is to spare.

Oh think not of my doubts and fears,
   My strivings with Thy grace divine;
Think upon Jesus' woes and tears,
   And let His merits stand for mine.

Thine eye, Thine ear, they are not dull;
   Thine arm can never shortened be;
Behold me here; my heart is full;
   Behold, and spare, and succor me!—H. F. Lyte.

THE SPIRIT OF PRAISE.

"BLESS the Lord, O my soul; and all that is within me, bless his holy name." Wake up, my *memory*, and find matter for the song. Tell what God has done for me in days gone by. Fly back, ye thoughts, to my childhood; sing of cradle-mercies. Review my youth and its early favors. Sing of long-suffering grace which followed my wanderings, and bore with my rebellions. Review before my eyes that gladsome hour when first I knew the Lord, and tell over again the matchless story of his mercy. Awake up, my *judgment*, and give measure to the music. Come forth, my *understanding*, and weigh his loving-kindness in the balance. See if thou canst count the small dust of his mercies. See if thou canst estimate the unsearchable riches which God hath given thee in his unspeakable gift of Christ Jesus. Recount his eternal love to thee. Reckon up the treasures of that everlasting covenant which he made on thy behalf, and which was "ordered in all things and sure." Sing aloud of that divine wisdom which contrived, of that love which planned, and of that grace which carried out the scheme of thy redemption. "Bless the Lord, O my soul!" For doth not all nature around me praise him? If

I were silent I should be an exception to the universe. Doth not the thunder praise him as it rolls like drums in the march of the God of Armies? Do not the mountains praise him when the woods upon their summits wave in adoration? Does not the lightning write his name in letters of fire upon the midnight darkness? Hath not the whole earth a voice, and shall I, can I be silent? "Bless the Lord, O my soul."—CHARLES SPURGEON.

LOSS AND GAIN.

DR. PAYSON, in his dying hours, said he could have saved himself much trouble in life if he had only believed that the Savior's presence was enough to fill him with joy if all worldly comforts were taken away. He found it so in sickness, but could not quite believe it in health. A poor simple man, with none of Payson's imagination or fancy, once said, in a similar spirit, with his dying words, "I have lost all my property; I have lost all my relations; my last son is dead; I have lost my hearing and my eyesight; I am all alone, old and poor; but it makes no difference: Christ never grows old; Christ never is poor; Christ never dies; and Christ never will forsake me."

OUR PILGRIMAGE.

WE are passing toward final rest. Do not regret it if the eyes grow dim. You will see better by-and-by. If the ear is growing heavy, do not be sorry. If your youth is passing, and your beauty fading, do not mourn. If your hand trembles, and your foot is unsteady with age, be not depressed in spirit. With every impediment, with every sign of the taking down of this tabernacle, remember that it is the striking of the tent that the march may begin, and when next you pitch your tabernacle it shall be on an undisturbed shore, and that there, with eyes unwet with tears, through an atmosphere undimmed by clouds, and before a God unveiled, and never to be wrapped in darkness any more—that there, looking back upon this world of ignorance, and suffering, and trouble, and upon the hardships of the way, you will, with full and discerning reason, lift up your voice, and give thanks to God and say, "There was not one trouble too much; there was not one sorrow too piercing." And you will thank God in that land for the very things that wring tears from your eyes in this. Look, then, to that better land, out of all the trouble of the way—sigh for it, pray for it, prepare for it, and enter into it.—*Anon.*

DANGER OF BACKSLIDING IN OLD AGE.

Did it ever occur to you that Christians were more apt to backslide and fall into open sin in the latter part of their religious course than in its earlier stages? It is a startling announcement, but I think you will find it true. Look at all the cases of backsliding recorded in the Bible. Did they not, *every one of them*, occur late in life? There was David. In the days of his youth and early manhood, a pattern of faith and devotion. In advanced life guilty of murder and adultery, and still later of pride and self-conceit in numbering the people. Look at Moses. The great sin of his life committed when just about to enter the promised land. Look at Hezekiah—the " good king Hezekiah." In his early days zealous and devout. The last fifteen years of his life (a special gift from his God, and therefore, one would think, to be specially consecrated to him) bringing "wrath upon himself and upon Jerusalem." So, too, with Josiah and with Solomon. Alas! "the strongest are weak and the wisest are fools when left to be sifted in Satan's sieve." It becometh the old as well as the young to watch and pray lest they enter into temptation.—*Anon.*

MY GRACE IS SUFFICIENT FOR THEE.

Your harps, ye trembling saints,
  Down from the willows take;
Loud to the praise of love divine
  Bid every string awake.

Though in a foreign land,
  We are not far from home,
And nearer to our house above
  We every moment come.

His grace will to the end
  Stronger and brighter shine,
Nor present things, nor things to come,
  Shall quench the spark divine.

When we in darkness walk,
  Nor feel the heavenly flame,
Then is the time to trust our God,
  And rest upon His name.

Soon shall our doubts and fears
  Subside at His control;
His loving kindness shall break through
  The midnight of the soul.

Bless'd is the man, O God,
  That stays himself on Thee!
Who waits for Thy salvation, Lord,
  Shall Thy salvation see.—TOPLADY.

THE TREATMENT OF THE GREAT PHYSICIAN.

LET us look at the bright side of life, and believe that God means us to be always ascending — always getting nearer to himself — always learning something new about him — always loving him better and better. To be sure, our souls are sick, and of themselves can't keep "ever on the wing;" but I have had some delightful thoughts of late from just hearing the title of a book, "*God's Method with the Maladies of a Soul.*" It gives one such a conception of the seeming ills of life to think of him as our Physician, the ills all REMEDIES, the deprivations only a wholesome regimen, the losses all gains. When, as I study this individual case and that, I see how patiently and persistently he tries now this remedy, now that, and how infallibly he cures the souls that submit to his remedies, I love him so! — I love him so! And I am so astonished that we are restive under his unerring hand! Think how he dealt with me. My soul was sick unto death — sick with worldliness, and self-pleasing, and folly. There was only one way of making me listen to reason, and that was just the way he took. He snatched me right out of the world, and shut me up in one room, crippled, helpless, and alone, and set me to thinking,

thinking, thinking, until I saw the emptiness and shallowness of all in which I had hitherto been involved. And then I was shown the realities of life, and he was revealed to me as my invisible, unknown Physician. Can I love him with half my heart? Can I be asking questions as to how much I am to pay toward the debt I owe him? — MRS. E. PRENTISS, "*Stepping Heavenward.*"

THE PRIESTHOOD OF HOLY SONG.

NEVER should it be forgotten that, among the royalties and beatitudes of that world of light and life, evermore the voice of holy psalm and glad hosanna thrills the happy spirits of its redeemed and rejoicing multitudes with an ecstasy of bliss altogether unknown to the denizens of this shadowy, sin-smitten world of ours. Would we, then, aspire to the true nobility of Christian life, while we cherish chiefly the rich treasury of divine truth enshrined in the sacred oracles, let us not hold in small esteem their spiritual teachings, conveyed to us by these beautiful translations into song:

"God sent His singers upon earth
 With song of sadness and of mirth,
 That they might touch the hearts of men,
 And bring them back to heaven again."

Then even as a wayside sacrament will these persuasive measures prove to us along our pilgrim path, brightening and beautifying our dark and shady places, and, as by a divine alchemy, transmuting our bitterest sorrows into serenest joys. Let memory be but true to her trust, and among the choicest of her spoils as a celestial benison will be the precious legacy thus bequeathed to us by the gifted and the good—the priesthood of holy song. Like some saintly evangel will these sweet lyrics ofttimes prove their potency by urging our dull souls, full panoplied for the warfare — with sandal shoon and pilgrim staff—onward and upward in the divine life, till, leaving the discordant accompaniments of earth all forgotten, we attain to where

"No groans shall mingle with the songs
Which warble from immortal tongues."

FREDERICK SAUNDERS.

FAITH.

FAITH IS THE EYE BY WHICH WE LOOK TO JESUS. A dim-sighted eye is still an eye; a weeping eye is still an eye.

FAITH IS THE HAND WITH WHICH WE LAY HOLD OF JESUS. A trembling hand is still a hand, and he is a believer whose heart within him trembles when he touches the hem of the Savior's garment that he may be healed.

FAITH IS THE TONGUE BY WHICH WE TASTE HOW GOOD THE LORD IS. A feverish tongue is nevertheless a tongue. And even then we may believe, when we are without the smallest portion of comfort; for our faith is founded, not upon feelings, but upon the promises of God.

FAITH IS THE FOOT BY WHICH WE GO TO JESUS. A lame foot is still a foot. He who comes slowly, nevertheless comes.—H. MÜLLER.

JEHOVAH JIREH.

ABRAHAM did not find the provision of God as soon as he left his house, or half way on his journey, or at the foot of the hill, or as soon as the altar was built, but just as soon as he was about to take away Isaac's life. At this crisis the voice of the angel was heard, the hand was arrested, and the ram seen awaiting him in the thicket. This shows that God provides for us in wisdom according to our necessities and circumstances. We have not the things of heaven on earth, but when our souls, through grace, ascend to the mount of God, the glory will be provided for us. We have not dying grace in the full enjoyment of health, but when we come to death, if we now live to him, dying grace will be awaiting us. We have not the grace of bereavement when we are rejoicing in the midst of unbroken circles; but when the enemy makes a breach, we shall find, as our day, our strength will be. God works upon this principle in nature as well as in grace. The harvest does not come in spring; then the husbandman has something else to do; he has to prepare for the harvest. When all the preparatory work is done, then harvest comes, as provided by the wisdom and goodness of God.—JOHN BATE.

ARISE, SHINE, FOR THY LIGHT IS COME.

WE are pilgrims to a dwelling-place of blessedness, and the light that streams through its open portals ought to suffice us as we approach them. An anticipated beatitude, a sanctity that even now breathes of Paradise, a grace which is already tinged with the richer lines of glory—these should mark the Christian disciple, and these, as he advances in years, should brighten and deepen upon and around him, until this distinction of earth and heaven is almost lost, and the spirit, in its placid and unearthly repose, is gone, as it were, before the body, and at rest already with its God. A being already invested with a deathless life, already adopted into the immediate family of God, already enrolled in the brotherhood of angels, yea, of the Lord of angels; a being who, amid the revolutions of earth and skies, feels and knows himself indestructible, capacitated to outlast the universe, a sharer in the immortality of God—what is there that can be said of such a one which falls not below the awful glory of his position? Oh, misery, that with such a calling, man should be the groveling thing he is! that, summoned but to pause for a while in the vestibule of the eternal Temple ere he be introduced into its sanctuaries, he should forget, in the dreams of his lethargy, the eternity that awaits him. Oh, wretchedness beyond words, that, surrounded by love, and invited to glory, he should have no heart for happiness, but should still cower in the dark, while light ineffable solicits him to behold and to enjoy it!—W. ARCHER BUTLER.

WHEN Egypt's king God's chosen tribe pursued,
In crystal walls the admiring waters stood;
When through the desert wild they took their way,
The rocks relented and poured forth a sea,
What limit can almighty goodness know,
When seas can harden, and when rocks can flow.
ALEXANDER POPE.

SABBATH HYMN FOR A SICK-CHAMBER.

Thousands, O Lord of Hosts! this day
  Around Thy altar meet,
And tens of thousands throng to pay
  Their homage at Thy feet.

They see Thy power and glory there,
  As I have seen them too;
They read, they hear, they join in prayer,
  As I was wont to do.

They sing Thy deeds, as I have sung,
  In sweet and solemn lays;
Were I among them, my glad tongue
  Might learn new themes of praise.

For Thou art in their midst to teach
  When on Thy name they call;
And Thou hast blessings, Lord, for each—
  Hast blessings, Lord, for all.

I, of such fellowship bereft,
  In spirit turn to Thee;
Oh! hast Thou not a blessing left—
  A blessing, Lord, for me?

The dew lies thick on all the ground;
  Shall my poor fleece be dry?
The manna rains from heaven around;
  Shall I of hunger die?

Behold Thy prisoner; loose my bands,
  If 'tis Thy gracious will;
If not, contented in Thy hands,
  Behold Thy prisoner still.

I may not to Thy house repair,
  Yet here Thou surely art;
Lord, consecrate a house of prayer
  In my surrendered heart.

To faith reveal the things unseen,
  To hope the joys unfold;
Let love, without a veil between,
  Thy glory now behold.

O make Thy face on me to shine,
  That doubt and fear may cease;
Lift up Thy countenance benign
  On me, and give me peace.

THINK OF THIS.

WHATEVER of our frailties and infirmities may be remembered by our surviving friends when the green sod is growing over us, let it not be said that we had within us unkind and churlish hearts. WE are borne with; let us bear with OTHERS; not forgetting the injunction of the apostle Peter, "Be pitiful, be courteous;" nor that of Paul, "Be kindly affectioned one to another."—GEORGE MOGRIDGE.

I AM.

When the Lord speaketh of himself with regard to his people, he saith I am. He doth not say I am their light, their life, their guide, their tower, or their strength, but only *I AM*. He sets his hand as it were to a blank, that his people might write under it what they please that is for their good. As if he should say, Are they weak? I am strength. Are they sick? I am health. Are they in trouble? I am comfort. Are they poor? I am riches. Are they dying? I am life. Have they nothing? I am all things. I am justice and mercy; I am grace and goodness; I am glory, beauty, holiness, eminency, supremacy, perfection, all-sufficiency, eternity, Jehovah—I am whatsoever is suitable to their nature, or convenient for them in their several conditions. I am whatsoever is amiable in itself or desirable to their souls. Whatsoever is pure or holy, whatsoever is great and pleasant, whatsoever is good and needful to make them happy, that I am. So that, in short, God here represents himself unto us as one universal good, and leaves us to make the application to ourselves, according to our several wants, capacities, and desires, by saying only in general I AM.—William Beveridge.

MEMORY OF KINDNESS.

AMONG the Alps, when the day is done, and twilight and darkness are creeping over fold and hamlet in the valleys below, Mont Rosa and Mont Blanc rise up far above the darkness, catching from the retreating sun something of his light, flushed with rose-color, exquisite beyond all words, or pencil, or paint, glowing like the gate of heaven.

And so past favors and kindnesses lift themselves up in the memory of noble natures, and long after the lower parts of life are darkened by neglect, or selfishness, or anger, former loves, high up above all clouds, glow with divine radiance, and seem to forbid the advance of night any further.—H. W. BEECHER.

LOOKING TO JESUS.

IN every enjoyment, O Christian, look unto Jesus; receive it as proceeding from his love, and purchased by his agonies. In every tribulation look unto Jesus; mark his gracious hand managing the scourge, or mingling the bitter cup; attempering it to a proper degree of severity; adjusting the time of its continuance, and ready to make these seeming disasters productive of real good. In every infirmity and failing look unto Jesus, thy merciful High-priest, pleading his atoning blood, and making intercession for transgressors. In every prayer look unto Jesus, thy prevailing Advocate, recommending thy devotions, and "bearing the iniquity of thy holy things." In every temptation look unto Jesus, the Author of thy strength and Captain of thy salvation, who alone is able to lift up the hands which hang down, to invigorate the enfeebled knees, and make thee more than conqueror over all thy enemies. But especially when the hour of thy departure approaches, and when thy flesh and thy heart fail, when all the springs of life are irreparably breaking, then look unto Jesus with a believing eye. Like expiring Stephen, behold him standing at the right hand of God on purpose to succor his people in this their last extremity.

Yes, my Christian friend, when thy journey through life is finished, and thou art arrived on the very verge of mortality; when thou art just launching out into the invisible world, and all before thee is vast eternity, then, oh then look unto Jesus. See by faith the Lord's Christ. View him as the only "Way" to the everlasting mansions; as the only " Door" to the abodes of bliss.—J. HERVEY.

LIGHT AT EVENTIDE.

At evening time let there be light:
  Life's little day draws near its close;
Around me fall the shades of night,
  The night of death, the grave's repose:
  To crown my joys, to end my woes,
At evening time let there be light.

At evening time let there be light:
  Stormy and dark hath been my day;
Yet rose the morn divinely bright,
  Dews, birds, and blossoms cheered the way;
  Oh for one sweet, one parting ray!
At evening time let there be light.

At evening time there *shall* be light,
  For God hath spoken—it must be;
Fear, doubt, and anguish take their flight—
  His glory now is risen on me,
  Mine eyes shall His salvation see.
'Tis evening time, and there *is* light.

I WILL FEAR NO EVIL.

The Lord my pasture shall prepare,
And feed me with a shepherd's care;
His presence shall my wants supply,
And guard me with a watchful eye;

My noon-day walks He shall attend,
And all my midnight hours defend.

When in the sultry glebe I faint,
Or on the thirsty mountain pant,
To fertile vales and dewy meads
My weary, wandering steps He leads,
Where peaceful rivers, soft and slow,
Amid the verdant landscape flow.

Though in the paths of death I tread,
With gloomy horrors overspread,
My steadfast heart shall fear no ill,
For Thou, O Lord, art with me still;
Thy friendly crook shall give me aid,
And guide me through the dreadful shade.

Though in a bare and rugged way,
Through devious lonely wilds I stray,
Thy bounty shall my wants beguile;
The barren wilderness shall smile,
With sudden greens and herbage crowned,
And streams shall murmur all around.

Joseph Addison.

To pass through life without sorrow would, naturally speaking, be good; but patiently to bear sorrow and profit by it is still better; the former is a temporary good, the latter eternal.

PRAYER AND TEMPTATION.

PRAYER is an action of likeness to the Holy Ghost, the spirit of gentleness and dove-like simplicity; an imitation of the holy Jesus, whose spirit is meek, up to the greatness of the biggest example; and a conformity to God, whose anger is always just, and marches slowly, and is without transportation, and often hindered, and never hasty, and is full of mercy: prayer is the peace of our spirit, the stillness of our thoughts, the evenness of recollection, the seat of meditation, the rest of our cares, and the calm of our tempest; prayer is the issue of a quiet mind, of untroubled thoughts; it is the daughter of charity, and the sister of meekness; and he that prays to God with an angry—that is, with a troubled and discomposed spirit, is like him that retires into a battle to meditate, and sets up his closet in the old quarters of an army, and chooses a frontier garrison to be wise in. Anger is a perfect alienation of the mind from prayer, and therefore is contrary to that attention which presents our prayers in a right line of God. For so have I seen a lark rising from his bed of grass, and soaring upward, singing as he rises, and hopes to get to heaven, and climb above the clouds; but the poor bird was beaten back with the loud sighings of an eastern wind, and his motion was made irregular and inconstant, descending more at every breath of the tempest than it could recover by the libration and frequent weighing of his wings, till the little creature was forced to sit down and pant, and stay till the storm was over; and then it made a prosperous flight, and did rise and sing as if it had learned music and motion from an angel as he passed sometimes through the air about his ministries here below. So is the prayer of a good man when his affairs have required business, and his business was matter of discipline, and his discipline was to pass upon a sinning person, or had a design of charity, his duties met with the infirmities of a man, and anger was its instrument, and the instrument became stronger than the prime agent, and raised a tempest, and overruled the man; and then his prayer was broken, and his thoughts were troubled, and his words went up toward a cloud, and his thoughts pulled them back again, and made them without intention; and the good man sighs for his infirmity, but must be content to lose the prayer, and he must recover it when his anger is removed, and his spirit is becalmed, made even as the brow of Jesus, and smooth like the heart of God; and then it ascends to heaven upon the wings of the holy dove, and dwells with God, till it returns, like the useful bee, laden with a blessing and the dew of heaven.—JEREMY TAYLOR.

REVIEW OF LIFE.

O THOU who, without respect of persons, judgest according to every man's work, have mercy upon me, and blot out of the book of thy remembrance the manifold transgressions of my life. It becometh me, O Lord, to take a review of the course in which I have walked; but oh, what a review it is! How many talents unimproved, and duties left undone, and sins committed does it discover!

I stand before thee inexcusable — self-condemned; but, blessed be thy name! not without hope, for there is mercy and forgiveness with thee. Thou hast provided a sacrifice for sins. Thou hast revealed a Savior who made reconciliation for iniquity. To him would I fly for refuge, humbly beseeching him to order our cause before the throne of the Most High, that mercy may proceed from thence instead of judgment, and that my soul may sing of abounding grace.

And ever, ever may the remembrance of my sins and of thy mercy abide with us. Recollecting that thou hast spared one whom thou couldst have destroyed, let the remainder of my life be considered as a grant of mercy made to me in order that I may bring forth fruits worthy of repentance. Give me grace, therefore, O Lord, not only to repent of past sins and omissions, but to make it much of the business of my remaining days to supply the deficiencies of my former ones. May I endeavor, in full dependence on thy grace, to be more faithful in all my duties. May I be careful to render unto all their dues; and, above all, let me remember what is due to thee, O blessed God, from whom I receive all my blessings, temporal, spiritual, and eternal.

O Thou who hast been pleased, notwithstanding all my sins, hitherto to preserve me, vouchsafe me thy help during the remainder of my earthly course. May thy gracious presence direct and support me. Should any false light appear, suffer me not to follow it. Should the enemy come in like a flood, enable me to lift up a standard against him. Thus, O Lord, be thou my light and my strength. I know not what a day may bring forth, nor need I be desirous of knowing; let it be enough for me that, without thy permission, not a sparrow falleth to the ground. Enable me to cast all my care on thee. Bless to me both my enjoyments and my sufferings. Let my soul derive benefit by every thing that happens to me. Whether my days be calm or stormy, bright or dark, make me to increase in faith, in holiness, in humility, patience, and charity, that I may be rich toward God, whatever I be in other respects. O Lord, hear this my prayer, for the sake of Christ Jesus my Redeemer. Amen.—JAMES BEAN.

PRAYER AGAINST THE FEAR OF DEATH.

O MOST gracious and merciful Father, give me grace to be always ready to obey thy summons, and willing to depart this life when thou callest. Forgive me all my sins, which are the sting of death, that I may prepare to meet it as a harmless thing that can not hurt me—as a release from those weaknesses and sorrows which render my life a burden to me. Keep me from being all my days in bondage to the fear of death. Let not my spirit be broken with dreadful apprehensions of dying under the frown of thy displeasure; but make me to remember thy infinite mercies, the inexhaustible treasures of thy goodness and clemency, so that the consideration thereof may fortify my mind against the horrors of a dying hour. Strengthen me with a comfortable hope in thee, a steadfast faith in thy Son's atoning blood, and the power of his resurrection. He has changed death into a sleep, and has promised to make the risen bodies of believers like unto his own glorified body. Enable me to exclaim with the triumphant apostle, "O death, where is thy sting? O grave, where is thy victory? Thanks be to God who giveth us the victory, through our Lord Jesus Christ." Let me, therefore, no longer be afraid of that which, through thy mercy, will be a happy passage into thy kingdom—the gate of everlasting bliss and glory. This I beg, through the merits of him who is the resurrection and the life. Amen.

CONSOLING IDEA OF DEATH.

"I CONGRATULATE you and myself," wrote John Foster to a friend, "that life is passing fast away. What a superlatively grand and consoling idea is that of Death! Without this radiant idea, this delightful morning-star, indicating that the luminary of eternity is going to rise, life would, to my view, darken into midnight melancholy. Oh! the expectation of living here, and living thus always, would be indeed a prospect of overwhelming despair. But thanks to that fatal decree that dooms us to die—thanks to that Gospel which opens the vision of an endless life; and thanks, above all, to that Savior-friend who has promised to conduct all the faithful through the sacred trance of death into scenes of paradise and everlasting delight."

THE MAN CHRIST JESUS.

PAYSON once wrote to a friend thus: "A man now fills the throne of heaven. And who is this man? Mark it well; it is a man who is not ashamed to call you 'brother.' You may not now know what he is doing with you, but you shall know hereafter; you shall see the reason of all the trials and temptations, the dark and comfortless hours, the long and tedious conflicts, and you will be convinced that not a sigh, not a single uneasy thought was allotted to you without a wise and gracious design."—*Anon.*

THE HAPPY OLD MAN.

ONE stormy winter day, the Rev. Mr. Young, of Jedburg, was visiting one of his people, an old man, who lived in great poverty in a lonely cottage. He found him sitting with the Bible open on his knees, but in outward circumstances of great discomfort—the snow drifting through the roof, and under the door, and scarce any fire on the hearth. "What are you about to-day, John?" was his question on entering. "Ah! sir," said the happy saint, "*I'm sitting under his shadow with great* delight!"—*Anon.*

ATTAINING HAPPINESS.

It is not so much by the symmetry of what we attain in this life that we are to be made happy, as by the enlivening hope of what we shall reach in the world to come. While a man is stringing a harp, he tries the strings, not for music, but for construction. When it is finished it shall be played for melodies. God is fashioning the human heart for future joy. He only sounds a string here and there to see how far his work has progressed.—H. W. Beecher.

NEARER TO THEE.

Nearer, my God, to Thee,
   Nearer to Thee!
E'en though it be a cross
   That raiseth me;
Still all my song shall be,
Nearer, my God, to Thee,
   Nearer to Thee!

Though like the wanderer,
   The sun gone down,
Darkness be over me,
   My rest a stone;
Yet in my dreams I'd be

Nearer, my God, to Thee,
   Nearer to Thee!

There let the way appear
   Steps unto Heaven;
All that Thou send'st to me
   In mercy given;
Angels to beckon me
Nearer, my God, to Thee,
   Nearer to Thee!

Then with my waking thoughts
   Bright with Thy praise,
Out of my stony griefs
   Bethel I'll raise;
So by my woes to be
Nearer, my God, to Thee,
   Nearer to Thee!

Or if on joyful wing
   Cleaving the sky,
Sun, moon, and stars forgot,
   Upward I fly,
Still all my song shall be,
Nearer, my God, to Thee,
   Nearer to Thee!—SARAH FLOWER ADAMS.

Autumn hath violets as well as spring,
And age its sweetness hath as well as youth.
                MARY MAYNARD.

A PRAYER FOR LONGER LIFE.

O spare me, that I may recover strength before I go hence, and be no more.—Psalm xxxix., 13.

WHY is it that we do not extremely hate that which we so desperately love—sin? For the deformity of itself is unspeakable; and, besides, it is the cause of all our woes. Sin hath opened the sluices, and let in the deluge of sorrows, which makes the life of poor man nothing else but vanity and misery, so that the meanest orator in the world may be eloquent enough on that subject. What is our life but a continual succession of many deaths? Though we should say nothing of all the bitterness and vexations that are hatched under the sweetest pleasures in the world, this one thing is enough—the multitude of diseases and pains, the variety of distempers that those houses we are lodged in are exposed to. Poor creatures are ofttimes tossed between two—the fear of death and the tediousness of life, and under these fears they can not tell which to choose. Holy men are not exempted from some apprehensions of God's displeasure because of their sins, and that may make them cry out with David, "O spare me, that I may recover strength before I go hence, and be no more." Or perhaps this may be a desire, not so much simply for the prolonging of life as for the intermitting of his pain, to have ease from the present smart. The extreme torment of some sickness may draw the most fixed and confident spirits to cry out very earnestly for a little breathing. Or, rather, if the words imply a desire of recovery, and the spinning out of the thread of his life a little longer, surely he intended to employ it for God and his service. But long life was suitable to the promises of that time. There is no doubt those holy men, under the law, knew somewhat of the state of immortality; their calling themselves "strangers on the earth" argued that they were no strangers to these thoughts. But it cannot be denied that the doctrine was but darkly laid out in those times. It is Christ Jesus who hath "brought life and immortality to light," who did illuminate life and immortality, which before stood in the dark.

Surely the desire of life is, for the most part, sensual and base, when men desire that they may still enjoy their animal pleasures, and are loth to be parted from them. They are pleased to term it a desire to live and repent, and yet few do it when they are spared; like evil debtors who desire forbearance from one term to another, but with no design at all to pay. But there is a natural desire of

S

life, something of abhorrence in nature against the dissolution of these tabernacles. We are loth to go forth, like children who are afraid to walk in the dark, not knowing what may be there. In some, such a desire of life may be very reasonable; being surprised by sickness, and apprehensions of death and sin unpardoned, they may desire a little time before they enter into eternity. For that change is not a thing to be hazarded upon for a few days or hours' preparation. I will not say that a death-bed repentance is altogether desperate, but certainly it is very dangerous and to be suspected, and therefore the desire of a little time longer, in such a case, may be very allowable. I will not deny but it is possible even for a believer to be taken in such a posture that it may be very uncomfortable to him to be carried off so, through the affrightments of death and his darkness as to his after-state. On the other hand, it is an argument of a good measure of spirituality and height of love to God to desire to depart and be dissolved in the midst of health and the affluence of worldly comforts. But for men to desire and wish to be dead when they are troubled and vexed with any thing is but a childish folly, flowing from a discontented mind, which being over, they desire nothing less than to die. It is true, there may be a natural desire of death, which at some time hath shined in the spirits of some natural men; and there is much reason for it, not only to be freed from the evils and troubles of this life, but even from those things which many of this foolish world account their happiness—sensual pleasures, to eat, and drink, and to be hungry again, and still to round that same course, which, to souls that are raised above sensual things, is burdensome and grievous.

But there is a spiritual desire of death, which is very becoming a Christian. For Jesus Christ hath not only opened very clearly the doctrine of life, but he himself hath passed through death, and lain down in the grave; he hath perfumed that passage, and warmed that bed for us, so that it is sweet and amiable for a Christian to pass through and follow him, and to be where he is. It is a strange thing that the souls of Christians have not a continual desire to go to that company which is above, finding so much discord and disagreement among the best of men that are here—to go to the spirits of just men made perfect, where there is light, and love, and nothing else—to go to the company of angels, a higher rank of blessed spirits; but, most of all, to go to God, and to Jesus, the Mediator of the New Testament. And, to say nothing positively of that glory (for, the truth is, we can say nothing of it), the very evils that death delivers the true Christian from may make him long for it; for such a one may say, "I shall die and go to a more excellent country, where I shall be happy forever — that is, I shall die no more, I shall sorrow no more, and shall be tempted no more; and, which is chiefest of all, I shall sin no more."—Robert Leighton.

A PRAYER ON PREPARATION FOR DEATH.

Lord, what is our life but a vapor, that appears for a little time and then vanisheth away! Even at the longest, how short! and at the strongest, how frail! and when we think ourselves most secure, yet we know not what a day may bring forth, nor how soon thou mayest come to call us to our last account. Quickly shall we be as water spilt on the ground, that can not be gathered up again; quickly snatched away from hence, and our place here shall know us no more forever. Our days, one after another, are spent apace; and we know not how near to us is our last day, when our bodies shall be laid in the grave, and our souls be called to appear at the tribunal of God, to receive their eternal doom. Yet how have I lived in this world, as if I should never leave it; how unmindful of my latter end!

LIGHT AT EVENING TIME. 269

how improvident of my time! how careless of my soul! how negligent in my preparation for my everlasting condition! so that thou mayest justly bring my last hour as a snare upon me, to surprise me in my sins, and to cut me off in my iniquities. But, O Father of mercies, remember not my sins against me; but remember thy own tender mercies and thy loving kindnesses, which have been ever of old. O remember how short my time is, and spare me, that I may recover strength before I go hence and be no more seen. Make me so wise as to consider my latter end, and teach me so to number my days that I may apply my heart to true wisdom. Lord, what have I to do in this world but to make ready for the world to come! O that I may be mindful of it, and be careful to finish my work before I finish my course!

In the days of my health and prosperity, oh that I may remember and provide for the time of trouble, and sickness, and death, when the world's enjoyments will shrink away from me, and prove utterly unable to support and comfort me. Let me never allow myself in any course of living wherein I would be loth or afraid to die; but let me see my corruptions mortified and subdued, that they may never rise up in judgment against me. Enable me so to die unto sin daily that I may not die for sin eternally.

Instruct me, good Lord, and assist me in my preparation for a dying hour, that I may not then be fully surprised, but may meet it with comfort and composure. Quicken me to a serious concern about that great work, and help me to perform it acceptably and with good success. Oh that I may be fitted for heaven ere I leave this world, and may have peace with God through Jesus Christ, before I depart hence into that state in which I must abide forever. O my Lord, make me so ready to meet thee at thy coming that thine appearance may be the matter of my hopes, and desires, and joyful expectations; that I may look and long for that blessed time when thou wilt put an everlasting period to all my troubles and temptations, and exchange my present state of infirmity and sin for a state of endless happiness and glory. O thou who art my life and my strength, help me so to live as, at the hour of death, I shall wish I had lived; and so to make ready for death all my days that, at my last day, I may have nothing to do but to die, and cheerfully to resign my spirit into thy gracious hands. O my Father, hear and answer my humble petitions, and let me find a merciful admission to thy favor and thy kingdom, for the sake of Jesus Christ. Amen.
—B. Jenks.

A PRAYER FOR ONE IN AFFLICTION.

"I KNOW, Lord, that thy judgments are right, and that thou of very faithfulness hast caused me to be troubled" (Psalm cxix., 75); for "before I was afflicted I went astray, but now have I kept thy word" (Psalm cxix., 6). Blessed be thy goodness for afflicting me.

I humbly beg of thee, O merciful Father, that this affliction may strengthen my faith, which thou sawest was growing weak; fix my hope, which was staggering; quicken my devotion, which was languishing; rekindle my charity, which was cooling; revive my zeal, which was dying; confirm my obedience, which was wavering; recover my patience, which was fainting; mortify my pride, which was presuming; and perfect my repentance, which was daily decaying; for all these and the like infirmities to which my soul is exposed, O make thy affliction my cure!

Grant, O my God, that this affliction thou hast in mercy laid on me may wean all my affections from the world, which I was apt to grow too fond of; rescue me from those occasions of evil of which I was in danger; secure me from those temptations which were ready to assault me; restrain me from those sins to which my nature was strongly inclined; preserve me from all those abuses of health I am apt to incur; and purify my soul from all that dross, and from all those vicious propensions which either my impenitence has left behind, or which I have since contracted.

O my God, let thy affliction produce my amendment, and all the happy effects in me which it is wont to do in thy children, and which thou in mercy dost design it should, and then continue thy affliction if it seem good in thy sight; behold, Lord, happy is the man whom thou has corrected (Job v., 7).

What is best for me, O my God, I know not; my flesh desires deliverance from this distemper, and if it be thy pleasure, O Lord, deliver me; my spirit desires that thou only wouldst choose for me, because thou art my Father, and out of thy fatherly tenderness wilt be sure to choose what is best for me. I resign my own will entirely to thine. Let me be enabled to say, after my gracious Savior's example, "Father, if thou be willing, remove this cup from me; nevertheless, not my will, but thine be done."

Hear, Lord, and have compassion on me, for the merits and sufferings of Jesus Christ, whose perfect resignation may I always imitate. Amen.—Thomas Ken.

A PRAYER FOR THE USE OF AN AGED PERSON.

O LORD of my life, thou hast been my God from my birth, my hope and trust from my youth. By thee was I brought into the world, and upon thee have I lived all my days. With what patience and long-suffering hast thou endured me! and with what loving kindness and tender mercies hast thou still followed and preserved me! How many have I seen snatched out of this life, and, as I fear, miserably unprepared for their death; whereas thou prolongest my days, and still addest new mercies to my life. Oh that the lengthening of my days may be a real benefit, so that the whole work which the Lord has given me to do may be finished. May I redeem the time, and improve all means and opportunities to the everlasting advantage of my soul. May my graces be as ripe as my years, and the remainder of my life be the best part of it. Though my sight is dim, let me not be blind to the things belonging to my peace. Though my ears are dull of hearing, let my heart be attentive to thy word, and let me hear thy voice while it is called "to-day." Though I can not, as formerly, relish the pleasures of meat and drink, yet let me still taste the grace of the Lord, and savor the things of the Spirit of God.

And though my limbs are weak, and my strength will not serve me to travel abroad as I have done, yet make me strong in the Lord to do thy work, to walk in thy ways, and to pursue my journey homeward to my house not made with mortal hands, eternal in the heavens. Oh let not the length of my life tempt me to forget that it must soon end, but let me keep my last day ever in near prospect. May I order all my concerns not only like a stranger and sojourner, but as a dying man preparing and waiting for the coming of the Lord. Oh that at thy coming thou mayest find me watching. And because I am old in sins as well as in years, O my gracious Lord, give me that repentance which needeth not to be repented of. Thou hast saved many old sinners; be merciful to me in spite of my numberless provocations. Put all my sins to the account of thy dear Son my Redeemer, and wash them all away in the fountain of his blood. Especially, O merciful Lord, pardon those sins which make the thoughts of death and judgment most painful to me. O give me some evidence that I have found mercy at thy hands, through the all-sufficient merits of my only Savior, Jesus Christ. Amen.—B. JENKS.

Temptations are instructions.

ALL ONE IN CHRIST.

Come, let us join our friends above,
   That have obtained the prize,
And on the eagle wings of love
   To joy celestial rise.
Let all the saints terrestrial sing
   With those to glory gone,
For all the servants of our King,
   In earth and heaven, are one.

One family, we dwell in Him,
   One Church, above, beneath,
Though now divided by the stream,
   The narrow stream of death.
One army of the living God,
   To His command we bow;
Part of His host hath crossed the flood,
   And part is crossing now.

Ten thousand to their endless home
   This solemn moment fly;
And we are to the margin come,
   And we expect to die;
His militant embodied host,
   With wishful looks we stand,
And long to see that happy coast,
   And reach that heavenly land.

Our old companions in distress
    We haste again to see,
And eager long for our release
    And full felicity:
Even now by faith we join our hands
    With those that went before,
And greet the blood-besprinkled bands
    On the eternal shore.

Our spirits, too, shall quickly join,
    Like theirs with glory crowned,
And shout to see our Captain's sign,
    To hear His trumpet sound.
Oh! that we now might grasp our Guide!
    Oh! that the word were given!
Come, Lord of hosts! the waves divide,
    And land us all in Heaven!—CHAS. WESLEY.

SING, FOR YOUR REDEMPTION IS NEAR.

A KING was once hunting alone in a wood, when he heard a very beautiful voice singing very sweetly; he went on, and saw it was a poor leper: "How can you sing," he said, "when you seem in so wretched a condition?" The leper replied, "It is because I am in this state I sing; for, as my body decays, I know that the hour of my deliverance draws nigh, when I shall leave this miserable world, and go to my Lord and my God."—RACHEL GRAY.

"TO BE WITH CHRIST."

"*To be with Christ.*" Who can comprehend this but the Christian? It is a heaven which worldlings care not for. They know not what a mass of glory is crowded into that one sentence—"To be with Christ." But to the believer the words are a concentration of bliss. Take only one of the many precious thoughts the words suggest—*the sight of Christ*. "Thine eye shall see the King in his beauty." We have heard of him, and can say, "Whom having not seen we love." But then we "*shall see him.*" Yes, we shall actually gaze upon the exalted Redeemer. Realize the thought. Is there not a heaven within it? Thou shalt see the hands which were nailed to the cross for thee; thou shalt see the thorn-crowned head, and with all the blood-washed throng shalt thou bow with lowly reverence before him who bowed in lowly abasement for thee. Faith is precious, but what must sight be? To view Jesus as the Lamb of God through the glass of faith makes the soul rejoice with joy unspeakable; but oh! to see him face to face, to look into those eyes, to hear that voice—rapture begins at the very mention of it. If even to *think* of it is so sweet, what must the *vision* be when we shall talk with him, "even as a man talketh with his friend"—for the vision of Christ implies *communion*. All that which the spouse desired in Solomon's Song we shall have, and ten thousand times more. Then will the prayer be fulfilled, "Let him kiss me with the kisses of his mouth; for thy love is better than wine." Then we shall be able to say, "His left hand is under my head, and his right hand doth embrace me." Then shall we experience the promise, "They shall walk with me in white, for they are worthy." And then we will pour out the song of gratitude, a song such as we have never sung on earth, tuneful, dulcet, pure, full of serenity and joy, no discord to mar its melody—a song rapt and seraphic. Happy day, when vision and communion shall be ours in fullness—when we shall know even as we are known!—CHARLES SPURGEON.

THE BIBLE.

THE new convert, dazzled over its pages with the ecstasy of his new-found hope, yet can not as deeply and ardently love it as he will do when, a gray-headed patriarch, years after, he turns afresh its wondrous leaves to adore the ever-full freshness of its lessons, and to remember all the lights it has cast upon his weary pathway.—W. R. WILLIAMS.

NEARING HEAVEN.

WE read that, in certain climates of the world, the gales that spring from the land carry a refreshing smell out to sea, and assure the watchful pilot that he is approaching a desirable and fruitful coast, when as yet he can not discern it with his eyes. And to take up the comparison of life to a voyage, in like manner it fares with those who have steadily and religiously pursued the course which heaven pointed out to them. We shall sometimes find, by their conversation towards the end of their days, that they are filled with peace, and hope, and joy, which, like refreshing gales and reviving odors to the seamen, are breathed forth from Paradise upon their souls, and give them to understand with certainty that God is bringing them into the desired haven.—J. TOWNSON.

HEAVEN A HOME.

HOME! oh, how sweet is that word! what beautiful and tender associations cluster thick around it; compared with it, house, mansion, palace are cold, heartless terms. But home! that word quickens the pulse, warms the heart, stirs the soul to its depths, makes age feel young again, rouses apathy into energy, sustains the sailor in his midnight watch, inspires the soldier with courage on the field of battle, and imparts patient endurance to the worn-down sons of toil. The thought of it has proved a sevenfold shield to virtue; the very name of it has a spell to call back the wanderer from the paths of vice; and far away, where myrtles bloom, and palm-trees wave, and the ocean sleeps upon coral strands, to the exile's fond fancy it clothes the naked rock, or stormy shore, or barren moor, or wild highland mountain with charms he weeps to think of, and longs once more to see. Grace sanctifies these lovely affections, and imparts a sacredness to the homes of earth by making them types of heaven. As a home the believer delights to think of it. Thus, when lately bending over a dying saint, and expressing our sorrow to see him lay so low, with the radiant countenance rather of one who had just left heaven than of one about to enter it, he raised and clasped his hands, and exclaimed in ecstasy, "I am going home."—THOMAS GUTHRIE.

EXTRAORDINARY afflictions are not always the punishment of extraordinary sins, but sometimes the trial of extraordinary graces.—MATTHEW HENRY.

THE GLORIOUS GOSPEL.

Preach the Gospel to every creature—that is, go tell every man, without exception, whatsoever his sins be, whatsoever his rebellions be—go and tell him these glad tidings, that if he will come in, Jesus will accept him, his sins shall be forgiven him, and he shall be saved.

The Gospel method of salvation resembles a well-drawn picture, which seems to look every person in the room in the face. In like manner, Gospel truth has something in it suitable to every one's case that reads or hears it, and that as particularly as if it spoke to every Gospel hearer by name.—W. Arnot.

ASLEEP AND AWAKE.

One should go to sleep at night as home-sick passengers do, saying, "Perhaps in the morning we shall see the shore." To us who are Christians, is it not a solemn, but a delightful thought, that perhaps nothing but the opaque bodily eye prevents us from beholding the gate which is open just before us, and nothing but the dull ear prevents us from hearing the ringing of those bells of joy which welcome us to the heavenly land?—H. W. Beecher.

LOVE A SAFEGUARD.

As we mix in life, there comes, especially to sensitive natures, a temptation to distrust. In young life we throw ourselves with unbounded and glorious confidence on such as we think well of—an error soon corrected, for we soon find out, too soon, that men and women are not what they seem. Then comes disappointment, and the danger is a reaction of desolating and universal distrust; for, if we look on the doings of man with a mere worldly eye, and pierce below the surface of character, we are apt to feel bitter scorn and disgust for our fellow-creatures. We have lived to see human hollowness; the ashes of the Dead Sea shore; the falseness of what seems so fair; the mouldering beneath whited sepulchres; and no wonder if we are tempted to think "friendship ALL a cheat; smiles, hypocrisy; words, deceit." And they who are what is called KNOWING in life contract by degrees, as the result of their experience, a hollow distrust of men, and learn to sneer at apparently good motives. That demoniacal sneer which we have seen, ay, perhaps felt, curling the lips at times, "Doth Job serve God for naught?"

The only preservation from this withering of the

heart is love. Love is its own perennial fount of strength. The strength of affection is a proof, not of the worthiness of the object, but of the largeness of the soul which loves. Love descends, not ascends. The might of a river depends not on the quality of the soil through which it passes, but on the inexhaustibleness and depth of the spring from which it proceeds. The greater mind cleaves to the smaller with more force than the other to it. A parent loves the child more than the child the parent; and partly because the parent's heart is larger, not because the child is worthier. The Savior loved his disciples infinitely more than his disciples him, because his heart was infinitely larger. Love trusts on—ever hopes and expects better things, and this a trust springing from itself and out of its own deeps alone.

Therefore, come what may, hold fast to love. Though men should rend your heart, let them not embitter or harden it. We win by tenderness; we conquer by forgiveness. Oh, strive to enter into something of that large celestial charity, which is meek, enduring, unretaliating, and which even the overbearing world can not withstand forever. Learn the new commandment of the Son of God. Not to love, but to love as he loved. Go forth in this spirit to your life-duties; go forth, children of the Cross, to carry every thing before you, and win victories for God by the conquering power of a love like his. —F. W. Robertson.

"*MORE THAN CONQUERORS.*"

The Christian is to be a conqueror at last. Do you think that we are forever to be the drudges and the slaves of sin, sighing for freedom, and yet never able to escape from its bondage? No! Soon the chains which confine me shall be broken, the doors of my prison shall be opened, and I shall mount to the glorious city, the abode of holiness, where I shall be entirely freed from sin. We who love the Lord are not to sojourn in Mesech for aye. The dust may defile our robes now, but the day is coming when we shall rise and shake ourselves from the dust, and put on our beautiful garments. It is true we are now like Israel in Canaan. Canaan is full of enemies; but the Canaanites shall and must be driven out, and the whole land from Dan to Beersheba shall be the Lord's. Christians, rejoice! You are soon to be perfect, soon to be free from sin, without one wrong inclination, one evil desire. You are soon to be as pure as the angels in light; nay, more, with your Master's garments on, you are to be "holy as the holy One." Can you think of that? Is it not the very sum of heaven, the rapture of bliss, the sonnet of the hill-tops of glory—that you are to be perfect? No temptation can reach you; nor, if the temptation could reach you, would you be hurt by it, for there will be nothing in you which could in any way foster sin. It would be as when a spark falls upon an ocean—your holiness would quench it in a moment. Yes, washed in the blood of Jesus, you are soon to walk the golden streets, white-robed and white-hearted too. Oh rejoice in the immediate prospect, and let it nerve you for the present conflict.—CHARLES SPURGEON.

MAKING GOD'S LAW OUR SONG.

Thy statutes have been my songs in the house of my pilgrimage.—Psalm cxix., 54.

COME, Christian pilgrim, and beguile your wearisome journey heavenward by "singing the Lord's song in this strange land." With the statutes of God in your hand and in your heart, you are furnished with a song for every step of your way: "The Lord is my shepherd; I shall not want. He maketh me to lie down in green pastures; he leadeth me beside the still waters. He restoreth my soul; he leadeth me in the paths of righteousness for his name's sake. Yea, though I walk through the valley of the shadow of death, I will fear no evil, for thou art with me; thy rod and thy staff they comfort me. Thou preparest a table before me in the presence of mine enemies; thou anointest my head with oil; my cup runneth over. Surely goodness and mercy shall follow me all the days of my life, and I will dwell in the house of the Lord forever." A song such as this can not fail to smooth your path, and reconcile you to the many inconveniences of the way, while the recollection that it is here only "the house of your pilgrimage," and not your home, and " that there remaineth a rest for the people of God," will support the exercise of faith and patience to the end. The same statutes, which are the yoke and burden of the worldly professor, are the subject of the believer's daily song and the source of his daily comfort, leading him from pleasure to pleasure, and, under the cherishing vigor of gracious communications, making his way and work easy and prosperous. Evidently, therefore, our knowledge of the Lord's statutes, and our delight in them, will furnish a decisive test of our real state before God. But what reason have we every moment to guard against that debasing, stupefying influence of the world, which makes us forget the proper character of a pilgrim! And what habitual conflict must be maintained with the sloth and aversion of a reluctant heart to maintain our progress in the journey toward Zion!

Reader, have you entered upon a pilgrim's life? Then what is your solace? What is your refreshment on the road? It is dull, heavy, wearisome to be a pilgrim without a "song;" and yet the Lord's statutes must be understood and felt in all their blessed experience before they will form our song. And "if you have tasted that the Lord is gracious"—if "he has put a new song into your mouth," oh! do not suffer any carelessness or neglect to rob you of this heavenly anticipation. Let not your lips be found mute. Seek to keep your heart in tune. Seek to maintain a lively contemplation of the place whither you are going—of him who, as your "forerunner," is for you entered thither—and of the prospect that, when he has "prepared a place for you, he will come again and take you to himself, that where he is, there you may be also." In this spirit, and in these hopes before you, you may take up your song, "O God! my heart is fixed; I will sing and give praise. I will bless the Lord at all times; his praise shall continually be in my mouth." Thus may you go on your pilgrimage "singing in the ways of the Lord," and commencing a song below, which, in the world of praise above, shall never, never cease.—CHARLES BRIDGES.

RESIGNATION.

Stricken, smitten, and afflicted,
  Savior, to Thy cross I cling;
Thou hast every blow directed,
  Thou alone canst healing bring.

Try me till no dross remaineth;
  And, whate'er the trial be,
While Thy gentle arm sustaineth,
  Closer will I cling to Thee.

Cheerfully the stern rod kissing,
  I will hush each murmuring cry;
Every doubt and fear dismissing,
  Passive in Thine arms will lie.

And when, through deep seas of sorrow,
  I have gained the heavenly shore,
Bliss from every wave I'll borrow,
  And for each will love Thee more.

THE FULL VISION AND ENJOYMENT OF CHRIST.

Make haste, my beloved, and take me to thyself; let me see thee face to face, and enjoy thee, thou dearest Jesus, whom my soul longeth after. It is good to live upon thee by faith, but to live with thee is best of all. I have found one day in thy courts, conversing sweetly with thee, better than a thousand; but this has only whetted my appetite; the more communion I have with thee, I hunger and thirst still for more. My soul panteth for nearer, still nearer communion with thee. When shall I come to appear before the presence of God? Oh thou light of my life, thou joy of my heart, thou knowest how I wish for the end of my faith, when I shall no longer see through a glass darkly, but with open face behold the glory of my Lord. Thou hast so endeared thyself to me, thou precious Immanuel, by ten thousand thousand kindnesses, that I can not be entirely satisfied, until I have the full vision and complete enjoyment of thyself. The day of our espousals has been a blessed time. Oh for the marriage of the Lamb, when I shall be presented as a chaste virgin to my heavenly bridegroom! How can I but long earnestly for this full enjoyment of thy everlasting love! Come, Lord Jesus, let me see thee as thou art. Come and make me like unto thee. I do love thee; I am now happy in thy love; but not so as I hope to be. I am often interrupted here, and never love thee so much as I desire; but these blessed spirits, standing now round thy throne, are perfected in love. Oh that I was once admitted to see, as they do, the glory of God in the face of Jesus Christ! Is not that the voice of my beloved which I hear answering, *Surely I come quickly?* Amen, say I; even so come, Lord Jesus. Make haste, my beloved, and be thou like to a roe, or to a young hart upon the mountains of spices.—WILLIAM ROMAINE.

"*I AM READY TO DIE.*"

THE Christian, at his death, should not be like the child who is forced by the rod to quit his play, but like the one who is wearied of it, and willing to go to bed. Neither ought he to be like the mariner whose vessel, by the violence of the tempest, is drifted from the shore, tossed to and fro upon the ocean, and at last suffers wreck and destruction, but like one who is ready for the voyage, and the moment the wind is favorable, cheerfully weighs anchor, and, full of hope and joy, launches forth into the deep. The pious monk, Staupitz, says, "Die as Christ did, and then, beyond all doubt, your death will be good and blessed." But how, then, did Christ die? "No man," he himself says, "taketh my life from me, but I lay it down of myself." And St. Luke tells us that "when the time was come that he should be received up, he steadfastly set his face to go to Jerusalem;" that is, he took the way to it with a confident and cheerful heart and an intrepid look. Let us follow this great forerunner; and that we may do it with alacrity and confidence, and be at all times ready, let us so order our affairs that when we come to die, we may have nothing else to do.—CHRISTIAN SCRIVER.

PILGRIM'S WAY TO HEAVEN.

THAT wonderful book (Pilgrim's Progress), while it obtains admiration from the most fastidious critics, is loved by those who are too simple to admire it. . . . . There is no ascent, no declivity, no resting-place, no turnstile with which we are not perfectly acquainted. The wicket-gate and the desolate swamp which separates it from the City of Destruction, the long line of road as straight as a rule can make it, the Interpreter's house and all its fair shows, the prisoner in the iron cage, the palace, at the doors of which armed men keep guard, and on the battlements of which walked persons clothed all in gold, the cross and the sepulchre, the steep hill and the pleasant arbor, the stately front of the house Beautiful by the wayside, the chained lions crouching in the porch, the low green valley of Humiliation, rich with grass and covered with flocks—all are as well known to us as the sights of our own street. Then we come to the narrow place where Apollyon strode right across the whole breadth of the way to stop the journey of Christian, and where afterwards the pillar was set up to testify how bravely the pilgrim had fought the good fight. As we advance, the valley becomes deeper and deeper, the shade of the precipices on both sides falls blacker and blacker. The clouds gather overhead. Doleful voices, the clanking of chains, the rushing of many feet to and fro, are heard through the darkness. The way, hardly discernible in the gloom, runs close by the mouth of the burning pit, which sends forth its flames, its noisome smoke, and its hideous shapes to terrify the traveler. Thence he goes on amidst the snares and pitfalls, with the mangled bodies of those who have perished in the ditch by his side. At the end of the long dark valley he passes the dens in which the old giants dwelt, amidst the bones of those whom they had slain.

Then the road passes straight on through a waste moor, till at length the towers of a distant city appear before the traveler, and soon he is in the midst of the innumerable multitudes of Vanity Fair. There are the jugglers and the apes, the shows and the puppet-shows. There are Italian Row, and French Row, and Spanish Row, and British Row, with their crowds of buyers, sellers, loungers, jabbering all the languages of the earth.

Thence we go on by the little hill of the silver mine, and through the meadow of lilies, along the bank of that pleasant river which is bordered on both sides by fruit-trees. On the left branches off the path leading to the horrible castle, the court-yard of which is paved with the skulls of pilgrims; and right onward are the sheep-folds and orchards of the Delectable Mountains.

From the Delectable Mountains the way lies through the fogs and briers of the enchanted ground, with here and there a bed of soft cushions spread under a green arbor. And beyond is the land of Beulah, where the flowers, the grapes, and the song of birds never cease, and where the sun shines night and day. Thence are plainly seen the golden pavements and streets of pearl on the other side of that black and cold river over which there is no bridge. —T. B. MACAULAY.

THE PILGRIM'S PRAYER.

GUIDE me, O Thou great Jehovah!
  Pilgrim through this barren land;
I am weak, but Thou art mighty;
  Hold me with Thy powerful hand!
    Bread of Heaven! Bread of Heaven!
Feed me now, and evermore.

Open now the crystal Fountain
　Whence the healing streams do flow;
Let the fiery, cloudy pillar
　Lead me all my journey through;
　　Strong Deliverer! Strong Deliverer!
Be Thou still my strength and shield.

When I tread the verge of Jordan,
　Bid my anxious fears subside;
Death of death, and Hell's destruction,
　Land me safe on Canaan's side;
　　Songs of praises, songs of praises,
I will ever give to Thee.—WILLIAM WILLIAMS.

BEGINNING OF HEAVEN.

THE joys of heaven will begin as soon as we attain the character of heaven and do its duties. That may begin to-day. It is everlasting life to know God—to have his spirit dwelling in you—yourself at one with him. Try that and prove its worth. Justice, usefulness, wisdom, religion, love, are the best things we hope for in heaven. Try them on—they will fit you here not less beseemingly. They are the best things of earth. Think no outlay of goodness and piety too great. You will find your reward begin here. As much goodness and piety, so much heaven. Men will not pay you—God will pay you now, pay you hereafter and forever.—T. PARKER.

THE DEATH OF THE BELIEVER.

THE death of the believer is always glorious, and the difference between the circumstances of the departure of the prophet Elijah and those of the servants of God in all ages is not so great as might at first be supposed. In the rapture of Elijah there was only *seen* a little more than usual of that which is true in fact, but which is concealed to the eye of sense in the death of every believer. The spirit of the departing saint is not left to wing a solitary flight to the distant regions of bliss, but an angel escort is sent even for the humblest. At the cotter's door— by the bedside of the prisoner in his lonely cell— amid the smoke and flame of the battle-field, or the darkness of the storms in mid-ocean, as well as in the peaceful dwelling or gilded palace, there stands in waiting for the expiring saint the shining escort —the chariot of fire and horses of fire, to waft the soul away to heaven. True, in the case of Elijah, as an especial honor to one who had especially honored him, God sent his flaming ministers a little farther on the road of life to receive him than he is accustomed to do for others; but the same dazzling chariot, the same flaming steeds stand in waiting, just outside the gates of sense, at the departure of every faithful servant of God; and the dying saint no sooner drops the mantle of his earthly body than, like Elijah, his soul steps into the shining equipage, and angel spirits hurry it with the speed of the whirlwind into the presence of the Lord.

You say this rapture of the glorified prophet was not death, and you say truly; and the departure of the believer is not death. It is said of him that he shall never see death. The believer in Jesus hath already entered upon life eternal. "He that believeth hath life"—yes, hath it already, and he can never see death.

> "No, no—it is not dying
> To go unto our God,
> This gloomy earth forsaking,
> Our journey homeward taking,
> Along the starry road."

No, this is not death. To many a Christian, we have reason to believe, the gates of Paradise stand open before the golden chain is broken, and he begins to enjoy conscious angelic companionship and felicity before his countenance changes or his heart ceases to beat. But with all alike the transition is instantaneous, and the moment the ear ceases to hear the sobs of mourning friends, it catches the hallelujahs of the world of glory.—JOHN STANFORD HOLME.

SPIRITUAL FELLOWSHIP WITH THE LOVED AND THE LOST.

THAT which is most valuable and lovely of life on earth—sanctified friendship—can not be said to die with those we love; but, through their death, it is rather raised to a higher and more influential life. By the transfer of our loved ones to heaven, our friendship becomes spiritualized and perpetuated. Our friends live in such circumstances, and in such relation to us, that their spirit, and faith, and love should exert more influence upon us than ever. "Being dead, they yet speak"—speak to us in such tones as should only the more command attention and charm the ear. A holy life has been compared to a song—a song of praise, and there is something not only beautiful, but very striking in the simile. A song hath its lower and its higher notes, but they are all pitched to one key; and so the life of the Christian hath its lower notes of sorrow and its higher notes of joy, but they, too, are all set to the one key-note—the love of God in Christ; and thus, together, they make up the melody of a holy life—a life in Christ.

This melody does not cease with this life, nor does it cease to awaken its echoes in the heart of loved ones when the singer is lost to sight through death; but it continues to come floating down to us from the heavenly world like the song of the skylark, only rendered more sweet and enchanting by distance. I shall never forget my own first impression of the morning song of the English skylark. In my zeal as a traveler to see all that could be seen, I had arisen with the sun, and had wandered off alone over the hills surrounding the old city of Winchester and its grand cathedral. The rays of the rising sun had changed the dew-drops into diamonds, and the early breeze had awakened the lark both to song and to flight; for as this almost spirit-bird begins to sing, it commences also mounting upon its wings, and, mounting, it continues to sing, and, singing, it continues to mount higher and still higher, as if it had truly bid adieu to earth, as Jeremy Taylor has it, and had gone to mingle with the choirs of heaven. At last I could no longer see the bird. Its form was entirely lost to my vision, but its song was still heard; its glad notes still came floating down from heaven like the music of an angel, and charmed my heart the more, since my eye could no longer discern the singer. Such is the song of a holy life; for the Christian, as he commences the song of the new life, commences his upward course, and his song grows sweeter as he rises; and it is never so sweet, so moving, so attractive as when the singer is lost to human vision, and the notes come floating down to us from the upper spirit-world. Listen! Can we not even now hear some notes of the life-song of some departed loved one? If the ear is too dull to catch the spirit-strains, can not the heart discern the melody, and is there not awakened within us kindred harmonies? They tell us that when two lutes are attuned to the same key, and placed near each other, when one is struck the other is heard to send forth notes and tones of kindred harmony. May not our spirits be thus so nearly attuned to the same key with those of our loved ones who have gone before to heaven, and may we not draw so near to them in spiritual union and sympathy that, even while we are yet upon the earth, our souls may send forth occasional strains at least of that song which fills all hearts, and occupies all voices in the choirs of the redeemed? Yes, yes, it is even so.

> "Their song to us descendeth;
> The spirit who in them did sing,
> To us his music lendeth;
> His song in them, in us, is one;
> We raise it high, we send it on—
> The song that never endeth."
>
> J. STANFORD HOLME.

COMMUNION WITH GOD A PREPARATION FOR DEATH.

It is, I believe, an undoubted truth that, in proportion as any one draws near to God, and thinks of him, and prays to him constantly and earnestly, so does he become familiar with the life beyond the grave, and finds it possible and natural to fix his faith there. For with God continually in our thoughts — God in Christ I mean, for a Christian knows God no otherwise than as approached through his Son — with God constantly thought of, praised, thanked, and served, it is impossible that death should any longer be so great a barrier, or the state beyond it so dark and cheerless. For to God there is no difference of time or state. He is, after our death as before it, before it as after it, in all respects the same. And death, which to him is absolutely nothing, becomes to us also less and less in proportion as we are more entirely his. So it is said that Enoch walked with God; and then it is added, "And he was not, for God took him." He walked with God on earth, and he walked with God in heaven, and the two became blended in one, and the barrier between them melted away into nothing. This is a true type, showing that the sense of death is destroyed by our consciousness of God. He who walks with God faithfully here, all that is said of him will be, "He was not, for God took him." He will be missed here by us, but to himself it is in a manner all but one life, the latter part the more perfect and the happier, yet both were passed with God.

Again, all that has been said tends to that same conclusion on which I have dwelt so often—the one conclusion, "Let us pray." Let us pray: if we have prayed hitherto, let us pray the more; if we have not, then let us begin to pray. Remember that we may pray not merely as God's creatures, but as his children. This is our Christian privilege; this Christ's death has purchased for us. We may pray to God as his children. Where, then, is fear? Where is doubt? Where ought to be coldness? More certainly than our fathers and mothers love us does God the Most High love us, even us—so humble, so sinful. And this is the most simple truth in the world, although it sounds like the loftiest flight of fancy — it is really and actually true. Wherefore let us pray to God in Christ continually; and so we shall learn, like the patriarchs, to live in faith and to die in faith.—THOMAS ARNOLD.

GRACE withereth without adversity.

A SIGHT WELL-PLEASING TO GOD.

To see a Christian mind encountering some great affliction, and conquering it; to see his valor in not sinking at the hardest distresses of life, this is a sight which God delights to behold. It were no hard condition to have a trial now and then, with long ease and prosperity between; but to be plied with one affliction at the heels of another; to have them come thronging in multitudes, and of different kinds, this is that which is often the portion of those who are the beloved of God.—ROBERT LEIGHTON.

HEAVEN A CITY.

A CITY never built with hands, nor hoary with the years of time; a city whose inhabitants no census has numbered; a city through whose streets rush no tide of business, nor nodding hearse creeps slowly with its burden to the tomb; a city without griefs or graves, without sins or sorrows, without births or burials, without marriages or mournings; a city which glories in having Jesus for its king, angels for its guards, saints for its citizens; whose walls are salvation, and whose gates are praise.—THOMAS GUTHRIE.

LAST VICTORY.

"THEN shall be brought to pass the saying that is written, *Death is swallowed up in victory.*" "So let all thine enemies perish, oh Christ;" and "let them that love thee be as the sun, when he goeth forth in his might." They shall *be* this, for they shall be sons of light, "being children of the resurrection, and shall shine as the stars, and as the brightness of the firmament, forever and ever." As a wreck may sink in the sea, and the ocean close over it so that not a vestige of its existence shall remain, nor a ripple on the surface tell that it was, so shall mortality be swallowed up of life—immortal life—life sinless, God-like, divine. Nor shall there be wanting the voice of rejoicing, as heard at the termination of successful war, for "death shall be swallowed up *in victory.*"—THOMAS BINNEY.

CARING FOR THE FUTURE.

MEN fall into the great mistake, on this subject, of supposing that to look forward must mean to look ANXIOUSLY forward. It is just as easy to look forward with hope as with sadness. And God's Word does not teach us that we are NOT to plan and forelook, but that we are not to plan and forelook with a spirit of anxious, mischievous, annoying fear. That is forbidden. Asceticism of every kind is against the Word of God. That is asceticism which leads a man to torment himself on account of the future—which leads a man to use the future as a whip to flagellate himself with. That is forbidden. It is not using the future; it is rather abusing it.—H. W. BEECHER.

THE DEATH OF ABRAHAM.

WHEN the days of Abraham, the man of God and hero of faith, drew toward a close, he laid himself down upon his quiet bed, full of years, and satisfied with life, and summoned his children and grandchildren; and they stood in a circle around him. Then the old man spake with serene aspect, and said, "My children, the God in whom I have believed now calls me to himself;" and he blessed them. His children, however, wept, saying, "Oh that the hour might never come!" But he replied, "No, my dears. I have walked as a child *before him* all the days of my life in truth and love; why should I now, when he calls, delay to *go to him?*" So saying, he bowed his head and gave up the ghost, and the form of death was as if one slumbered.—F. W. KRUMMACHER.

BEAUTY OF OLD AGE.

The scathed and leafless tree may seem
    Old age's mournful sign,
Yet on its bark may sunshine gleam,
    And moonlight softly shine.

Thus on the cheek of age shall rest
    The light of days gone by,
Calm as the glories of the West,
    When night is drawing nigh.

As round the scathèd trunk fondly clings
    The ivy green and strong,
Repaying, by the grace it brings,
    The succor granted long,

So round benevolent old age
    May objects yet survive,
Whose greenness can the heart engage,
    And keep the soul alive.—Bernard Barton.

AGED AND HELPLESS.

In age and feebleness extreme,
Who shall a helpless worm redeem?
Jesus, my only hope Thou art,
Strength of my failing flesh and heart;
Oh, could I catch a smile from Thee,
And drop into eternity!

HEAVEN LOOKED FORWARD TO.

There is a land of pure delight,
    Where saints immortal reign,
Infinite day excludes the night,
    And pleasures banish pain.

There everlasting spring abides,
    And never withering flowers;
Death, like a narrow sea, divides
    This heavenly land from ours.

Sweet fields beyond the swelling flood
    Stand dressed in living green;
So to the Jews old Canaan stood,
    While Jordan rolled between.

But timorous mortals start and shrink
    To cross this narrow sea,
And linger shivering on the brink,
    And fear to launch away.

Oh, could we make our doubts remove,
    These gloomy doubts that rise,
And see the Canaan that we love
    With unbeclouded eyes;

Could we but climb where Moses stood,
    And view the landscape o'er,
Not Jordan's stream, nor death's cold flood,
    Should fright us from the shore.—Isaac Watts.

NEARNESS OF HEAVEN.

THE nearness of heaven is suggested by the epithet "veil." Christians, there is only a veil between us and heaven! A veil is the thinnest and frailest of all conceivable partitions. It is but a fine tissue, a delicate fabric of embroidery. It waves in the wind; the touch of a child may stir it, and accident may rend it; the silent action of time will moulder it away. The veil that conceals heaven is only our embodied existence, and, though fearfully and wonderfully made, it is only wrought out of our frail mortality. So slight is it that the puncture of a thorn, the touch of an insect's sting, the breath of an infected atmosphere, may make it shake and fall. In a bound, in a moment, in the twinkling of an eye, in the throb of a pulse, in the flash of a thought, we may start into disembodied spirits, glide unabashed into the company of great and mighty angels, pass into the light and amazement of eternity, know the great secret, gaze upon splendors which flesh and blood could not sustain, and which no words lawful for man to utter could describe! Brethren in Christ, there is but a step between you and death; between you and heaven there is but a veil.—C. STANFORD.

GAIN OF DYING.

THROUGHOUT the Bible it is declared that the things that we are permitted to see in this life are but imitations, glimpses of what we shall see hereafter. "It doth not yet appear what we shall be." There are times when it seems as though our circumstances, our nature, all the processes of our being, conspired to make us joyful here, yet the apostle says we now see "through a glass darkly." What, then, must be the vision which we shall behold when we go to that place above where we shall see face to face? What a land of glory have you sent your babies into! What a land of delight have you sent your children and companions into! What a land of blessedness are you yourselves coming to by-and-by! Men talk about dying as though it was going toward a desolate place. All the past in a man's life is down hill and toward gloom, and all the future of man's life is up hill and toward glorious sunrising. There is but one luminous point, and that is the home toward which we are tending, above all storms, above all sin and peril. Dying is glorious crowning; living is yet toiling. If God be yours, all things are yours. Live while you must, yet yearn for the day of consummation, when the door shall be thrown open,

and the bird may fly out of his netted cage, and be heard singing in higher spheres and diviner realms.
—H. W. BEECHER.

THOUGHTS OF HEAVEN.

AND there truly is nothing which should keep your desires from heaven. No; not that delightful circle of home where the parent's eye may glisten as he looks upon his child, and the child may smile with joy because it gazes on its father; or, more loving still, when it looks upon its mother—there is naught even there which can abstract the desires from heaven; and the only modification of that desire should be that children, and parents, and brethren, and sisters should all meet in heaven. No; there is nothing, when here we meet round the table of the Lord, and Christian comes by Christian to taste the bread and wine which shows forth the Lord's death till he comes—till we all meet as by one electric impulse upon the spirit—till we all blend together in one, being members of his body, and his flesh, and his bone—there is nothing here that can abstract the desires from heaven; the only modification of that desire must be that those who break the bread and drink the wine may have fulfilled at last the glorious promise, "Verily, I will no more taste of the fruit of the vine until that day when I drink it new with you in my Father's kingdom." Onward and onward still, from year to year, and from day to day, must the Christian spirit press in its desire toward heaven. It will be, my brethren, but a little longer, and then that desire shall be fulfilled, and mortality will be swallowed up in life. The portal shall be entered, and the spirit shall gaze round on the wonders of its completed salvation. What pearly gates are these? What jasper walls are these? What golden streets are these? What splendid palaces are these? What immortal trees are these? What crystal streams are these? What amaranthine bowers are these? These are the spirits of the just, and I see my parents, my partner, and my children, and they beckon to the entrance. There is Jesus, whom my soul hath loved, and now I behold him with the glory of his Godhead. And there is the overshadowing splendor of everlasting happiness, which breathes blessings on all beneath it. And this—*this* is heaven! Earth, I have nothing to do with thee, with thy dull days and thy nights of darkness. I have left thee, with thy storms and tempests—with thy distressing temptations and thy polluting scenes. I have left thee, with thy sorrows, thy bereavements, thy diseases, and thy destinies. This—*this* is heaven! Am I come there?

Then redemption and immortality are mine. Oh, brethren, in the body or out of the body, can we tell? Have not your desires expanded and extended till even now you listen to the song, and inhale the atmosphere of heaven? We must come back again to earth till the will of God removes us; but as we descend to the world of mortality, and of sorrow, and of sin, in which we must breathe a little longer, we can not but send our desires to him who has gone before us, "When shall I come and appear before God?" "Oh that I had the wings of a dove, then I would flee away and be at rest!"— JAMES PARSONS.

THE MUSIC OF HEAVEN.

WE may judge by the saints here, when they are in a fit disposition to praise God, what fervors they feel in their united praises of him in heaven. The psalmist, in an ecstasy, calls to all the parts of the world to join with him: "The Lord reigns; let the heavens rejoice, and the earth be glad; let the sea roar, let the fields be joyful, and all that dwell therein." He desires that nature should be elevated above itself, that the dead parts be inspired with life, the insensible feel motions of joy, and those that want a voice break forth in praises to adorn the divine triumph. With what life and alacrity will the saints in the blessed communion celebrate the object of their love and praises! The seraphim about the throne "cried to one another" to express their zeal and joy in celebrating his eternal purity and power, and the glory of his goodness. Oh! the unspeakable pleasure of this concert, when every soul is harmonious, and contributes his part to the full music of heaven! Oh, could we hear but some echo of those songs wherewith the heaven of heavens resounds, some remains of those voices wherewith the saints above "triumph in the praises" in the solemn adoration of the King of Spirits, how would it inflame our desires to be joined with them? "Blessed are those that are in thy house; they always praise thee."—WILLIAM BATES.

SERVICE OF HEAVEN.

THEY serve God. "They cry with a loud voice, saying, Salvation to our God which sitteth upon the throne, and unto the Lamb!" They are before the throne of God, and "serve him day and night in his temple." Adoration at the throne, activity in the temple—the worship of the heart, the worship of the voice, the worship of the hands, the whole being consecrated and devoted to God—those are the services of the upper sanctuary. Here the flesh is often wearied with an hour of worship; there "they rest not day and night, saying, Holy, holy, holy, Lord God Almighty, which was, and is, and is to come." Here a week will often see us weary in well doing; there they are drawn on by its own deliciousness to larger and larger fulfillments of Jehovah's will. Here we must lure ourselves to work by the prospect of rest hereafter; there the toil is luxury, and the labor recreation, and nothing but jubilees of praise, and holidays of higher service, are wanted to diversify the long and industrious Sabbath of the skies; and it matters not though sometimes the celestial citizens are represented as always singing, and sometimes as always flying; sometimes as always working, sometimes as always resting, for there work is rest, and every moment song; and the "many mansions" may be one temple, and the whole being of its worshipers one tune —one mighty anthem, long as eternity, and large as its burden, the praise of the great Three-One—the self-renewing and ever-sounding hymn, in which the flight of every seraph, of every raptured spirit, is a several note, and repeats ever over again, "Holy, holy, holy, Lord God Almighty, which was, and is, and is to come."—J. HAMILTON.

X

I WILL NEVER LEAVE THEE NOR FORSAKE THEE.

How firm a foundation, ye saints of the Lord,
Is laid for your faith in His excellent Word;
What more can He say than to you He hath said,
Who unto the Savior for refuge have fled:

Fear not, I am with thee; oh be not dismayed,
For I am thy God, and will still give thee aid;
I'll strengthen thee, help thee, and cause thee to stand,
Upheld by My righteous, omnipotent hand.

When through the deep waters I call thee to go,
The rivers of sorrow shall not overflow;
For I will be with thee thy trials to bless,
And sanctify to thee thy deepest distress.

When through fiery trials thy pathway shall lie,
My grace, all-sufficient, shall be thy supply;
The flame shall not hurt thee; I only design
Thy dross to consume, and thy gold to refine.

E'en down to old age all my people shall prove
My sovereign, eternal, unchangeable love;
And then, when gray hairs shall their temples adorn,
Like lambs they shall still in my bosom be borne.

The soul that on Jesus hath leaned for repose,
I will not—I will not desert to his foes;
That soul, though all hell should endeavor to shake,
I'll never—no, never—no, never forsake.

THE CHAMBER OF SICKNESS.

CHAMBER of sickness! much to thee I owe,
    Though dark thou be;
The lessons it imports me most to know
    I owe to thee.
A sacred seminary thou hast been,
I trust, to train me to a happier scene.

Chamber of sickness! suffering and alone,
    My friends withdrawn,
The blessed beams of heavenly truth have shone
    On me forlorn
With such a hallowed vividness and power
As ne'er were granted to a brighter hour.

Chamber of sickness! midst thy silence oft
    A voice is heard,
Which, though it falls like dew on flowers, so soft
    Yet speaks each word
Into the aching heart's unseen recess,
With power no earthly accents could possess.

Chamber of sickness! in that bright abode
    Where is no pain,
If, through the merits of my Savior God,
    A seat I gain,
This theme shall tune my golden harp's soft lays,
That in thy shelter passed my early days.—*Anon.*

WAYS OF GOD.

God often lets his people reach the shore as on planks of a shipwrecked vessel. He deprives us of the cisterns, in order to make us drink out of the fountains of waters. He frequently takes away our supports, not that we may fall to the ground, but that he may himself become our rod and our staff. The embarrassments of his people are only the festive scaffoldings on which his might, his faithfulness, and his mercy celebrate their triumphs.—F. W. KRUMMACHER.

PAUL'S ESTIMATE OF HEAVEN.

"I RECKON," he says, like a man skilled in spiritual arithmetic, "I reckon," after a due estimate of their comparative value, "that the sufferings of this present time are not worthy to be compared with the glory that shall be revealed."

No man was ever so well qualified to make this estimate. Of the sufferings of the present world he had shared more largely than any other man. Of the glory that shall be revealed, he had a glimpse granted to no other man. He had heard the words of God, and seen the vision of the Almighty, and the result of this privileged experience was, he "desired to depart and be with Christ;" he desired to escape from this valley of tears; he was impatient to recover the celestial vision, eager to perpetuate the momentary foretaste of the glories of immortality.—HANNAH MORE.

NOT IMPATIENT, BUT READY.

"ARE you not weary for your heavenly rest?" said Whitefield one day to an old clergyman. "No, certainly not," he replied. "Why not?" "Why, my good friend," said the old minister, "if you were to send your servant into the fields to do a certain portion of work for you, and promised to give him rest and refreshment in the evening, what would you say if you found him languid and discontented in the middle of the day, and murmuring, 'Would God it were evening?' Would you not bid him be up and doing, and finish his work, and then go home and get the promised rest? Just so does God say to you."

Let us take the full comfort of this *fact*, that we are servants, and have really no work of our own to do—nothing which we are striving to accomplish on our own account.—*Anon.*

DAVID'S HARP (A PARABLE).

ONE day David, the king of Israel, sat on the hill of Sion; his harp rested before him, and he leaned his head on the harp.

The Prophet Gad came to him and said, "Of what are you thinking, my king?"

David answered and said, "Of my perpetually changing lot. How many hymns of thanksgiving and rejoicing, but, also, how many plaintive and mournful odes, have I sung with this harp!"

"Be thou like thy harp!" said the prophet.

"What do you mean?" asked the king.

"Behold," answered the man of God, "thy sorrow, as thy joy, elicited heavenly tones from thy harp, and animated its strings; so may sorrow and joy form thy heart and life to the heavenly harp."

Then David arose and struck the strings.—F. W. KRUMMACHER.

INQUIRIES ABOUT HEAVEN.

"MY chief conception of heaven," said Robert Hall to Wilberforce, "is REST." "Mine," said Wilberforce, "is LOVE." Perhaps both conceptions were true; and union of perfect love with perfect rest conveys our best idea of heaven, considered simply as a state. But what is the manner of existence there, and what is the true physical theory of another life? How shall we see without these eyes, hear without these ears, act without this material instrument of being? What are the visions, the emotions, the specific employment of heaven? Where and what is the region itself? Is it a star? Is it a sun? Is it a vast and splendid cluster of worlds, or is it some spacious, magnificent, and unlimited continent of light and beauty? Where are "the holy places not made with hands?" Where are the "many mansions of our Father's house?" Where is the grand metropolis of God's moral rule, whence his laws go forth, and whither the tribes go up, "the tribes of the Lord," from every realm of earth, and every age of time? Where stands that throne before which, at this solemn instant, the innumerable companies of the glorified bend in an ecstasy of adoration? The Heir of Glory dies—"he giveth up the ghost, and where is he?" These questions are unanswered and unanswerable.

"He that hath found some fledged bird's nest may know
    At first sight if the bird be flown;
But what fair field or grove he sings in now,
    That is to him unknown."

C. STANFORD.

FRIENDSHIPS OF HEAVEN.

MAN is constituted to be happy in society. Place him in solitude, and, however exciting and felicitous are his circumstances in other respects, he will wither and pine away. But above, we shall be with many that shall come from the east and west, and north and south, and shall sit down with Abraham, Isaac, and Jacob. The entire heaven of angels, and the whole host of the redeemed, we shall have sweet and improving fellowship with forever! The wise and the good, the great and the pure, the benevolent and active, from every region, will be our companions and associates, with whom we shall live, and love, and know, and obey, through one eternally enduring day. Of all the afflictions to which we are liable, there is none so painful as the death of our friends. And oh! what a consoling balm is the doctrine that we shall, in the realms above, be restored to their fellowship. This doctrine is involved in many passages of Scripture: in the account of the last judgment day—in the language of David on the occasion of the death of his infant child by Bathsheba—in the parable of the rich man and Lazarus —in the consolation which our Savior gives to the penitent sinner on the cross—in the assurance ad-

ministered by the apostle St. Paul to the Thessalonian believers, that they should be his joy and crown of rejoicing in the presence of our Lord Jesus Christ at his coming, and in the same apostle forbidding them to sorrow for such as had fallen asleep as though they had no hope of being united with them, and of being together with the Lord—and in the general use which the sacred writers make of the word SLEEP for death—a simile which would be flagrantly incorrect if our recollections, our friendships and affections, were not renewed in a future state. And, in general, the same doctrine is taught also through the whole book of the Revelations of St. John. Happy prospect, that exalts friendship into religion! What blest society there will be above!
—J. BEAUMONT.

FORETOKENS OF HEAVEN.

LET the traveler, however remote his stray, find something congenial to his own latitude and country, and the sense of alienation is redeemed. Should he unexpectedly discover the daisy of his native fields, or catch the wood-note that had caroled from his native groves — should he hear his mother tongue—should he enjoy the right and protection of some institution at which his youthful heart had learned to bound — though the earth's diameter struck through between his sojourn and his own land, even that sojourn would be less to him than home. And the Christian has now much akin to heaven. His heart is there. Eternal life abides in him. Now he possesses the principles which heaven but matures, and cherishes the affections which it but expands.—R. W. HAMILTON.

"IT IS WELL."

A POOR wayfarer, leading by the hand
   A little child, had halted by a well,
To wash from off her feet the clinging sand,
And tell the tired boy of that bright land
   Where, this long journey past, they longed to dwell.

When, lo! the Lord who many mansions had,
   Drew near, and looked upon the suffering twain:
Then pitying spoke: "Give me the little lad;
In strength renewed, and glorious beauty clad,
   I'll bring him with me when I come again."

Did she make answer selfishly and wrong—
   "Nay, but the woes I feel he too must share!"
Oh rather, bursting into grateful song,
She went her way rejoicing, and made strong
   To struggle on, since he was freed from care.
                                     Anon.

I WOULD NOT LIVE ALWAY.

I would not live alway: I ask not to stay
Where storm after storm rises dark o'er the way;
The few lurid mornings that dawn on us here,
Are enough for life's woes, full enough for its cheer.

I would not live alway; no—welcome the tomb,
Since Jesus hath lain there, I dread not its gloom;
There, sweet be my rest, till He bid me arise
To hail Him in triumph descending the skies.

Who, who would live alway, away from his God;
Away from yon heaven, that blissful abode,
Where the rivers of pleasure flow o'er the bright plains,
And the noontide of glory eternally reigns:

Where the saints of all ages in harmony meet,
Their Savior and brethren, transported to greet;
While the anthems of rapture unceasingly roll,
And the smile of the Lord is the feast of the soul!
Wm. A. Muhlenburg.

FULLNESS OF JOY AT GOD'S RIGHT HAND.

I have found it an interesting thing to stand on the edge of a noble rolling river, and to think that, although it has been flowing on for six thousand years, watering the fields, and slaking the thirst of a hundred generations, it shows no signs of waste or want; and when I have watched the rise of the sun as he shot above the crest of the mountain, or in a sky draped with golden curtains sprang up from his ocean bed, I have wondered to think that he has melted the snows of so many winters, and renewed the verdure of so many springs, and painted the flowers of so many summers, and ripened the golden harvests of so many autumns, and yet shines as brilliant as ever, his eye not dim, nor his natural strength abated, nor his floods of light less full for centuries of boundless profusion. Yet what are these but images of the fullness that is in Christ? Let that feed your hopes, and cheer your hearts, and brighten your faith, and send you away this day happy and rejoicing. For when judgment flames have licked up that flowing stream, and the light of that glorious sun shall be quenched in darkness, or veiled in the smoke of a burning world, the fullness that is in Christ shall flow on throughout eternity in the bliss of the redeemed. Blessed Savior, image of God, divine Redeemer, in thy presence is fullness of joy, at thy right hand there are pleasures for evermore. What thou hast gone to heaven to prepare, may we be called up at death to enjoy.—T. Guthrie.

LONGING FOR HEAVEN.

It appears from the life of the poet Southey that he had at times a wish to leave the world, but it seems to have been chiefly for the sake of enjoying the intellectual society of a future state. Heaven was, in his view, the home of genius, where all the gifted spirits of our race hold exalted fellowship. He longed to see and converse with Shakspeare, Dante, and Chaucer. John Foster, a man whose character and thoughts were cast in a far different mould, felt in this world that he was under restraint; that the great secrets of the spiritual universe were hid from him; that death would break down the barrier, and would give his spirit free scope to plunge into the mysteries of truth. His sublime soul was like a courser panting to leap the barrier; like an eagle dragging at its chain, and longing to soar above the clouds. Leighton's desire was strictly and simply spiritual. It was a longing for purity, love, perfection, Christ, and God. He felt this was a dark world because a sinful one, and he longed for a holy heaven more than they who watch for the morning, saying, "The utmost we poor mortals can attain to is to lie awake in the dark; and a great piece of art and patience is to while away the hours of night." He delighted in the old apothegm, "The day which you fear as the death-day of time is the birthday of eternity." His alacrity to depart resulted from his earnest desire to see and enjoy perfection, in the perfect sense of it, which he could not do and live.—J. STOUGHTON.

UNANSWERED PRAYER.

THE case of the apostle is an undoubted instance of "the effectual fervent prayer of a righteous man" not "availing" for the object desired; in other words, it teaches us that the precept of our Lord, "Ask, and it shall be given you," must not be understood as promising a direct answer to every prayer, but as expressing the certainty that he who knows our infirmities before we ask, and our ignorance in asking, will, in the end, supply our needs with all that we require, though not with all that we desire, or think that we require.

The apostle prayed not for wealth, or honor, or wisdom, but simply that a great impediment to his usefulness might be removed; and even this was not granted. And, in like manner, a greater than the apostle had "offered up prayers and supplications with strong crying and tears," earnestly and in an agony, and the sweat, as it were great drops of blood, falling down to the ground, saying, "Father, if it be possible, let this cup pass from me," and yet the cup was not removed, and the prayer was not granted. If the prayer of Paul and the prayer of Christ were refused, none need complain or be perplexed.—ARTHUR P. STANLEY.

"*THE CLOUD OF WITNESSES.*"

SURROUNDED by the great cloud of witnesses, which includes all the illustrious dead, cheered by the presence of angels and glorified spirits, fanned and wafted by the wing of some brighter seraph, with the glory of the throne streaming upon our vision, and with the melody of heaven falling upon our ears, let us rise and hasten forward in our course. If it be that, in the new song of that world—the song of redemption—the sweet singer of Israel " is sweeping a harp far more melodious and tuneful than the one he swept with a master hand on earth; if Elijah is there, pouring " his soul of fire into it ;" if Isaiah, rapt in seraphic flame, is giving to it " a loftier echo ;" if Paul is there, mingling his mighty ascriptions of glory and of praise; if John is ever breathing into it his full heart of love ; if " the martyrs, those witnesses for the truth who passed through the flames for their reward," are furnishing " new accession to its strength;" if all the redeemed are adding to its volume and its grandeur, then let us never pause till our feet shall stand on that mount of God, and our voices blend in that one sweetest of all notes, "Unto him that loved us, and hath washed us from our sins in his blood, and hath made us kings and priests unto God, even his Father—unto him be glory and dominion forever and ever. Amen."—R. FERGUSON.

CAST THY BURDEN ON THE LORD.

Hast thou a care whose pressure dread
Repels sweet slumber from thy bed?
To thy Redeemer take that care,
And change anxiety to prayer.

Hast thou a hope from which thy heart
Would feel it almost death to part?
Entreat the Lord that hope to crown,
Or give thee strength to lay it down.

Hast thou a friend whose image dear
May prove an idol worshiped here?
Implore the Lord that naught may be
A shadow between heaven and thee.

Whate'er the care that breaks thy rest,
Whate'er the wish that swells thy breast,
Spread before God that wish, that care,
And change anxiety to prayer.

THE BEACON LIGHT.

While on life's stormy sea
　My bark is driven,
From a far coast to me
　Sweet light is given,
Gleaming around my way,
Changing dark night to day,
Blending its golden ray
　With hues of heaven.

That beacon light I have,
　And lose all fear;
The Savior walks the wave—
　His voice I hear—
My precious, perfect Guide,
Bidding the storm subside,
Showing, beyond the tide,
　Skies heavenly clear.

I feel thy magnet powers,
　Bright world to come!
Faith sees thy glorious bowers,
　Where angels roam;
Where loved ones, gone before,
Now beckon from the shore,
And make me long the more
　For them and home.—S. D. Phelps.

COMFORT FOR THE HOUR OF DEATH.

AFTER having dwelt much on the graces and duties of the believer, I would remind the reader of one unspeakable privilege connected with all our graces, all our duties, and all our works. It was the privilege which comforted the devout Herbert on his dying bed. On the day of his death, when reminded of his many acts of mercy, he replied, "They be good works if they be sprinkled with the blood of Christ, and not otherwise." There is not only for us the blessed truths to be believed, that Jesus has loved us, and washed us from our sins in his own blood, and that our persons are accepted in him, but there is also for us the daily privilege of offering up all our services in his name: "These are they that came out of great tribulation, and have washed their robes, and made them white in the precious blood of the Lamb." What Christian is not burdened and humbled to the dust by the sins of his best doings? All our spiritual clothing, our humility, our charity, our prayers, our kindness to others, our gifts of every character, all our robes of righteousness imparted to us, as worn by us are soon polluted, and need the continual application of the blood of the Son of God, which cleanseth from all sin, that they may be made white. Thus shall we be found at the last among those who are before the throne of God, and serve him day and night in his temple.—EDWARD BICKERSTETH.

HEAVENLY ASPIRATION.

WE foresee, by faith, that happy day. We see, by faith, the new Jerusalem; the innumerable angels; the perfect spirits of the just; their glorious light, their flaming love, their perfect harmony. We hear, by faith, their joyful songs of thanks and praise. Lately they were as low and sad as we—in sins and sorrows, in manifold weaknesses, sufferings, and fears; but by faith and patience we desire to follow our Lord and them. The time is near; this flesh will quickly turn to dust, our delivered souls shall come to thee; our life is short, and our sins and sorrows will be short; then we shall have light; we shall no more groan, and cry out in darkness, oh that we could know the Lord! then shall we love thee with pure, unmixed, perfect love, and need no more to groan and cry, oh that our souls were inflamed with thy love! then shall we praise thee with thankful alacrity and joy, which will exceed our present apprehensions and desires.

Oh blessed streams of light and love, which will

flow from thy opened, glorious face upon our souls forever! How far will that everlasting Sabbath and those perfect praises excel these poor and dull endeavors? as far as that triumphant city of God excelleth this imperfect, childish, discomposed church!

Quicken, Lord, our longing for that blessed state and day! O come, Lord Jesus, come quickly, and fulfill thy word, that we may be with thee where thou art, and may behold thy glory!—R. BAXTER.

ACTIVITY IN HEAVEN.

EXCEPTING exemption from sin, intense, vigorous, untiring action is the greatest pleasure of the mind. I could hardly wish to enter heaven did I believe its inhabitants were idly to sit by purling streams, fanned by balmy airs. Heaven, to be a place of happiness, must be a place of activity. Has the far-reaching mind of Newton ceased its profound investigations? Has David hung up his harp as useless as the dusty arms in Westminster Abbey? Has Paul, glowing with God-like enthusiasm, ceased itinerating the universe of God? Are Peter, and Cyprian, and Edwards, and Payson, and Evarts idling away eternity in mere psalm-singing? Heaven is a place of restless activity, the abode of never-tiring thought. David and Isaiah will sweep nobler and loftier strains in eternity, and the minds of the saints, unclogged by cumbersome clay, will forever feast on the banquet of rich and glorious thought. My friends, go on, then; you will never get through. An eternity of untiring action is before you, and the universe of thought is your field.—HENRY WARD BEECHER.

THE SHINING SHORE.

My days are gliding swiftly by,
  And I, a pilgrim stranger,
Would not detain them as they fly—
  Those hours of toil and danger.
    For oh! we stand on Jordan's strand,
      Our friends are passing over,
    And just before, the shining shore,
      We may almost discover.

We'll gird our loins, my brethren dear,
  Our distant home discerning;
Our absent Lord has left us word,
  Let every lamp be burning.
    For oh! we, etc.

Should coming days be cold and dark,
  We need not cease our singing;
That perfect rest naught can molest,
Where golden harps are ringing.
    For oh! we, etc.

> Let sorrow's rudest tempest blow,
>   Each cord on earth to sever;
> Our King says, Come! and there's our home
>   Forever, oh! forever!
>   For oh! we, etc.

NEARING THE GATES.

Now, while they were thus drawing towards the gates, behold a company of the heavenly host came out to meet them, to whom it was said by the other two shining ones, "These are the men that have loved our Lord when they were in the world, and that have left all for HIS HOLY NAME, and he hath sent us to fetch them, and we have brought them thus far on their desired journey, that they may go in and look their Redeemer in the face with joy." . . . .

And now were these two men, as it were, in heaven before they came at it, being swallowed up with a sight of angels, and with hearing of their melodious notes. . . . But, above all, the warm and joyful thoughts that they had about their own dwelling there with such company, and that forever and ever — oh! by what tongue or pen can these glorious joys be expressed? . . . .

Now, just as the gates were opened to let in the men, I looked in after them, and behold, the city shone like the sun; the streets were also paved with gold, and in them walked many men with crowns on their heads, palms in their hands, and golden harps to sing praises withal. And after that they shut up the gates, which when I had seen, I wished myself amongst them.—JOHN BUNYAN.

A VISION OF GLORY.

Child. But oh! what means this weakness, and this dim bewilderment, for I feel as though some mighty change were working in me? The former things are past away, and behold all things are becoming new! I see no more the world and the glories of it, as they appear unto the eye of mortal man, but in a light so clear and awful! Surely it beameth from eternity itself! How vain and perishing hath that world become, thus suddenly unveiled to me!

Divine Master. Rise up, my child, my faithful one, and come away; for lo, the winter is past, the rain is over and gone, the shadows depart of thy mortal life, and the day is dawning that never shall fade. It is past—it is gone—the dark time of thy conflict and trial. . . . . The time of the singing of angels is come for thee, and the voice of the seraphim is heard in that land. Thou hast wrestled with sin till the breaking of the day; thou hast toiled all night, but the morning is nigh. Arise up, then, my child, my faithful one, and come away; let us haste and be gone, for the dawn is bright on the everlasting hills.

Child. Oh, my Lord, in the time past of my life there was a great strong wind that rent my soul, and brake in pieces all my hopes in this world. .... But thou wert not in the wind. .... And after the wind there was an earthquake. .... All the fair things of earth I had sought to repose in gave way beneath my feet, and I knew of what dust they were made. .... But thou wert not in the earthquake. .... Then there was a fire, the searching flame of suffering, fierce and intense. .... But thou wert not in the fire. .... and I still lived on; and now there is a still small voice. ....

Divine Master. And I am here! Thy Master is come, and calleth for thee. .... My child, the day breaketh, and we must depart; the shadow of death is darkening on thine eyelids, and the radiance of earthly suns hath passed from them forever. .... But the hand that once opened the eyes of the blind is laid upon thine; and through thy soul, already trembling on the threshold of a new existence, the light of eternity is dawning, ere yet the silver cord that binds thy mortal life is altogether loosed. Look up—what seest thou?

Child. I see worlds floating in the infinite glory of God, like motes in the sunshine. I see the centuries falling into the ocean of eternity, swift as the rain-drops in summer.

Divine Master. Look again—what seest thou?

Child. The Word—the Word is fulfilled. Mine eyes behold the King in his beauty. Oh God, *Thou art love!*

TO DEPART AND BE WITH CHRIST—FAR BETTER.

NOT only the dead are the living, but, since they have died, they live a better life than ours. . . . In what particulars is their life now higher than it was? First, they have close fellowship with Christ; then, they are separated from this present body of weakness, of dishonor, of corruption; then, they are withdrawn from all the trouble, and toil, and care of this present life; and then, and surely not least, they have got death behind them, not having that awful figure standing on their horizon waiting for them to come up with it. . . . They are closer to Christ; they are delivered from the body as a source of weakness; as a hinderer of knowledge; as a dragger-down of all the aspiring tendencies of the soul; as a source of sin; as a source of pain; they are delivered from all the necessity of labor which is agony, of labor which is disproportionate to strength, of labor which often ends in disappointment, of labor which is wasted so often in mere keeping life in, of labor which at the best is a curse, though it be a merciful curse too; they are delivered from that "fear of death" which, though it be stripped of its sting, is never extinguished in any soul of man that lives; and they can smile at the way in which that narrow and inevitable passage bulked so large before them all their days, and, after all, when they come to it was so slight and small. If these be parts of the life of them that "sleep in Jesus;" if they are fuller of knowledge, fuller of wisdom, fuller of love, and capacity of love, and object of love; fuller of holiness, fuller of energy, and yet full of rest from head to foot; if all the hot tumult of earthly experience is stilled and quieted, all the fever beating of this blood of ours ever at an end; all the "whips and arrows of outrageous fortune" done with forever, and if the calm face which we looked upon, and out of which the lines of sorrow, and pain, and sickness melted away, giving it back a nobler nobleness than we had ever seen upon it in life, is only an image of the restful and more blessed being into which they have passed—if the dead are thus, then "Blessed are the dead."—A. McLaren.

FROM SHADOW INTO SUNSHINE AT LAST.

THERE he waits for his release,
There in God finds perfect peace;
Till the long years end at last,
And he too at length has past
From the sorrows and the fears,
From the anguish and the tears,
From the desolate distress
Of this world's great loneliness,
From its withering and its blight,
From the shadows of its night,
Into God's pure sunshine bright.
    RICHARD CHENEVIX TRENCH.

THE REST OF FAITH.

FOR a long time I felt myself to be a lost sheep, not knowing on whom to rely; and now, with the deepest consciousness that I have at last attained rest, I exclaim, "The Lord is my Shepherd!" What is there that can harm me? I have reached the harbor, and storms can no more drive my little vessel afloat upon the wide sea. And as I look forward into the future, I exclaim with David, "I shall not want."—AUGUSTUS THOLUCK.

THE SHORE OF ETERNITY.

ALONE! to land alone upon that shore,
With no one sight that we have seen before;
    Things of a different hue,
    And the sounds all new,
And fragrances so sweet the soul may faint.
Alone! Oh, that first hour of being a saint!

Alone! to land alone upon that shore,
On which no wavelets lisp, no billows roar,
    Perhaps no shape of ground,
    Perhaps no sight or sound,
No forms of earth our fancies to arrange—
But to begin alone that mighty change!

Alone! to land alone upon that shore,
Knowing so well we can return no more;
    No voice or face of friend,
    None with us to attend
Our disembarking on that awful strand,
But to arrive alone in such a land!

Alone! to land alone upon that shore!
To begin alone to live forevermore,
    To have no one to teach
    The manners of the speech
Of that new life, or put us at our ease;
Oh that we might die in pairs or companies!

Alone? the God we know is on that shore,
The God of whose attractions we know more
    Than of those who may appear
    Nearest and dearest here;
Oh, is He not the life-long friend we know
More privately than any friend below?

Alone? the God we trust is on that shore,
The Faithful One whom we have trusted more
    In trials and in woes
    Than we have trusted those
On whom we leaned most in our earthly strife:
Oh, we shall trust Him more in that new life!

Alone? the God we love is on that shore—
Love not enough, yet whom we love far more,
    And whom we loved all through,
    And with a love more true
Than other loves—yet now shall love Him more:
True love of Him begins upon that shore!

So not alone we land upon that shore;
'Twill be as though we had been there before;
    We shall meet more we know
    Than we can meet below,
And find our rest like some returning dove,
And be at home at once with our Eternal love!
F. W. Faber.

"Thou hast dealt well with thy servant."

THE REUNION.

As it was the first Adam that broke creation into fragments, so it is the second Adam that is to restore creation in all its parts and regions, and make it *one* again. The good and the evil then are parted forever, but the good and the good are brought into perfect oneness — a oneness so complete, so abiding, as more than to compensate for brokenness and separation here.

The soul and the body come together and form one glorified man. The ten thousand members of the church come together and form one glorified church. The scattered stones come together and form one living temple. The Bride and the Bridegroom meet. *Here* it has been one Lord, one faith, one baptism; *there* it shall be one body, one bride, one vine, one temple, one family, one city, one kingdom.

The broken fruitfulness, the fitful inconstancy of the cursed earth, shall pass into the unbroken beauty of the new creation. The discord of the troubled elements shall be laid, and harmony return. The warring animals shall lie down in peace.

Then shall heaven and earth come together into one. That which we call distance is annihilated, and the curtain drawn by sin is withdrawn from between the upper and lower glory, and the fields of a paradise that was never lost are brought into happy neighborhood with the fields of paradise regained, God's purpose developing itself in the oneness of a twofold glory—the rulers and the ruled, the risen and the unrisen, the celestial and the terrestrial, the glory that is in the heaven above, the glory that is in the earth beneath; for "there are celestial bodies and bodies terrestrial, but the glory of the celestial is one, and the glory of the terrestrial is another."

Such scenes we need to dwell upon, that, as our tribulations abound, so also our consolations may abound. Our wounds here are long in healing. Bereavements keep the heart long bleeding. Melancthon, with a tender simplicity so like himself, refers to his feelings when his child was taken from him by death. He wept as he recalled the past. It pierced his soul to remember the time when once, as he sat weeping, his little one with its napkin wiped the tears from his cheeks.

Recollections like these haunt us through life, ever and anon newly brought up by passing scenes. Some summer morning's sun recalls, with stinging freshness, the hour when that same sun streamed in through our window upon a dying infant's cradle, as if to bring out all the beauty of the parting smile, and engrave it upon our hearts forever. Or it is a funeral scene that cometh to memory—a funeral scene that had but a few days before been a bridal one—and never on earth can we forget the outburst of our grief when we saw the bridal flowers laid upon the new-made tomb. Or some wintry noon recalls the time and the scene when we laid a parent's dust within its resting-place, and left it to sleep in winter's grave of snows. These memories haunt us, pierce us, and make us feel what a desolate place this is, and what an infinitely desirable thing it would be to meet these lost ones again, where the meeting shall be eternal.

Hence the tidings of this reunion in the many mansions are like home-greetings. They relieve the smitten heart. They bid us be of good cheer, for the separation is but brief, and the meeting to which we look forward will be the happiest ever enjoyed. The time of sorrowful recollections will soon pass, and no remembrance remain but that which will make our joy to overflow.

Every thing connected with this reunion is fitted to enhance its blessedness. To meet again any where, or any how, or at any time, would be blessed; how much more at such a time, in such circumstances, and in such a home! The dark past lies behind us like a prison from which we have come forth, or like a wreck from which we have escaped in safety and landed in a quiet haven. We meet where separation is an impossibility, where distance no more tries fidelity, or pains the spirit, or mars the joy of loving. We meet in a kingdom. We meet at a marriage-table. We meet in the "prepared city," the new Jerusalem. We meet under the shadow of the tree of life, and on the banks of the river of life. We meet to keep festival and sing the songs of triumph. It was blessed to meet here for a day; how much more to meet in the kingdom forever! It was blessed to meet, even with parting full in view; how much more so when no such cloud overhangs our future! It was blessed to meet in the wilderness and the land of graves; how much more in paradise, and in the land where death enters not! It was blessed to meet "in the night," though chill and dark; how much more in the morning, when light has risen, and the troubled sky is cleared, and joy is spreading itself around us like a new atmosphere from which every element of sorrow has disappeared!—HORATIUS BONAR.

THERE is not a more repulsive spectacle than the old man who will not forsake the world which has already forsaken him.—AUGUSTUS THOLUCK.

FOREVER WITH THE LORD.

"Forever with the Lord!"
    So, Jesus, let it be;
Life from the dead is in that word—
    'Tis immortality.

Here in the body pent,
    Absent from Thee I roam;
Yet nightly pitch my moving tent
    A day's march nearer home.

"Forever with the Lord!"
    Savior, if 'tis Thy will,
The promise of that faithful word
    E'en here to me fulfill.

So when my latest breath
    Shall rend the veil in twain,
By death I shall escape from death,
    And life eternal gain.

Knowing as I am known,
    How shall I love that word,
And oft repeat before the throne,
    "Forever with the Lord!"

                JAMES MONTGOMERY.

Although the day be ne'er so long,
  At last it ringeth to even song.

INDEX OF AUTHORS.

Adam, T., 223.
Adams, Sarah F., 262.
Adams, William, 140, 214.
Addison, Joseph, 254.
À Kempis, Thomas, 169.
Alexander, James W., 9.
Arnold, Thomas, 300.
Arnot, William, 281.
Augustine, 150.
Barrow, J., 56.
Barton, Bernard, 142, 305.
Bate, John, 245.
Bates, William, 311.
Batty, Thomas, 208.
Baxter, Richard, 115, 331.
Bean, James, 259.
Beaumont, J., 320.
Beecher, H. W., 48, 83, 117, 120, 180, 251, 262, 281, 303, 308, 332.
Beveridge, William, 250.
Bickersteth, Edward, 330.
Binney, Thomas, 303.
Blunt, Henry, 96, 133, 143, 207.
Bonar, Horatius, 53, 148, 342.
Boyd, A. K. H. ("Country Parson"), 24.
Bridges, Charles, 285.
Brooks, Thomas, 48, 180.
Bunyan, John, 47, 142, 194, 334.
Burlingham, A. H., 85.
Butler, W. Archer, 246.

Byrom, John, 161.
Caird, John, 61, 157.
Campbell, Hope, 90.
Cameron, Andrew, 135.
Cheever, George B., 203.
Cheever, H. T., 77.
Chrysostom, 98, 100.
Coley, S., 83.
Crosby, Howard, 154.
Davies, Edwin, 87.
Davies, Samuel, 231.
Elliott, Charlotte, 228.
Faber, F. W., 340.
Ferguson, R., 327.
Flavel, John, 198.
Foster, John, 49.
Fry, Caroline, 94.
Gasparin, Madame de, 190, 194, 207.
Gill, John, 166.
Gray, Rachael, 276.
Guthrie, Thomas, 89, 93, 121, 279, 302, 323.
Hall, John, 170, 173, 174, 176, 177, 194.
Hall, Joseph, 22, 76.
Hamilton, James, 70, 104, 312.
Hamilton, R. W., 321.
Hawker, Robert, 34.
Henry, Matthew, 136, 179, 280.
Henry, Philip, 202.

INDEX OF AUTHORS.

Hervey, James, 73, 251.
Hoge, W. J., 128.
Holme, John Stanford, 295, 297.
Hood, Edwin Paxton, 227.
Howe, John, 182.
Hullett, J., 145.
Jay, William, 187.
Jenks, Benjamin, 268, 273.
Kelly, Thomas, 118, 168.
Ken, Thomas, 271.
Krummacher, F. W., 31, 37, 84, 128, 304, 316, 318.
Leighton, Robert, 92, 130, 221, 264, 302.
Longfellow, H. W., 134.
Lyte, Henry Francis, 71, 127, 236.
Macaulay, T. B., 291.
Macduff, J. R., 79, 160.
Maclaurin, J., 70.
Magoon, E. L., 88.
Manning, H. E., 30.
Martyn, Henry, 55.
Maynard, Mary, 263.
McCheyne, R. M., 235.
McLauren, 337.
Milton, John, 52.
Montgomery, James, 346.
More, Hannah, 316.
Mogridge, George ("Old Humphrey"), 249.
Muhlenburg, William A., 323.
Müller, H., 244.
Newman, John Henry, 149.
Newton, John, 114, 191.
Palmer, Ray, 63.
Parker, T., 294.
Parsons, James, 309.
Pascal, Jacqueline, 146.

Phelps, S. Dryden, 329.
Pope, Alexander, 247.
Prentiss, Mrs. E., 46, 219, 225, 242.
Pulsford, J., 36.
Punshon, William M., 146, 188, 205.
Ramsay, E. B., 125.
Ridgaway, H. B., 198.
Robertson, Frederick W., 32, 38, 44, 59, 68, 91, 164, 196, 219, 232, 282.
Romaine, William, 288.
Ruskin, John, 119.
Rutherford, Samuel, 80, 113, 190.
Saunders, Frederick, 243.
Scriver, Christian, 158, 290.
Sibbes, Richard, 153, 211.
Spurgeon, Charles, 57, 162, 230, 237, 277, 284.
Stanford, C., 307, 318.
Stanley, Arthur P., 326.
Stoughton, J., 325.
Taylor, Jeremy, 255.
Tholuck, Augustus, 41, 339, 345.
Toplady, A. M., 40, 241.
Townson, J., 279.
Trench, Richard Chenevix, 132, 339.
Vaughan, C. J., 209.
Watson, Richard, 122.
Watts, Isaac, 82, 131, 306.
Wesley, Charles, 181, 275.
Wesley, John, 106, 225.
Wesleys, The Mother of the, 112.
Whitecross, J., 195.
Whittier, John G., 97.
Wilberforce, William, 187.
Williams, William, 293.
Williams, William R., 65, 81, 278.
Willmott, R. A., 138.
Winslow, Mrs. Mary, 39.

INDEX OF SUBJECTS.

Abide with us, 127.
Abraham, the Death of, 304.
Active Life, aged Christians still in, 12.
Advent, the, 82.
Affliction, 126.
Affliction, a Prayer for one in, 271.
Affliction, Uses of, 132.
Age, Happiness of, 36.
Aged and Helpless, 305.
Aged, a Psalm for the, 41.
Aged Christian, Testimony of an, 51.
Aged Person, a Prayer for the Use of an, 273.
Aged Person, Letter to an, 113.
Arise, Shine, for thy Light is come, 246.
Asleep and Awake, 281.
Autumn and Spring, 263.

Beacon Light, the, 329.
Believer, Death of the, 295.
Best as it is, 143.
Bible, the, 231, 278.
Bible, the Old Man's, 140.
Bitter, the, with the Sweet, 64.
Blindness, Milton on his, 52.
Building, 120.

Care upon Christ, cast all your, 205.
"Casting all your Care upon him," 115.
Cheer, Words of, 195.

Christ a Fountain, 83.
Christ, all from, 76.
Christ, all One in, 275.
Christ in the Christian, 85.
Christ, joint Heirs with, 98.
Christ, Looking to, 169.
Christ, the full Vision of, 288.
Christ, to be with, 277.
Christ, to depart and be with—far better, 337.
Christian Progress, 32.
Christian, the trembling, 136.
Christian, Trial of the worldly, 196.
City, the abiding, 168.
Clouds, 227.
Communion with God, 300.
Compensation, the Bible a History of, 138.
Conquerors, more than, 284.
Contentment, 112.
Cross-bearing, 207.
Cross, before the, 208.
Cross, Glory of the, 69.
Cross, Taking up the, 71.
Crown of Glory, the hoary Head a, 22.

David's Harp, 318.
Death, a Preparation for, 300.
Death, Comfort for the Hour of, 330.
Death, consoling Idea of, 260.
Death, the Believer's, 166.
Death, the Fear of, 18.
Death, the Worldling's Notion of, 21.

INDEX OF SUBJECTS.

Death welcome, 157.
Delight in God, the Saint's, 182.
Dependence, a Life of, 176.
Dependence of the Soul, God the only, 68.
Depression, Religious, 164.
Difficulties solved, 194.
Due Time, the, 130.
Dying, Gain of, 308.

Enduring unto the End, 49, 75.
Entrance, the abundant, 154.
Eventide, Light at, 253.

Faint not, ye shall Reap if ye, 68.
Faith, 244.
Faith, Fidelity to the, 79.
Faith, Life of, 82.
Faith, Living by, 63.
Faith, Magnetism of, 77.
Faith, Simple, 36.
Faith, Simplicity of, 89.
Faith, the riper Fruits of, 137.
Faith, the Trial of our, 106.
Faith, the Walk of, 39.
Fear of Death, Prayer against the, 259.
Feelings, Changeful, 180.
Fidelity in Persecution, 88.
Forever with the Lord, 346.
Fullness of Joy at God's right Hand, 323.
Future, Caring for the, 303.
Future, Ignorance of the, 87.

Glory, a Vision of, 335.
God, Access to, 104.
God a Friend, 84.
God a Rock, 135.
God, Dependence upon, 145.
God hath led me all these Years, 209.

God, Love of, 160.
God, Rest only in, 161.
God, Silence of, 117.
God unchangeable, 48.
God, upheld by, 73.
God, Ways of, 316.
Goodness, personal, 192.
Gospel, the Glorious, 281.
Gospel, the, not gloomy, 128.
Grace, saved by, 195.
Grace, the Teachings of, 179.
Gratitude, Memorial of, 147.
Great Physician, Treatment of the, 242.
Guide, the Holy Spirit our, 211.

Hand, Divine, upheld by the, 73.
Happiness, attaining, 262.
Hearer, not a Forgetful, 234.
Hearing and Doing, 125.
Heart, hardening the, 235.
Heaven a City, 302.
Heaven, Activity in, 332.
Heaven, Beginning of, 294.
Heaven, Foretokens of, 321.
Heaven, Friendships of, 320.
Heaven, Inquiries about, 318.
Heaven, Longing for, 325.
Heaven looked forward to, 306.
Heaven, nearness of, 307.
Heaven, Paul's Estimate of, 316.
Heaven, Service of, 312.
Heaven, the Music of, 311.
Heaven, the Suburbs of, 20.
Heaven, Thoughts of, 309.
Heavenly Aspiration, 331.
Holy Song, Priesthood of, 243.
Home, a humble, 70.
Home, Heaven a, 279.
Home, Heaven our, 153.

I AM, 250.
"I am ready to die," 290.

INDEX OF SUBJECTS.

Indemnities, Christianity a System of, 15.
Inheritance, Glory of our, 100.
"It is well," 322.
I will fear no Evil, 253.
I will never leave thee nor forsake thee, 314.
I would not live alway, 323.

Jehovah Jireh, 245.
Jerusalem, the Holy, 50.
Jesus, Looking to, 251.
Jesus, Sight of, 93.
Jesus, Sympathy of, 91.
Job, a Parable, 37.
Just as I am, 228.

Keep the Heart alive, 142.
Kindness, Memory of, 251.

Last Hours of Life, Occupation for the, 219.
Lead, kindly Light, 149.
Life in the Flesh, a, 173.
Life, Review of, 257.
Life, the Discouragements of, 96.
Life, the Troubles of, 191.
Life to come, Happiness of the, 221.
Life's Changes, 144.
Light and Dark, 122.
Light, at Evening Time it shall be, 24.
Light, through Darkness to, 192.
Light through Tears, 124.
Lives, some noble, 170.
Longer Life, a Prayer for, 264.
Look on Jesus, not on the Waves, 133.
Look up, 92.
Look within, 123.
Looking Westward, 51.
Lord, cast thy Burden on the, 328.
Loss and Gain, 238.

Love a Safeguard, 282.

Making God's Law our Song, 285.
Man Christ Jesus, the, 261.
Meditation, Importance of, 202.
Memories of the Way, 146.
Mercy, Cloud of, 81.
Morning, Evening often pleasanter than, 57.
Mourners, Comfort for, 231.
My Grace is sufficient for thee, 241.

Nearer Heaven, 224.
Nearer to Thee, 262.
Nearing Heaven, 279.
Nearing the Gates, 334.
Night of Sorrow—Morning of Joy, 121.
Night-watch, the, 53.
Not impatient, but ready, 317.
Not my Will, but Thine, 148.

Old Age, a Parable, 31.
Old Age, Beauty of, 305.
Old Age, blessed Work for, 229.
Old Age, Backsliding in, 240.
Old Age, a happy, 198.
Old Age, Sin forgiven in, 162.
Old Man, the, 207.
Old Man, the happy, 261.
One in Christ, 40.
Opened Gates, the, 224.

Parable, a, 128.
Path of the Just, the, 203.
Patience, Angel of, 97.
Patience, Motives to, 65.
Patient Waiting, 191.
Paul the Aged, such a one as, 34.
Perseverance, Christian, 47.
Perseverance, Christian, Necessity of, 48.
Pilgrimage, our, 239.

INDEX OF SUBJECTS.

Pilgrim's Prayer, the, 293.
Pilgrim's Way to Heaven, 291.
Portion, God our, 61.
Poverty in Old Age, 187.
Praise, 56.
Praise, the Spirit of, 237.
Prayer and Temptation, 255.
Prayer, unanswered, 326.
Preparation for Death, a Prayer on, 268.
Progress, Christian, 32.

Reaching forward, 38.
Remember Lot's Wife, 30.
Resignation, 288.
Rest, Entering into, 190.
Retiring from Business, 11.
Retrospect and Prospect, 214.
Reunion, the, 342.
Rock, Build on the, 80.
Rod, the, 158.

Self-denying Effort, a Life of, 174.
Seventy-first Psalm, a Commentary on the, 41.
Shadow into Sunshine, from, 339.
Shore of Eternity, the, 340.
Sick-chamber Sabbath Hymn, 248.
Sickness of Elisha, 187.
Sickness, the Chamber of, 315.
Sight well-pleasing to God, a, 302.
Simply Trusting, 95.
Sing, for your Redemption is near, 276.
Sinner, a, be merciful to me, 236.
Sorrow, the Lessons of, 232.
Spiritual Fellowship with departed Friends, 297.
Strength of Age, the, Joy of the Lord, the, 17.
Submitting to what? 141.

Suffering a higher Path than Doing, 167.
Sufficiency, the Believer's, 188.
Sun of Righteousness, the Soul mounting toward the, 14.
Sunlight sent by the Lord, 90.
Suspense, 46.
Swift Ships, like the, 230.

Taking Rest, 59.
Temple, the Finishing of the, 55.
The Day, Strength sufficient for, 54.
The Past, Oblivion of, 44.
The Rest of Faith, 339.
The Shining Shore, 333.
The Vision of God and a Knowledge of Heavenly Mysteries, 150.
Think of this, 249.
Thoughts, Wandering, 225.
Through Darkness to Light, 119, 192.
Time, Sanctification a Work of, 146.
Time, the Due, 130.
Trials, our, 114.
Tribulation, Comfort in, 116.
Tribulations, we glory in, also, 131.
Truly noble Life, a, 177.

Unbelief, evil Effects of, 198.

Victory, Last, 303.

Waiting Times, 180.
Wanderer, the returning, 181.
Way to God, we are on our, 118.
Welsh Peasant, the, 94.
"When Egypt's King," 247.
Witnesses, the Cloud of, 327.
Work, Finish thy, 197.

Youth renewed in Age, 9.

THE END.

PUBLICATIONS OF THE AMERICAN TRACT SOCIETY
A Major Project from Solid Ground Christian Books

This is a Six Volume Set of over 2400 pages and 194 Tracts from the most gifted writers of the church including: as John Bunyan, Jonathan Edwards, Joseph Alleine, Archibald Alexander, J.W. Alexander, John Flavel, John Witherspoon, John Newton, Robert Hall, James Hervey, Richard Cecil, John Owen, Philip Doddridge, Timothy Dwight, Richard Baxter, Isaac Watts, Legh Richmond, Thomas Goodwin, Gardiner Spring, William Cowper, Edward Payson, Ashbel Green, Andrew Fuller, Benjamin Rush, Cesar Malan and many more.

"The American Tract Society publications are of enduring and superlative quality. They represent the cream of the best writers in the Reformed world from the sixteenth to the nineteenth century, such as John Flavel, Jonathan Edwards, and Archibald Alexander. Almost without exception, these tracts, which range from four to forty-eight pages each and cover a remarkable variety of subjects, interface biblical, doctrinal, and experiential material in practically helpful ways. Having often perused these volumes in my own study with considerable profit for nearly four decades, I am so grateful to SGCB for bringing them back into print again. Here is truly a case where 'the old is better'!" - **Dr. Joel R. Beeke**, Puritan Reformed Theological Seminary, Grand Rapids, Michigan

"The early publications of the American Tract Society are as valuable as they are varied. The individual pieces were written by well-seasoned Christians and abound in sweet seasoning for the soul. Something here for everyone."- **Dr. Robert P. Martin**, Pastor of Emmanuel Reformed Baptist Church, Seattle, Washington and Editor of Reformed Baptist Theological Review

"The collected tracts are a veritable treasure chest of good sound doctrine from the greatest proclaimers of gospel truth the church has had for the last 300 years. You would be doing your soul a tremendous disservice if you fail to obtain these gems!"
- **Dr. Don Kistler**, founder of Soli Deo Gloria and now Northampton Publications

Call us Toll Free at **1-866-789-7423**
Send an e-mail to us at **sgcb@charter.net**
Visit our web site at **www.solid-ground-books.com**

www.ingramcontent.com/pod-product-compliance
Lightning Source LLC
Chambersburg PA
CBHW060107170426
43198CB00010B/802